# SCOTLAND'S NOSTRADAMUS

*A quest for the Brahan Seer*

The author above Castle Leod, in August 1982
(courtesy of Kevin McKenzie)

Human nature is not exclusively displayed in the histories of only great countries, or in the actions of only celebrated men; and human nature may be suffered to assert its claim on the attention of the beings who partake of it, even though the specimens exhibited be furnished by the traditions of an obscure village.

Hugh Miller, *Scenes and Legends of the North of Scotland: Or the Traditional History of Cromarty*, 1834, p. 10

**In memory of my much-adored parents, Patricia and John McKenzie, who first encouraged my love of both storytelling and history.**

'Bring me the two most precious things in the City', said God to one of His Angels.

Oscar Wilde, *The Happy Prince*, 1888, p. 24

# SCOTLAND'S NOSTRADAMUS

*A quest for the Brahan Seer*

Witchcraft, Folklore, Collective Trauma and
Conspiracy Theory in the Scottish Highlands

## Andrew McKenzie

UNICORN

Published in 2024 by
Unicorn, an imprint of Unicorn Publishing Group
Charleston Studio
Meadow Business Centre
Lewes BN8 5RW
www.unicornpublishing.org

Text copyright © 2024 Andrew McKenzie

All rights reserved. No part of the contents of this book may be reproduced,
stored in or introduced into a retrieval system, or transmitted, in any form
or by any means (electronic, mechanical, photocopying, recording or
otherwise), without the prior written permission of the copyright holder
and the above publisher of this book.

Every effort has been made to trace copyright holders and to obtain their
permission for the use of copyrighted material. The publisher apologises
for any errors or omissions and would be grateful to be notified of any
corrections that should be incorporated in future reprints or editions of this
book.

ISBN  978 1 916846 44 9
10 9 8 7 6 5 4 3 2 1

Design by newtonworks.uk
Printed and bound in Great Britain by Bell & Bain Ltd, Glasgow

Frontispiece: Historiated initial with portrait of Michael Scot from *Liber particularis; Liber
de Physiognomia*. Thirteenth-century Italy © Bodleian Libraries, University of Oxford

# Contents

| | |
|---|---|
| Preface | viii |
| | |
| The Legend | 1 |
| Second Sight in the Highlands and its Background | 6 |
| Coinneach *Odhar* and Scotland's Witch-Craze | 20 |
| | |
| Plate Section | 34 |
| | |
| A Superstitious Highland Backwater? | 44 |
| An Occult Laboratory: Part One | 57 |
| A Land of Myth and Legend | 64 |
| Dante's Scholar Wizard | 75 |
| The Highlands as a Treasury of Wonder Tales | 84 |
| | |
| Plate Section | 91 |
| | |
| An Occult Laboratory: Part Two | 99 |
| 'Seaforth's Doom' | 106 |
| A Highland Conspiracy Theory | 123 |
| 'I see into the far future ...': Prophecies Believed to Have Been as Yet Unfulfilled | 134 |
| | |
| Conclusions | 148 |
| Selected Bibliography | 154 |
| Index | 161 |

# Preface

> I see into the far future, and I read the doom of the race of my oppressor. The long-descended line of Seaforth will, ere many generations have passed, end in extinction and in sorrow. I see a chief, the last of his house, both deaf and dumb. He will be the father of four fair sons, all of whom he will follow to the tomb. He will live careworn and die mourning, knowing that the honours of his line are to be extinguished for ever.

These are the dramatic words of Coinneach *Odhar* (or 'Sallow' Kenneth) Mackenzie, known as the Brahan Seer, which he was supposed to have uttered after being sentenced to death by his clan chief's wife, Isobel Mackenzie, Countess of Seaforth. This particular prediction, known as 'Seaforth's Doom', was preserved as the concluding chapter in the legend of his life, but other famous prophecies attributed to him include the Battle of Culloden, the Highland Clearances, the demise of the traditional landowning classes that meant the end of the clan system, the construction of the Caledonian Canal, the coming of the railways and even the Second World War. Therefore, as a McKenzie (the spelling has varied over time and I retain my own spelling in this book for my particular ancestors) who has spent my adult life researching the history of this family, it would be remiss of me not to make a special study of one of this clan's most famous sons.

I first became familiar with the Seer's story as a teenager when I read the late Earl of Cromartie's Highland History, immediately after its publication in 1979. This book held a special fascination for me, since it combined my two early loves: history and folklore. Shortly afterwards, when I was seventeen years old, at the first opportunity in 1982, my brother, Kevin, and I made our way to Castle Leod, the Earl's ancient seat, where the hospitable clan chief showed us round his home in this enchanting sixteenth-century pink sandstone tower house, just to the north of Inverness. A decorated hero in the Second World War, Earl Rorie lived up to an earlier age's expectations of what a patriarchal Edwardian aristocrat in his stately old castle should be. As someone who had a true passion for his family's heritage, he was at pains to share with a wider audience that love for the history of his homeland. He had no trouble inspiring me, since, to my teenage imagination, the Highland legends that were preserved in oral tradition were every bit as magical to me as the stories of C.S. Lewis and J.R.R. Tolkien. In fact, one of the Seer's predictions – that 'the Mackenzies one day would be so reduced in numbers that women will fight over a pock-marked, squint-eyed tailor, and the sole surviving members of the family will finally return to the land in the

*Preface*

west, from whence they came, in an open fishing boat' – reminded me of the end of *The Lord of the Rings*, and in my mind I pictured my very own family in that single boat. That family in my imagination inevitably included my (probably very anxious) mother and grandmother, albeit that they were not Mackenzies by birth, but they surely possessed the same unassuming yet heroic nature that secured Frodo and Bilbo Baggins their well-deserved places alongside the Elves on board the vessel that ultimately took them west to Middle-earth's Isles of the Blessed. And behind all of this was the Brahan Seer: apparently a wise and all-seeing wizard, who in my eyes undoubtedly wore a long white beard and held a gnarled staff, just like Gandalf!

Shortly after that first visit to Castle Leod, I was then to spend a contented summer in Edinburgh, researching the life of Francis Humberston Mackenzie, the object of the Brahan Seer's most famous prediction, known as 'Seaforth's Doom', which was the subject of my undergraduate degree dissertation. Coinciding with the Edinburgh Festival, which allowed me to spend my evenings watching the performances of thespian friends from college taking part in Fringe events, I would find my daytimes equally entertaining, spending them at the Scottish Record Office in Robert Adam's elegant Register House, poring over the papers of Francis, the 'Last of the Seaforths'. It was with some affection that I got to know this remarkable man. Frank, as he was known to his intimate family and friends, defied the handicaps of being first deaf and subsequently dumb, by following a distinguished political career as an MP, Lord Lieutenant, Colonel of a regiment and Governor of Barbados, which allowed him to revive his family's fortunes, repairing the damage caused by the upheavals that beset his forebears during the Jacobite Rebellions earlier on in the eighteenth century. That summer, I then paid a second visit to Castle Leod, this time with my elder brother, Chris, and I can remember being plied yet again with large glasses of Glenmorangie's single-malt whisky in the study at Castle Leod, before the Earl of Cromartie drove us over the steep slope of the Cat's Back opposite the Castle to what had formerly been the Mackenzie chief's seat at Brahan, and where nearby we visited the memorial to Francis's daughter, the Hon. Caroline Mackenzie, which marked the fulfilment of the Seer's prediction that the male line of the Seaforth Mackenzies, who had for centuries presided over the whole of Ross-shire, would come to an end, and a 'white-coiffed lassie from the East' would kill her sister, thus cementing the curse of 'Seaforth's Doom', when the daughter of the 'Last Seaforth', Lady Hood, would kill her younger sister in a carriage accident.

Several years later, after 2001, when Kevin and I began to delve more deeply into the history of our own direct ancestors, this not only led to my writing a wider history of the family (entitled *May we be Britons? A History of the Mackenzies*), but, during the course of all this research, we discovered that the family of our direct ancestor, Bishop Murdo McKenzie's wife, Margaret MacAulay, was from Uig on the Isle of Lewis. Uig was where the Brahan Seer was supposed to

ix

*Scotland's Nostradamus*

have been born; and their grandson, Daniel McKenzie, was a kind of secretary cum right-hand-man to Frances Herbert, Countess of Seaforth, who was a fierce rival to her equally formidable mother-in-law, Countess Isobel. Countess Isobel was none other than the Brahan Seer's nemesis: the woman who was purported to have sentenced Coinneach *Odhar* to death by being burned in a spiked barrel of tar on Chanonry Point. This she supposedly enacted in a fit of rage after the Seer's gift of second sight enabled him to inform her about her philandering husband's activities when he was away in Paris. My ancestor Daniel was even described at one point as having lived with Frances at Brahan Castle. Over the years, time and again, I kept coming across the people and places associated with the Brahan Seer when I was looking into the history of my own family. This ever-closer familiarity with this family at this crucial time in its history added yet more to my fascination with this intriguing and shadowy character.

And it was later, in 2022, that I was interviewed for a number of podcasts, including two about the Brahan Seer, by my friend in the United States, Jared Smart, with whom I had previously served on the Committee of the Clan Mackenzie Society of Scotland and the UK. In the first of these, Jared asked the question whether the Brahan Seer was fact or fiction, effectively asking whether the Highland prophet was a real historical person. I was interviewed alongside Phyllis Hannah from the Ross and Cromarty Heritage Society. My view at the time was entirely sceptical of the idea that there was a genuine local seer who was a labourer on the Brahan estate living in the seventeenth century, as described by Alexander Mackenzie. That was the view suggested by Elizabeth Sutherland in her 1977 edition of Alexander Mackenzie's *The Prophecies of the Brahan Seer*. As you will see, following my subsequent research, I have come to refine my opinion.

Another one of Jared's podcasts concerned the Landmark Trust's renovation at that time of Fairburn Tower (built by yet another direct ancestor of mine, John Mackenzie, First Laird of Fairburn, in the mid-sixteenth century). Its ruin, the Seer had famously foreseen, along with his prediction that a cow would give birth on the topmost floor of this once splendid fortress. Caroline Stanford, the highly knowledgeable historian working for the Landmark Trust, made the observation in that podcast that it was interesting how much longer a belief in second sight persisted (and perhaps persists) in Scotland.

This book is in many ways a response to the two questions that arose in these podcasts.

The interesting point is that it was not, as we might expect, during the height of Scotland's 'witch-craze', in the seventeenth century, that the apparent fulfilment of Coinneach *Odhar*'s prophecies were being excitedly discussed and believed, but notably in the aftermath of the 'Age of Reason', at a time when the Highlands had undergone far-reaching modernisation, during the nineteenth century, and then later still again, into the twentieth century and even into my own lifetime. An example of a casual reference to a Brahan Seer prophecy occurs

x

*Preface*

in a letter written to the factor of the Knoydart Estate in June 1902 from an iron-monger in Beauly, which is now kept in the Highland Council Archives. This is a prophecy that a king would reign over Britain but would not be crowned, which had not by 1902 been realised. While the writer of the letter believed that it might apply to King Edward VII, then undergoing an operation for appendicitis, prior to his coronation, it has since been applied to Edward VIII, who, thirty years later, did indeed famously 'reign over Britain, but would not be crowned'.

In 1932, when a small airship made an emergency landing, when it dropped a grapnel that became entangled in the spire of the new church in Strathpeffer, this was thought to fulfil the story of how the Seer had pointed to a field that was far from seashore, loch or river, and said that a ship would anchor there one day: 'A village with four churches will get another spire,' said *Coinneach*, 'and a ship will come from the sky and moor at it.' At the start of the twentieth century, when it was first proposed that an Episcopal church should be built in Strathpeffer, the inhabitants had even presented a petition to the rector asking that he should not include a spire in the new building for fear that the prophecy would come to fulfilment.

In August 1939, with the construction of a fifth bridge over the River Ness, Coinneach was again cited for predicting that, when there were five bridges built over the river, there would be 'worldwide chaos'. Shortly afterwards, Hitler invaded Poland and the Second World War commenced. Similarly, the Brahan Seer declared that when a ninth bridge would be constructed over the River Ness, then 'fire, blood and calamity' would ensue. This ninth bridge was finished in 1987 and the following year the Piper Alpha disaster took place.

The survival into the twentieth century of beliefs in the Seer's prophecies is recorded in an article I came across by chance, as I was beginning to write up my initial notes about the Brahan Seer. This was published on 25 June 2023 in *The Guardian* and written by the *Observer*'s art correspondent, Laura Cumming. In it, she mentions how her artist father, James Cumming, spent time on the Isle of Lewis in the late 1940s and was inspired to make a painting of the Brahan Seer. On this island, in Laura's words:

> The past was present everywhere and to everyone; and to some people, so were events in the future. He encountered many islanders with the foretelling gift known on Lewis as second sight. They included the minister who wished to be rid of what he regarded as its curse, the carpenter who bleakly knew the dimensions of each coffin before a death had even occurred, the woman with second sight who brought milk to Callanish in an iron urn ... All of these prophecies take the form of visions – specifically, pictures. The Seer has need of these because he lives in a place without much writing, at a time when very few people can read; pictures will lodge best in memory. There is a great beauty to the Seer's pictures, of skies and glens and rowan berries, of seas and lochs, of

crofters tilling the land and trawling their nets through the water. And eventually, when he is somewhere between historic figure and deathless legend, the Brahan Seer becomes a picture himself.

It just so happened that I knew Laura from when she interviewed me in 2013 regarding a newly discovered portrait that we sold at Bonhams, where I have worked as an Old Master Paintings specialist, by the great seventeenth-century Spanish artist Diego Velázquez. She writes superbly, so I felt very privileged when she went on to acknowledge me in 2016 in her excellent book, *The Vanishing Man*, about a lost portrait of King Charles I by Velázquez. After reading her latest article, I got in touch again and she told me about the fascination with the Brahan Seer and second sight that she shared with her father, and also kindly gave me permission to illustrate his particularly striking painting in this book. I believe this is what is known as 'serendipity', but since the Brahan Seer is involved, some might suggest there may have been other occult forces at work!

We have also been told that Coinneach *Odhar* more recently spoke of the day when Scotland would once again have its own Parliament. This would only come, he said, when men could walk dry shod from England to France. The opening of the Channel Tunnel in 1994 was followed a few years later by the inauguration of the first Scottish Parliament since 1707.

And, as late as 1995, when the ferry between Ullapool and Stornoway was named the 'Isle of Lewis', there were fears that the ship's name might explain how the Seer's seemingly unlikely foretelling that 'The Day will come when the Isle of Lewis will sink beneath the waves' might be fulfilled. It was said that this would happen once the building of the road between Tolsta and Ness on Lewis was complete. So seriously was this prophecy taken that there have been no calls to complete the road while that ferry was operational!

An easy inference might, of course, be that beliefs in the Highlands remained 'backward' and that the region's remoteness might have allowed the survival of superstition. In this investigation, however, I intend to show that explanation to be much too simplistic and in many ways a hangover from the prejudices of the Jacobite period in the eighteenth century, when it served the Hanoverian side to paint their enemies as uncivilised. I will show such a picture to be very far from the truth.

Having come to an acceptance that belief in second sight was not some kind of mediaeval survival in a supposed Highland backwater, another factor that came to shape my thinking about this subject was the recent preponderance of discussions on the subject of conspiracy theories in the aftermath of the COVID-19 pandemic in particular. It struck me immediately that the same willingness to accept irrational explanations when feeling helpless in the face of enormous upheaval might equally account for a belief in second sight in what was not after all such an uncivilised part of the world. Armed with my awareness of all of this, and combined with what over the years had amounted to an exceptionally

*Preface*

thorough knowledge of the Brahan Seer's immediate background, I felt a strong urge to readdress a story that I had long known, but had now come to see with fresh eyes.

~·~·~

In all of this, I wish to acknowledge my debt to a number of people. Foremost, I would like to mention my parents, Patricia and John McKenzie, who fostered my initial love of the subjects that inspired this book. Those subjects are also ones that I shared with both my brothers, Chris and Kevin, particularly the latter, who has worked closely with me over the last two decades in exploring in enormous depth our ancestors' past. I am also grateful to John and Eve Cromartie, who have not only also shared many of those interests with me, but have been very kind in accommodating me at Castle Leod on a number of those occasions in which I have visited 'Mackenzie country' (to coin a term employed by Queen Victoria). In shaping my overall approach to the historical background, I am also enormously grateful to those inspirational historians with whom I have enjoyed maintaining ties after they first taught me during my undergraduate degree at Cambridge: Professor Sir David Cannadine and Professor Peter Burke; along with my subsequent fortunate encounter with Professor Hugh Cheape, whose support and sympathetic approach to the history of the Highlands and Islands has been invaluable. I would also like to thank Jared Smart, whose *Clan Mackenzie* podcasts inspired me to start writing this book; Julian Roup, who drew my attention to Siener van Rensburg, as well as being a huge support in all my current writing projects; and Laura Cumming for kindly allowing me to reproduce her father's splendid painting, *The Brahan Seer*.

# The Legend

The first mention that I can find of the man who came to be known as the Brahan Seer is in Thomas Pennant's *A Tour in Scotland*, in 1769: 'Every country has its prophets ... And the Highlands their Kenneth Oaur.' He is later mentioned in the *Bannatyne Manuscript* history of the MacLeods, which dates from about 1832, in which he was said to predict the downfall of the MacLeods, placing him as a native of Ness in the Isle of Lewis, and born in the sixteenth century. The first extensive literary reference to the Brahan Seer, however, was made by the folklorist and geologist from the Black Isle in Ross-shire, Hugh Miller, first published in 1831 and based on material largely collected between fifteen and twenty years earlier, in his *Scenes and Legends of the North of Scotland: Or The Traditional History of Cromarty*. According to Miller, 'when serving as a field labourer with a wealthy clansman who resided somewhere near Brahan Castle', Kenneth Ore,

> made himself so formidable to the clansman's wife by his shrewd, sarcastic humour, that she resolved on destroying him by poison. With this design, she mixed a preparation of noxious herbs with his food, when he was one day employed in digging turf in a solitary morass, and brought it to him in a pitcher. She found him lying asleep on one of those conical fairy hillocks which abound in some parts of the Highlands, and her courage failing her, instead of awaking him, she set down the pitcher by his side and returned home. He woke shortly after, and, seeing the food, would have begun his repast, but feeling something press heavily against his heart, he opened his waistcoat and found a beautiful smooth stone, resembling a pearl, but much larger, which had apparently been dropped into his breast while he slept. He gazed at it in admiration, and became conscious as he gazed, that a strange faculty of seeing the future as distinctly as the present, and men's real designs and motives as clearly as their actions, was miraculously imparted to him; and it is well for him that he should become so knowing at such a crisis, for the first secret he became acquainted with was that of the treachery practised against him by his mistress. But he derived little advantage of the faculty ever after, for he led, it is said, till extreme old age, an unsettled, unhappy kind of life, wandering from place to place, a prophet only of evil, or of little trifling events, fitted to attract notice when they occurred, merely from the circumstances of their having been fulfilled.

Of Kenneth's predictions, Miller went on to inform us:

There was a time of evil, he said, coming over the Highlands, when all things would appear fair and promising, and yet be both bad in themselves, and the beginnings of what would prove worse. A road would be opened upon the hills, from sea to sea, and a bridge built over every stream; but the people would be degenerating as their country was growing better; there would be ministers among them without grace, and maidens without shame; and the clans would have become so heartless, that they would flee out of their country before an army of sheep. Moss and muir would be converted into corn-land, and yet hunger press as sorely upon the poor as ever. Darker days would follow, for there would arise a terrible persecution, during which a ford in the River Oickel, at the head of the Dornoch Firth, would render a passage over the dead bodies of men, attired in the plaid and bonnet; and on the hill of *Finnbheim* in Sutherlandshire, a raven would drink her full of human blood three times a day for three successive days. The greater part of this prophecy belongs to the future; but almost all his minor ones are said to have met their fulfilment. He predicted, it is affirmed, that there would be dram-shops at the end of almost every furrow; that a cow would calve on the top of the old tower of Fairburn; that a cub would rear a litter of calves on the hearth-stone of Castle Downie; that another animal of the same species, but white as snow, would be killed on the western coast of Sutherlandshire; that a wild deer would be taken alive at Fortrose Point; that a rivulet in Wester Ross would be dried up in winter; and that there would be a deaf Seaforth.

Just under half a century later, what has since been regarded as the definitive collection of the Seer's prophecies was first published by Alexander Mackenzie in 1877 in his *The Prophecies of the Brahan Seer, Coinneach Odhar Fiosaiche*. Known by the nickname of 'Clach' (derived from his clothes shop business in Clach na Cudainn House), Mackenzie was a writer and politician who campaigned for security of tenure for crofters and who became the Editor and Publisher of the *Celtic Magazine*, and the *Scottish Highlander*, as well as writing several clan histories. As with Hugh Miller's account of 'Kenneth Ore', it is worthwhile quoting here Mackenzie's introduction to what he had recorded surrounding the folklore that he said was then being repeated at the time in local oral tradition. This is because, surprising though it might at first seem, there is more to these stories than being simply pretty fairytales and I will show in due course that a thorough historical investigation can uncover certain elements in them that were firmly rooted in an amalgamation of authentic collective memories:

Kenneth Mackenzie, better known as Coinneach Odhar, the Brahan Seer (according to Mr. Maclennan), was born at Baile-na-Cille, in the Parish of Uig and Island of Lews, about the beginning of the seventeenth century. Nothing particular is recorded of his early life, but when he

*The Legend*

had just entered his teens, he received a stone in the following manner, by which he could reveal the future destiny of man: – While his mother was one evening tending her cattle in a summer shealing on the side of a ridge called Cnoceothail, which overlooks the burying-ground of Baile-na-Cille, in Uig, she saw, about the still hour of midnight, the whole of the graves in the churchyard opening, and a vast multitude of people of every age, from the newly born babe to the grey-haired sage, rising from their graves, and going away in every conceivable direction. In about an hour they began to return, and were all soon after back in their graves, which closed upon them as before. But, on scanning the burying-place more closely, Kenneth's mother observed one grave, near the side, still open. Being a courageous woman, she determined to ascertain the cause of this singular circumstance, so, hastening to the grave, and placing her 'cuigeal' (distaff) athwart its mouth (for she had heard it said that the spirit could not enter the grave again while that instrument was upon it), she watched the result. She had not to wait long, for in a minute or two she noticed a fair lady coming in the direction of the churchyard, rushing through the air, from the north. On her arrival, the fair one addressed her thus – 'Lift thy distaff from off my grave, and let me enter my dwelling of the dead.' 'I shall do so,' answered the other, 'when you explain to me what detained you so long after your neighbours.' 'That you shall soon hear,' the ghost replied; 'My journey was much longer than theirs – I had to go all the way to Norway.' She then addressed her: – 'I am a daughter of the King of Norway; I was drowned while bathing in that country; my body was found on the beach close to where we now stand, and I was interred in this grave. In remembrance of me, and as a small reward for your intrepidity and courage, I shall possess you of a valuable secret – go and find in yonder lake a small round blue stone, which give to your son, Kenneth, who by it shall reveal future events.' She did as requested, found the stone, and gave it to her son, Kenneth. No sooner had he thus received the gift of divination than his fame spread far and wide. He was sought after by the gentry throughout the length and breadth of the land, and no special assembly of theirs was complete unless Coinneach Odhar was amongst them. Being born on the lands of Seaforth, in the Lews, he was more associated with that family than with any other in the country, and he latterly removed to the neighbourhood of Loch Ussie, on the Brahan estate, where he worked as a common labourer on a neighbouring farm. He was very shrewd and clear-headed, for one in his menial position; was always ready with a smart answer, and if any attempted to raise the laugh at his expense, seldom or ever did he fail to turn it against his tormentors.

There are various other versions of the manner in which he became possessed of the power of divination. According to one – His mistress, the farmer's wife, was

*Scotland's Nostradamus*

unusually exacting with him, and he, in return, continually teased, and, on many occasions, expended much of his natural wit upon her, much to her annoyance and chagrin. Latterly, his conduct became so unbearable that she decided upon disposing of him in a manner which would save her any future annoyance. On one occasion, his master having sent him away to cut peats, which in those days were, as they now are in more remote districts, the common article of fuel, it was necessary to send him his dinner, he being too far from the house to come home to his meals, and the farmer's wife so far carried out her intention of destroying him, that she poisoned his dinner. It was somewhat late in arriving, and the future prophet feeling exhausted from his honest exertions in his masters interest and from want of food, lay down on the heath and fell into a heavy slumber. In this position he was suddenly awakened by feeling something cold in his breast; which on examination he found to be a small white stone, with a hole through the centre. He looked through it, when a vision appeared to him which revealed the treachery and diabolical intention of his mistress. To test the truth of the vision, he gave the dinner intended for himself to his faithful collie; the poor brute writhed, and died soon after in the greatest agony.

The following version is supplied by Mr. Macintyre, teacher, Arpafeelie: – Although the various accounts as to the manner in which Coinneach Odhar became gifted with second-sight differ in some respects, yet they generally agree in this, that it was acquired while he was engaged in the humble occupation of cutting peats or divots, which were in his day, and still are in many places, used as fuel throughout the Highlands of Scotland. On the occasion referred to, being somewhat fatigued, he lay down, resting his head upon a little knoll, and waited the arrival of his wife with his dinner, whereupon he fell fast asleep. On awaking, he felt something hard under his head, and examining the cause of the uneasiness, discovered a small round stone with a hole through the middle. He picked it up, and looking through it, saw by the aid of this prophetic stone that his wife was coming to him with a dinner consisting of sowans and milk, polluted, though unknown to her, in a manner which, as well as several other particulars connected with it, we forbear to mention. But Coinneach found that though this stone was the means by which a supernatural power had been conferred upon him, it had, on its very first application, deprived him of the sight of that eye with which he looked through it, and he continued ever afterwards *cam*, or blind of an eye.

It would appear from this account that the intended murderer made use of the Seer's wife to convey the poison to her own husband, thus adding to her diabolical and murderous intention, by making her who would feel the loss the keenest, the medium by which her husband was to lose his life.

~·~·~

According to Mackenzie, the Brahan Seer

> is beyond comparison the most distinguished of all our Highland Seers, and his prophecies have been known throughout the whole country for

*The Legend*

more than two centuries. The popular faith in them has been, and still continues to be, strong and wide-spread. Sir Walter Scott, Sir Humphrey Davy, Mr. Morritt, Lockhart, and other eminent contemporaries of the 'Last of the Seaforths' firmly believed in them. Many of them were well known, and recited from generation to generation, centuries before they were fulfilled. Some of them have been fulfilled in our own day, and many are still unfulfilled.

In his account the Clach dated the most celebrated of the Seer's prophecies – that of 'Seaforth's Doom', which foretold how the last of his house who would be deaf and dumb and whose sons would predecease him – to the middle of the seventeenth century. The story was supposedly uttered at Brahan Castle, the chief seat of the Seaforth chiefs of Clan Mackenzie, near Dingwall, after the Seer had been condemned to death by Lady Seaforth for informing her, by virtue of his second sight, that her husband had been unfaithful while in Paris. Before he was famously burned to death in a spiked barrel of tar on Chanonry Point, near Fortrose on the Black Isle, Coinneach declared to Lady Seaforth that he would go to Heaven, but she would never reach it. As a sign of this, he also foretold that when he was burned, a raven and a dove would hasten towards his ashes. If the dove was the first to arrive it would be proved his hope was well founded. And so it was, and so also his prediction regarding the future fate of the House of Seaforth was shown to have been correct when Lord Seaforth died in 1815 and the elder male line of the Mackenzies came to an end.

In the following chapters I shall explore the historical background behind these popular oral legends that Hugh Miller and Alexander Mackenzie first recorded for the benefit of the wider world in the nineteenth century and whose stories largely dovetail. In doing so, I will attempt to explain why so many people living in the relatively enlightened nineteenth and twentieth centuries appear to have believed what to us today would seem extremely far-fetched fairy stories.

# Second Sight in the Highlands and its Background

Prophecy has had a long history. The earliest source that mentions sibyls was by Heraclitus, around 500 BC, when he described how the 'sibyl with frenzied lips, uttering words mirthless, unembellished unperfumed, penetrates through a thousand years with her voice'. Her oracular utterances were said to have been delivered in a state of delirium owing to the gases arising from the floor of the shrine of the temple at Delphi. Both Julius Caesar and Tacitus recorded that the gift of forecasting the future was especially well-known to exist among the Germanic races; while the earliest extant Scandinavian literature celebrates the 'Song of the prophetess', known as the *Voluspa*. We are also familiar with those of the Bible, and later with Shakespeare's Three Weird Sisters in *MacBeth*. But perhaps the most common seer that Coinneach *Odhar* has been compared to is Nostradamus, who does indeed bear comparison in some respects. While I shall show that the methodology for predicting the future that was claimed by Nostradamus was quite different from that which the Seer was purported to have practised, there were notable similarities in the nature of his prophecies, and there are indeed a number of particular comparisons that are worth our attention.

A protégé of the French Queen Catherine de' Medici, Michel de Nostradame, whose name is usually Latinised as Nostradamus, was a French astrologer, apothecary and reputed seer, who is best known for his book *Les Prophéties*, which was published in 1555. This was a collection of 942 poetic quatrains, allegedly predicting future occurrences: in particular 'divers calamities, weepings and mornings' and 'civil sedition and mutination of the lowest against the highest'. These included such disasters as plagues, earthquakes, wars, floods, invasions, murders, droughts and battles. A major underlying theme that ran through Nostradamus's prophecies was an impending invasion of Europe by Muslim forces from farther east and south, headed by the expected Antichrist, famously originally foretold in the Bible's Book of Revelation. More famous today, however, are the claims, for example, that he predicted the Great Fire of London, the French Revolution, the rise of both Napoleon and of Adolf Hitler, both world wars and the nuclear destruction of Hiroshima and Nagasaki. Even more recently, popular authors have claimed that the sixteenth-century French seer predicted such major newsworthy events as the Apollo moon landing in 1969, the Space Shuttle *Challenger* disaster in 1986, the death of Diana, Princess of Wales in 1997 and the September 11 attacks on the World Trade Center in 2001.

In the years since the publication of *Les Prophéties*, Nostradamus has attracted many apologists, who, along with some of the popular press, credit him with having accurately predicted many such major world events. Of course, more academic approaches have rejected the notion that Nostradamus had any genuine supernatural prophetic abilities and maintain that the associations made between world events and Nostradamus's quatrains are the result of (sometimes deliberate) misinterpretations or mistranslations. These academics also argue that Nostradamus's predictions are characteristically vague, meaning they could be applied to virtually anything, and are useless for determining whether their author had any real prophetic powers. Research suggests that much of his prophetic work paraphrases collections of ancient end-of-the-world prophecies (mainly Bible-based), supplemented with references to historical events and anthologies of omens, and then inserts those into the future, sometimes with the aid of comparative astrology, although astrology itself is mentioned only twice in Nostradamus's *Preface*, while at one point he specifically attacked astrologers.

Despite such strong criticism, following the attack on the World Trade Center on 11 September 2001 there was renewed interest in Nostradamus and his prophecies. One anonymous email message that was widely circulated in the United States claimed that Nostradamus foretold the destruction in some detail and included the following quatrain:

> In the City of God there will be a great thunder,
> Two Brothers torn apart by Chaos,
> While the fortress endures, the great leader will succumb.
> The third big war will begin when the big city is burning.

It was claimed that the 'two brothers' refers to the Twin Towers of the World Trade Center, the 'fortress' refers to the Pentagon, the 'great leader' refers to President Bush and 'the big city' refers to New York. Other people then added even more lines to it, supposedly from Nostradamus, as the message made its way around the Internet. One version described 'metal birds' crashing into 'two tall statues'; others referred to 'the city of York'; and another widespread message included these lines:

> In the year of the new century and nine months,
> From the sky will come a great King of Terror.
> The sky will burn at forty-five degrees.
> Fire approaches the great new city.

It was argued that the references to fire and terror from the sky fit with the aerial attack; and New York City is around 40° 5' N latitude (relatively close to 'forty-five degrees'). The date is also not far off. Additionally, several other quatrains refer to an Antichrist figure called Mabus, who supposedly will start a world war. The letters in Mabus can be rearranged to spell Usam B, leading some to believe Nostradamus saw the coming of Osama bin Laden.

*Scotland's Nostradamus*

More recently, since the terrorist attack on the World Trade Center, there was one rumour circulating in 2020 that Nostradamus had accurately predicted the COVID-19 pandemic; while his supposed foretelling that a 'feeble man' would 'rule the western world with a jezebel' after the plague was taken by some Americans to be a reference to either Donald Trump or to Joe Biden, depending on their political persuasion.

~·~·~

In the sixteenth century, the prophecies of Nostradamus were by no means an isolated phenomenon. When I was writing up my university dissertation at Cambridge in the autumn of 1986 about Francis Humberston Mackenzie (who, as we have seen, was the subject of the Brahan Seer's most celebrated prophecy of 'Seaforth's Doom'), I happened to attend a visiting lecture by the eminent Oxford historian Sir Keith Thomas. Having admired Thomas's seminal *Religion and the Decline of Magic*, I made a particular point of hearing him speak, even though the subject of his lecture did not coincide with the specific syllabus I was then studying. In Thomas's wide-ranging analysis of early modern Europe, he revealed how prophecies of one kind or another were employed in virtually every rebellion or popular rising that disturbed the Tudor state, for example. The Spanish Armada gave retrospective justification to the widely disseminated forecast, attributed to the German astronomer Johannes Müller von Königsberg (better known as Regiomontanus), that 1588 would be an *annus mirabilis*; while prophecies had circulated among northern Roman Catholic supporters of Mary, Queen of Scots in England since the beginning of Elizabeth's reign and included a copy of one owned by the conspirator Anthony Babington of a prophecy attributed to Merlin. Once deemed a rather exotic maverick and intellectual outlier, Elizabeth I's colourful crystal-gazing astrologer John Dee is now being recognised by historians as having fulfilled a role at the very heart of the Elizabethan court, and to have been a figure of national significance in an age with a belief system very different from our own today. Both Elizabeth and her politically astute chief adviser William Cecil Lord Burghley employed Dee to counter the predictions of Nostradamus, which the French used in their propaganda against the English queen. In the following century the Interregnum and the Restoration of Charles II were discovered to have been foreshadowed by ancient prophetic utterances and we know from Pepys that interest in Mother Shipton, the sixteenth century soothsayer from North Yorkshire, was renewed with the Fire of London in 1666, when he quoted Prince Rupert's remark that 'now Shipton's prophecy was out'. As Thomas observed:

> This was also a period when Nostradamus resumed his career as a prognosticator of English history. Later his utterances were to be adapted to fit the American War of Independence and the French revolution. Other prophets were invoked to explain the 1688 Revolution and the triumph of William III. The Jacobites also had their prophecies. As late

8

as 1745 the Duke of Gordon was identified with the Cock of the North mentioned in the fourteenth-century prophecy of Bridlington.

Of particular significance to the wider European historical context in which the actors involved in the Brahan Seer's story can be placed was the role prophecy played during the Thirty Years' War. In the second quarter of the seventeenth century, the conquests of Gustavus Adolphus were justified by a reference to a prediction about the 'Lion from the North' destined to defeat the Eagle (the Habsburg's symbol), which was said to fulfil Paracelsus's 'prognostication' that referenced the Book of Jeremiah 5:6. In her fascinating exploration of the Scientific Revolution, entitled *The Rosicrucian Enlightenment*, Frances Yates discusses a curious book called 'Light in Darkness', or *Lux in tenebris*, which contains the outpourings of three prophets, three visionaries who claimed to make revelations about coming apocalyptic events, the end of the reign of the Antichrist, and the return of light after the darkness of his rule. One of the prophets, Christopher Kotter, promised a future restoration of Frederick of the Palatinate to the Kingdom of Bohemia. A variety of visions by Kotter saw four lions – the heraldic symbols of the Palatinate, of Bohemia, of Great Britain and of the Netherlands – bringing down an Eagle. It was the Second Earl of Seaforth's brother-in-law, Lord Reay, who raised a regiment to fight for Frederick and Gustavus Adolphus's cause at this time, in which served the Earl's brother, Captain Thomas Mackenzie of Pluscarden, alongside the author's ancestor Murdo McKenzie as chaplain, together with a number of other Mackenzies and Munros from Easter Ross. The Second Earl had a particularly notable devotion to Frederick's wife, Elizabeth, the sister of the British King Charles I and former Queen of Bohemia, who was a regular correspondent of Seaforth, referring to him in a letter to the Marquis of Montrose as 'My Highlander'; on Seaforth's death 'the Royall Elizabeth giving her speciall direction of the forme and manner of his burial'.

Prophecy was employed in this period, not only further afield in Europe, but also more widely still, across the Atlantic. In Spanish America, prophecies circulating among the Indians prepared the ground for both the invasions of the Spanish *conquistador*, Hernán Cortés in the sixteenth century, and that of Cromwell in the seventeenth. Thus, prior to the arrival of the Spaniards, beginning in 1509, Montezuma believed that there were eight omens predicting the end of the Aztec civilisation, which amounted to them as the end of the world. The last of eight omens in 1517 reported to Montezuma was the sighting of 'men with two heads', which were interpreted as the horse-back riding men of Juan de Grijalva's expedition. This, moreover, coincided with the arrival of Cortés on the traditional birthday of the Aztec god, Quetzalcoatl, which was during the year of the end of the fifty-two-year cycle of the Aztec calendar.

~·~·~

The most comparable recorded example of an instance of prophecy in the Highlands from the time in which the Brahan Seer was purported to have lived was

*Scotland's Nostradamus*

written down in the contemporary account known as the Wardlaw Manuscript by the Rev. James Fraser, minister of Wardlaw (now the parish of Kirkhill in Inverness-shire), a socially well-connected man who recorded contemporary life in Easter Ross and Inverness-shire and who died in 1705. The full title of this family history is *Chronicle of the Frasers, The Wardlaw Manuscript, entitled 'Polichronicon Se Policratica Temporum, or The True Genealogy of the Frasers' 916–1674.* One citation of a prophecy in this account has remarkable similarities to the prediction that the promising sons of the 'Last Seaforth' will predecease him and that his line will end. This prophecy both draws on Biblical precedents and, like Coinneach *Odhar*'s most celebrated prediction, foretells the fate of the chiefly family. It was made by Hugh Fraser, Seventh Lord Lovat (who was a cousin of the Third Earl of Seaforth via his mother, Catherine Mackenzie), on his deathbed in 1645. In the minister of Wardlaw's words, Hugh Fraser was 'a true prophet, and fortold me what is come to pass in my famely, and I must trust his predictions'. Quoting from Genesis 49.1, and Joshua 23.14, the Rev. James Fraser goes on to tell how 'My Lord called his children before the ministers, and gravely declares with Jacob, I call yow together my sones, gather yourselves together that I may tell yow that which shall befall yow in the last dayes. I shall say with Joshua, I go this day the way of all the earth.'

Lovat began by advising his sons to 'Be sober and temperat, chast and continent; as yow would wish others to doe, even the same doe ye. Fear God, honor the King, and medle not with those that are given to changes.' He then went on to predict,

> My sone Alexander, thou wilt be great, and have many advantages, and a happy, peaceable, flourishing time; but its my feare thow'el want mannagement and improvement: easiness and credulity is the bane of many. Give a deafe ear to sicophants; let not those gloworms hand on yow; what was your brothers ruin I am affraied may be thine [his two elder brothers, Simon and Hugh, had both recently died before reaching their twenties]; prepare to die young, for yow will never reach my days. My sone Tome, thou wilt wrestle with the world, but thowle be the man yet, live long and see many dayes. Since Lord Thomas his time thow wilt live longest; thow shalt have the name and honor, but little or no profit; but from thy loines shall they come who will doe great things. I see yow will die a violent death; but thy temperance and moderation shall lengthen thy days, for thou wilt not incline to excess. My sone James, thow art my youngest, thow wilt have projects, and curage to prosecut; thow wilt take a flight; thowl appeare upon the stage, and evanish, *filius noctis*, or *unius diei oriens et moriens*, thow'l be separat from thy bretheren. But Tomm shall survive yow all, and be the last of my famely. The very line will be almost [extinct?], yet at length their [line?], which had long lain buried in their own ashes, will yet begin to revive and flourish, being wearied of the

*Second Sight in the Highlands and its Background*

insulting tyranny of O.C. [Oliver Cromwell], begin to take fresh spirit, and to seeke one of their own native race to rule over them. I must go, but leave yow my sones, a ball to be tossed about in fortunes tennis court, but which your brother Hugh hath woven? Yow will see happy, serene, halcion days yet, when the sword is sheathed which now rages.

The minister of Wardlaw then concluded: 'After all these sentiments, reflections, expostulations, and declarations to his famely and friends, and many other excellent advices, which I had and heard from an eye and ear witnes, this good man dyed in peace at Lovat the 17 day of December, being Tusday, in the 55 yeare of his age, *anno Domini* 1645.'

~·~·~

The Rev. James Fraser is also valuable to us in telling of another local Highland prophecy that is more in keeping with the distinctively Highland nature of second sight that was much repeated in the seventeenth century. According to the Wardlaw Manuscript, when the Seventh Lord Lovat was staying at Dunrobin Castle in Sutherland, Sir John Sinclair of Dunbeath proposed marriage to Lovat's daughter, Catherine. Dunbeath being 'a harsh, unpleasant man', the 'young lady would not wild, but weept and mournd continually, full of greef and melancholy, and would often say she rather dye than marry Dunbeath'. However, when she was descending the hillside beneath the Castle, Catherine encountered a servant called Donald Glasshach (or Donald from Strathglass), who 'accosted Lady Kathrin, checking her severely for her willfulness, speaking in Irish to her (having no other language) *Cathrin, ha tu toishach* [you are a foolish woman], yow are unwise, marry the great Laird of Dunbeath, he will make yow a wealthy woman and leave yow happy, for I see a lord uppon each shoulder of yow, whom yow will marry after Dunbeath's death. This man had the second sight, and could forsee anything that happened about the place.' Donald Glasshach's prediction did indeed come to pass, since Catherine was persuaded to marry the Laird of Dunbeath, Lord Lovat staying on at Dunrobin until the marriage was consummated, and James Fraser was able to confirm that Catherine went on to 'have two lords after Dunbeath's death. I was in her house at Bervy, being Lady Arbuthnot, and after his death she married the famous and renouned Lord Fraser of Muchel, for I payed her a visit, living in the great house Carnbuilg in Buchan, being then Lady Fraser.'

In Scotland and the Scottish Highlands in particular, there was such a tradition of prophecies that had its own particular character. Rather than those predictions that I have described, that were largely founded on ancient religious texts, or astrological charts, the Highlands was famous for its individuals who claimed to possess the gift of 'second sight'. Different parts of Scotland celebrated their own particular local seers, such as *Mac a' Chreachair* in Barra, the White Lady of Lawers in Perthshire, and, in Isla, *Am Fiosaiche Ileach*, otherwise known as *Guala Chrosta.*, or simply as the Isla Seer. *The phantasm or vision seen by the seer is called in Gaelic taibhs (pronounced 'taish'); the person seeing it taibhsear; and the gift of vision, in addition to its name of second sight, is taibhsearachd' (a number of words in Galic referring to spirits and ghosts begin with the syllable 'ta').* In Francis Thompson's *The Supernatural Highlands*, published in 1999, he explains:

> The Gaelic word for second sight is *da-shealladh*, which means 'two sights', perhaps conveying the idea that a vision of the world of sense is one sight, but a vision of another world, populated by people living, but not within the actual sight of the seer, or living but in another time, is another, rarer, sight. Through this faculty, seers can 'see' the dead returned to earth, revisiting the physical world for some purpose, and wraiths, fetches, doubles or apparitions of the living, either in the present time or in a future time. These visions seem to fall into two general categories: those which involve living people, contemporary with the seer and often his or her own close friends or relations, who appear as wraiths and might be taken as 'precognition' – the ability to foretell events about to happen, and which do occur within a short time of the forecast; the other category contains visions of events which often involve those not yet born and which are more difficult both to explain in contemporary language, images and meanings, and also to establish their time. The latter sights are contained in the visions of the true seer: the person able to project far into the future, and, though he or she has no means of knowing whether the vision will come to pass, are sufficiently convinced of their gift that the details of it are set down and recorded.

As we shall see, the traditions associated with the Brahan Seer suggest that he was believed to possess both forms of second sight.

In fact, a great deal of interest has been taken in Highland second sight for some time, and many cases have been described, ever since the second half of the seventeenth century, by such men of learning as the Welsh-born Oxford naturalist, linguist and Celtic scholar Edward Lhuyd, who among other achievements was also responsible for the first scientific description and naming of what we would now recognise as a dinosaur. Thanks to funding from his friend Sir Isaac Newton, Lhuyd was able to travel widely in order to investigate his various interests and, in the autumn of 1699, he visited Argyllshire, describing some of the characteristic prognostications he encountered there as follows:

> Men with the second sight see a man with a light like the light of the glow-worm, or with fish [scales] over his hair and his clothes, if he is to be drowned; bloody if he is to be wounded; in his shroud if he is to die in his bed; with his sweetheart on his right hand if he is to marry [her]. But on his left hand if he is not to win his sweetheart.

Other English intellectuals and luminaries of the Royal Society who remarked on this phenomenon included John Aubrey, Robert Wodrow and Robert Boyle.

They also began to perceive that the Gaelic-speaking Highlands of Scotland contained a remarkably interesting repository of customs and beliefs, and they actively began to gather information about them. This information given to them about second sight included the following points:

1. Even by 1700 it was said that it was not so common as it used to be; it was a 'trouble to most of them who are subject to it, and they would be rid of it [at] any rate if they could'.It was not a gift acquired in consequence of any pact with the Evil One, being of its nature spontaneous (this was a matter of importance in the seventeenth century, when trials for witchcraft still occurred in Scotland: had it been held that the seers owed their powers to any pacts, they could have been in serious trouble).

2. Whether the gift of second sight was hereditary or not is something on which the authorities were not in agreement.

It was then in 1703 that Martin Martin made the most extensive analysis of Highland second sight to date. In his *A Description of the Western Islands of Scotland*, Martin defined the phenomenon as follows:

The Second-sight is a singular Faculty of Seeing an otherwise invisible Object, without an previous Means us'd by the Person that sees it for that end; the Vision makes such a lively impression upon the Seers, that they neither see nor think of anything else, except the Vision, as long as it continues; and then they appear pensive or jovial, according to the Object which was represented to them.

He also observed that *'the gift of second sight was not looked upon as something to be envied or desired. Frequently seers wished they had no such gift, but often, perhaps because it ran in the family, they were dogged with it ... The gift was not voluntarily controlled, rather it came and went without the option of the seer'*. The Seers, Martin explained, are generally illiterate, and well meaning People, and altogether devoid of design, nor could I ever learn that any of them made the least gain by it, neither is it reputable among 'em to have that Faculty: because the People of the Isles are not so credulous as to believe implicitly, before the thing foretold is accomplished; but when it actually comes to pass afterwards, it is not in their power to deny it, without offering violence to their Senses or Reason.

For Martin, the fact that no learned man had come up with a valid explanation to account for second sight was no reason to question its existence: 'If every thing for which the Learned are not able to give satisfying account be condemn'd as impossible, we may find other things generally believed that must be rejected as false by this Rule', words that anticipate what Carl Jung wrote of the 'shallow positivism' with which Freud rejected the possibility of psychic phenomena two hundred years later.

*Scotland's Nostradamus*

Martin also pointed out that the faculty was not confined to one corner of the Hebrides, nor even to the Western Isles themselves, but was also known to other places, such as Wales, the Isle of Man and Holland. Indeed, in his *A Tour in Scotland*, published in 1769, Thomas Pennant was to write: 'Every country has its prophets .... And the Highlands their Kenneth Oaur.' This is, to my knowledge, the first historical reference to Coinneach *Odhar* that describes him as a seer.

Martin went on to discuss this faculty, giving about thirty cases, mostly from the Isle of Skye, and an account of the significance of the signs perceived by the seers, such as had been given earlier by Lhuyd. Martin outlined a number of patterns that he had observed when gathering information regarding second sight, which are worth summarising here:

1. When a shroud was perceived about one, it was a sure prognostic of death. The time was judged according to the height of it about the person. If not seen above the middle, death was not expected for the space of a year, and perhaps some months longer; and as it was frequently seen to ascend higher towards the head, death was concluded to be at hand within a few days, if not hours.

2. If a woman was seen standing at a man's left hand, it was a presage that she would be his wife, whether they were married to others, or unmarried at the time of the apparition.

3. If two or three women were seen at once standing near to a man's left hand, she that was next to him would undoubtedly be his wife first, and so on, whether all three, or the man, were single or married at the time of the vision or not.

4. It was usual for the Seers to see any man that was shortly to arrive at the house. If unknown to the Seer he would give such a description of the person he saw as to make him to be at once recognised upon his arrival. On the other hand, if the Seer knew the person he saw in the vision, he would tell his name, and know by the expression of his countenance whether he came in a good or bad humour.

5. The Seers often saw houses, gardens and trees in places where there were none, but in the course of time these places became covered with them.

6. To see a spark of fire fall upon one's arm or breast was a forerunner of a dead child to be seen in the arms of those persons. To see a seat empty when one was sitting on it was a presage of that person's immediate death.

The folklorist Isabel Grant writes, 'The visions of people who had the Second Sight were largely concerned with a future death.' The prediction of future death

*Second Sight in the Highlands and its Background*

was a major concern for the pre-industrial Scots: a wide variety of signs and portents of death were known and eagerly watched for, including visions of funeral processions or coffins being made; the eerie sound of glasses rattling at wakes; apparitions of the wraiths or physical doubles of those soon to die, encounters with crows or ravens, for example. And, as Emma Wilby explains in *The Visions of Isobel Gowdie*, death-divination was not delivered as hysterical doommongering, but as precise and considered assessments based on specific visible signs. With regard to the seer's ability to determine the time of a man's demise by the position of his death shroud, Robert Kirk, in his collections of Scottish folklore made from 1691 to 1692, published in 1815 under the title *The Secret Commonwealth of Elves, Fauns and Fairies*, noted that the seer saw a winding-shroud creep up on a walking healthfull persons legs, till it came to the knee, and afterwards it came to the middle, then to the shoulders, and at last over the head, which was visible to no other person. And by observing the spaces of time betwixt the several stages, he easily guess'd how long the man was to live who wore the shroud, for when it approached his head, he told that such a person was ripe for the Grave.

Two accounts of Highland second sight that I encountered when researching my own particular ancestors took my attention, since they directly relate to my family's members during this period. A letter that was published by Martin Martin, dated 'Old Aberdene May 4 – 94', is from James Garden, Professor of Theology at King's College, to the Royal Society's John Aubrey. It explained how Andrew MacPherson of Cluny, in pursuit of the hand in marriage of the Mackenzie Laird of Gairloch's daughter, had travelled to Gairloch in Wester Ross. When Lady Gairloch made the observation to her attendants, 'that yonder was Clunie, going to see his Mistris', at which point it was said that one who possessed the second sight in her company 'replied and said: if yon be he unless he marie within 6 moneths, he'l never marie'. When the lady asked how he knew that, he said 'very well, for I see him saith be, all inclosed in his winding-sheet, except his nostrils & his mouth, which will also close up withing 6 moneths'. As Professor Garden explained to Aubrey, this came about, just as the man had foretold, so that within the said time he died, and his brother, Duncan MacPherson, succeeded to the Cluny estate.

Another account sourced from my own forebears concerns Bishop Murdo McKenzie's nephew, Alexander McKenzie, who was a tenant of their cousin, Donald MacKay, First Lord Reay in Strathnaver in Sutherland. It recounts that two men were in Alexander's house discoursing by the fireside when one of them began to weep and cry out regarding a particular gentlewoman who lived five or six miles away who had been for some days before in a fever, saying: 'Alas! Such a woman is either dead or presently expiring.' But, the other man, who was a 'gentleman, being somewhat better expert in their facultie' was able to contradict him. 'O saith the gentleman I see her as well as you doe; but do you not see her linens all wett which is her sweat, she being presently cooling of the feaver.' It was

*Scotland's Nostradamus*

Alexander's son, the Rev. Hector McKenzie, minister of Inverness, who conveyed this account to Professor Garden.

~·~·~

A renewed interest in second sight can be found half a century after Martin, in both the correspondence between Henry Baker and Archibald Blair in the late 1740s; then in 'Theophilus Insulanus', aka the Rev. Donald McLeod of Hamer in Skye's *A Treatise on the Second Sight, Dreams and Apparitions*, published in 1763. Perhaps more famously, though, it received the particular attention of Dr Samuel Johnson and his biographer, James Boswell, when the two men toured the Western Isles in the autumn of 1773.

Under the date of 7 September 1773 in Boswell's *Journal of a Tour to the Hebrides*, Boswell recorded that he and Johnson were at Corrichatachin, in the Broadford district of Skye and wrote that Johnson inquired here, if there were any remains of the Second-Sight. Mr Macpherson, minister of Slate, said, he was resolved not to believe it, because it was founded on no principle. Johnson – 'There are many things then, which we are sure are true, that you will not believe. What principle is there, why a loadstone attracts iron? why an egg produces a chicken by heat? why a tree grows upwards, when the natural tendency of all things is downwards? Sir, it depends upon the degree of evidence that you have.' Young Mr Mackinnon mentioned one Mackenzie, who is still alive; who had often fainted in his presence, and when he recovered, mentioned visions which had been presented to him. He told Mr Mackinnon, that at such a place he should meet a funeral, and that such and such people would be the bearers, naming four; and three weeks afterwards he saw what Mackenzie had predicted.

Boswell further recounted how Mrs Mackinnon, who is a daughter of old [MacDonald of] Kingsburgh, told us that her father was one day riding in Skye, and some women, who were at work in a field on the side of the road, said to him, they had heard two 'taischs' (that is two voices of persons about to die), and what was remarkable, one of them was an 'English taisch', which they never heard before. When he returned, he at that very place met two funerals, and one of them was that of a woman who had come from the mainland, and could speak only English. This, she remarked, made a great impression on her father.

On 16 September, wrote Boswell,

Macquarrie told us a strong instance of the Second-Sight. He had gone to Edinburgh, and taken a man-servant along with him. An old woman, who was in the house, said one day, 'Macquarrie will be at home to-morrow, and will bring two gentlemen with him, and his servant had a new red and green livery', which Macquarrie had bought for him in Edinburgh, upon a sudden thought, not having the least intention when he left home to put his servant in livery; so that the old woman could not have had heard any previous mention of it. This, he assured us, was a true story.

16

*Second Sight in the Highlands and its Background*

In his *A Journey to the Western Islands of Scotland*, at first Johnson speaks with apparent scepticism in the following lines: 'Strong reasons for incredulity will readily occur. This faculty of seeing things out of sight is local, and commonly useless. It is a breach of the common order of things, without any visible reason or perceptible benefit. It is ascribed only to a people very little enlightened; and among them, for the most part, to the mean and the ignorant.' Yet he was nonetheless to come to the following view:

> To the confidence of these objections it may be replied, that by presuming to determine what is fit, and what is beneficial, they presuppose more knowledge of the universal system than man has attained; and therefore depend upon principles too complicated and extensive for our comprehension; and that there can be no security in the consequence, when the premises are not understood; that the Second-Sight is only wonderful because it is rare, for considered in itself, it involves no more difficulty than dreams, or perhaps than the regular exercise of the cogitative faculty; that a general opinion of communicative impulses, or visionary representations, has prevailed in all ages and all nations; that particular instances have been given, with such evidence as neither Bacon nor Bayle has been able to resist; that sudden impressions, which the event has verified, have been felt by more than own or publish them; that the Second-Sight of the Hebrides implies only the local frequency for a power which is nowhere totally unknown; and that where we are unable to decide by antecedent reasons, we must be content to yield to the force of testimony.

By pretension to Second-Sight, no profit was ever sought or gained. It is an involuntary affection, in which neither hope nor fear are known to have any part. Those who profess to feel it do not boast of it as a privilege, nor are considered by others as advantageously distinguished. They have no temptation to feign; and their hearers have no motive to encourage the imposture.

General MacLeod, one of Johnson's hosts on his travels, remarked in his *Memoirs* that Johnson 'listened to all the fables of the nature which abound in the Highlands; and though no one fact was so well vouched as to command its particular belief, he held that the thing was not impossible; and that the number of facts alleged a favourable presumption'. And this was a judgement that was confirmed when Dr Johnson concluded in his *A Journey to the Western Islands of Scotland*: 'To collect sufficient testimonies for the satisfaction of the publick, or of ourselves, would have required more time than we could bestow ... I never could advance my curiosity to conviction; but came away at last only willing to believe.'

Nevertheless, by 1785, in his own *Journal of a Tour* to the Hebrides, Boswell chose to distance himself from any earlier indication of open-mindedness when he wrote:

17

*Scotland's Nostradamus*

> I own, I returned from the *Hebrides* with a considerable degree of faith in
> the many stories of that kind which I heard with a too easy acquiescence,
> without any close examination of the evidence: but, since that time,
> my belief in those stories has been much weakened, by reflecting on
> the careless inaccuracy of narrative in common matters, from which
> we may certainly conclude that there may be the same in what is more
> extraordinary.

And the phenomenon was still well recognised as a particularly Highland trait by 1822, when the 'most known and the most general superstition of the Gaels is that which they call *Taishitaraugh* [*Taibhhseadaireachd*]', according to the Swiss scientist Albertine-Adrienne Necker de Saussure in his *A Voyage to the Hebrides*, published in 1822. De Saussure, who was sceptical about the faculty himself, quoted Martin Martin's description of the seers and their visions in his book and mentions, as did Thomas Pennant before him, what was one of the most famous cases of second sight, which is that of Lord President Forbes foretelling at the time of the Battle of Prestonpans that the Jacobite rising would end at Culloden.

Interest in Highland second sight then received something of a further renaissance in 1894 when, as reported by the *Oban Times*:

> We understand that several members of the Society of Psychical Research
> are at present on a tour of the West Highlands and Islands collecting
> information from the natives in regard to that peculiar faculty said to be
> possessed by many people, especially in the Highlands, and popularly
> known as 'second sight', as well as kindred subjects.

The Society circulated some 2,000 potential individuals in the region whom they thought might offer some information on the occurrence, belief, current prevalence and practice of the gift. The Society of Psychical Research thus had the time, which Dr Johnson lacked in the previous century, to satisfy itself and the public by launching a thorough empirical study, and those cases that Martin had described in 1703 are very similar to those findings that were recorded by Father Allan McDonald from November 1895 to June 1897, and published in John L. Campbell and Trevor H. Hall's book *Strange Things*. Although the investigation came up against a number of obstacles, and the Society eventually failed to produce the promised, and eagerly awaited, reports of the Second Sight Enquiry in the Highlands, Francis Thompson concluded in 1999: 'Even so, the Society deserved credit for recognising, in its role and status of a learned body, that there existed interesting facets of Highland oral culture, however folk-based, and that this was worthy of serious investigation.'

As late as 1909 the popular writer Andrew Lang wrote in his introduction to that year's edition of Alexander Mackenzie's *Prophecies*:

> I can unblushingly confess the belief that there probably are occasional
> instances of second sight, that is, of 'premonitions.' I know too many

examples among persons of my acquaintance, mostly Lowlanders or English, to have any doubt about the matter. Hegel was of the same opinion, and was not ashamed to include second sight in his vast philosophic system. As to the modus of second sight, 'how it is done,' in fact, I have no theory. If there is a psychical element in man, if there is something more than a mechanical result of physical processes in nerve, brain, and blood, then we cannot set any limit to the range of 'knowledge super-normally acquired.' 'Time and space are only hallucinations,' as a philosopher has audaciously remarked. They may be transcended by the spirit in man, *et voilà pourquoi votre fille est muette!* This explanation, of course, is of the vaguest, but I have no better to suggest.

Even today, as I write, the *Electric Scotland* website, which is currently online, is evidently unable to avoid the, not altogether dismissive, conclusion, 'There are few persons, if any, who pretend to this faculty, and the belief in it is almost generally exploded. Yet it cannot be denied that apparent proofs of its existence have been adduced which have staggered minds not prone to superstition.' How, then, can this strong and longstanding belief in second sight and in the Brahan Seer's prophecies be explained?

# Coinneach *Odhar* and Scotland's Witch-Craze

William Matheson, the eminent twentieth-century folklorist, was the first to question core elements in the Brahan Seer's story as it had been published prior to the twentieth century, when he pointed out that there was in fact a genuine 'Keanoch/Coinneach *Odhar*', who was mentioned in a Scottish Parliament writ for his arrest, dated 1577, and who is again on record in 1578 as the 'principal Enchanter' in Katherine Ross's trial for witchcraft. Albeit that the two known records that exist concerning him date from the sixteenth, rather than the sixteenth, century, and that his fate is not known, the interesting point about him is that three of his accomplices, who were accused of witchcraft, were, just like the Brahan Seer, burned for their part in the crime at Chanonry. In the light of this, he also questioned Hugh Miller and Alexander Mackenzie's versions of the story with their alleged tradition of the Seer's association with an Earl and Countess of Seaforth, which were titles that did not exist until 1623; the traditions on which these folklorists were relying were reputed to be those that were preserved and transmitted by the 'tradition-bearers' in Gaelic, while the title of Earl of Seaforth (which in Gaelic would be *Iarla Shìoford*) was not employed among Gaelic speakers, who instead continued to use what was to them the much more significant designation *Mac Coinnich*, which was the 'style' of the Mackenzie chiefs for Gaelic speakers over the centuries.

A commission of justiciary, dated at Holyroodhouse, 25 October 1577, to Walter Urquhart, Sheriff of Cromarty, and Robert Munro of Foulis, authorised them to search for and apprehend six men and twenty-six women, charged with the diabolical practices of magic, enchantment, murder, homicide and other offences within the bounds of the Earldom of Ross, the lordship of Ardmanach (the Black Isle), and other parts of the Sheriffdom of Inverness. The places of abode of those charged were Daan, Assynt (in Easter Ross), Glastullich, Ardross, Chanonry, Nigg, Tain, Logie Easter, Calrossie and Ord House, all places in Easter Ross. Among those to be apprehended were Thomas McAnemoir McAllan McHenrik, alias Cassindonisch, Mariota Neynaine McAlester, alias Loskoir Longert, and Cristina Milla, daughter of Robert Milla.

The last name on the list is Keanoch Ower (Coinneach *Odhar*), described as 'the leading or principal enchantress' (presumably the clerk who drew up the document knew no Gaelic and failed to realise that Keanoch was a man's name).

The second commission, also dated at Hoyroodouse, was three months later, on 23 January 1578, appointing Lachlan Mackintosh of Dunachton, Colin

Mackenzie of Kintail, Robert Munro of Foulis, Walter Urquhart, Sherriff of Cromarty, Hugh Rose of Kilravock and Alexander Falconer of Halkertson, justiciaries within the bounds of the earldoms of Ross and Moray and lordship of Ardmanach, and other parts within the sheriffdoms of Inverness, Elgin, Forres and Nairn, to apprehend, imprison and try Kenneth, alias Kennoch Owir, principal or leader of the art of magic ... Neyneane Makallester alias Losgoloukart [*Losgadh-lùchairt*], and Marjory Millar, daughter of Robert Millar, smith in Assynt, and all other men and women using and exercising the diabolical, iniquitous and odious crimes of the art of magic, sorcery and incantations within the said bounds who shall be named by the ministers within the bounds of foresaid, each for his own parish.

This woman appears prominently, sometimes as Marjory and sometimes as Marion Neyne McAllester alias Laskie Loncart, in the records of a particularly celebrated witchcraft trial: that of Katherine Ross, Lady Munro of Foulis, in 1590. (William Matheson observed that 'Losgoloukart' was a nickname that could be translated as 'Burn-the-castle', and presumably referred to some exploit in which she was supposed to be involved: in the south of Scotland and elsewhere similar appellatives are attached to the names of people accused of witchcraft.)

The witchcraft trial of Katherine Ross, which was notorious at the time, took place at Chanonry (otherwise known as Fortrose) Cathedral, on 22 July 1590. Katherine was the second wife of Robert Munro, the chief of the Munro Clan, whose close Munro cousins I recently discovered among my own ancestors. Those direct ancestors of mine must have been heavily impacted by the dramatic events at that time. Katherine was accused of using poison and witchcraft in 1576 and 1577. Her intended victims were Marjory Campbell, the young wife of Katherine's brother; George Ross of Balnagown; and her stepson, Robert Munro. This was, as seems most likely, to aid her brother George Ross to gain possession of the highly desirable Munro of Foulis lands. While a colourful account was also given by Sir Walter Scott in his *Letters on Demonology and Witchcraft*, Robert Pitcairn's 1833 *Criminal Trials in Scotland* contains more precise details of twenty-nine accusations against Katherine Ross, where she is accused of consulting with fairies and using witchcraft and poisons in her attempts to kill her proposed victims. The opening statement of the trial reads as follows: 'Katherine Ross Lady Fowlis, you are accused, of the unnatural abusing of yourself, contrary the laws of God, and exercising and using yourself most ungodly and wickedly, by perverse enchantments, Witchcraft, Devilry, Incantations and Sorcery, with the craft of poison.'

It is perhaps notable that Scott, who was, of course, part of Francis Lord Seaforth's circle and was known to have believed in the fulfilment of 'Seaforth's Doom', gave us the background to the trial as follows:

Katherine Munro, Lady Fowlis, by birth Katherine Ross of Balnagowan, of high rank, both by her own family and that of her husband, who was

*Scotland's Nostradamus*

the fifteenth Baron of Fowlis, and chief of the warlike clan of Munro, had a stepmother's quarrel with Robert Munro, eldest son of her husband, which she gratified by forming a scheme for compassing his death by unlawful arts. Her proposed advantage in this was, that the widow of Robert, when he was thus removed, should marry with her brother, George Ross of Balnagowan; and for this Purpose, her sister-in-law, the present Lady Balnagowan, was also to be removed.

The first accusation against Katherine Ross took place at the house of Christian Ross Malcomson. Katherine, together with the 'Tain Witch Marjory Nein McAllister, alias Lonskie Loncart', was accused of attempting to cast a voodoo-like curse on her intended victims:

> In the first, you are accused, for the making of two images of clay, in company with the said Christian Ross and Marjory Nein McAllister alias Lonskie Loncart, in the said Christian Ross's western chamber in Canorth; one made for the destruction and consumption of the young Laird of Fowlis, and the other for the young Lady Balnagown; to the effect that one of them should be put at the Bridgend of Fowlis, and the other at Ardmore, for the destruction of the said young Laird and Lady: And this should have been performed at Alhallowmes, in the year of God 1577: These two pictures, being set on the north side of the chamber, the said Loskie Loncart took two elf arrowheads and gave one to you Katherine, and another the said Christian Ross Malcomson held in her own hand; and you shot twice with the said arrowhead, at the said Lady Balnagown, and Loskie Loncart shot three shot at the said young Laird of Fowlis.

The spell, apparently, did not have the desired result, even though more 'elf arrowheads' (which we know today as in reality Neolithic flint arrowheads) were purchased, and another attempt at a similar spell was made. Many of the other accusations concern Katherine's attempts to make, purchase and use poisons. She was accused of buying various poisons and a 'box of witchcraft' from William MacGillivray and sending a jar of poison with her nurse to attempt to poison many of the leading figures of the Munro Clan and their young children. These attempts were said to have only resulted in 'the cruel slaughter, by your craft of poison, of Marie Murdoch More's daughter, your nurse, who died after the tasting from the jar of poison, which was sent by you'.

While the contemporary take on the crime may have invoked witchcraft, Katherine's methods in reality do not appear to have been dissimilar to those with which we are familiar in more recent cases of murder, in which the most readily available forms of poison were employed. One of the last accusations is the poisoning of the dinner party being hosted at Ardmore by young Lady Balnagown:

> That Katherine Neynday passing out of the said town of Fowlis, took with her at your command, rat poison to Ardmore, and delivered it to the cook,

to mix it with the food, which the young Lady Balnagown and her company took that night: And Katherine Neynday, being in Ardmore that time, scunnered with it, she said, that it was the sorest and most cruel sight that she has ever seen, seeing the vomit and vexation that was on the young Lady Balnagown and her company; taking the poison, the young Lady Balnagown contracted a deadly sickness, where she remains yet incurable.

Marjory Campbell is said to have died not long afterwards, having never fully recovered from the poisoning.

When Katherine's accomplices were arrested on charges of 'magic enchantment, murder, homicide, and other horrible crimes', and very likely tortured by sleep deprivation into confessing the whole affair, she is said to have fled to Caithness, where her uncle, the Earl of Caithness, had the King's Justice, thus avoiding arrest for almost a year. Christian Ross, Agnes Roy and William Macgillivray, however, stood trial for witchcraft 'within the Cathedral Kirk of Roiss', on 28 November 1577, where they were found guilty and sentenced to death. Katherine's own trial for witchcraft did not take place until thirteen years later, after the death of her husband, Robert Munro of Foulis. The jury was comprised of Rosses and Munros, and the next case to be heard that day was a counter-accusation of witchcraft against her accuser, Hector Munro, now laird of Foulis. Katherine was found innocent of all the charges. Pitcairn remarked that the jury, 'being composed of subordinate persons not suitable to the rank or family of the person tried, has all the appearance of having been packed on purpose for acquittal'. It was also observed that, 'since the enchantment was performed in January, 1588, and the deceased was only taken ill of his fatal disease in April 1590, the distance between the events might seem too great to admit the former being regarded as the cause of the latter'.

Unfortunately, the full Chanonry Cathedral records for this period are missing (it's been suggested that they were lost in the Vatican archives). We are unable, therefore, to establish direct proof that Coinneach *Odhar* was ever caught and sentenced; but it was recorded regarding two of the others who were accused along with him that Christian Ross, alias Malcolmson, was burned, and that Thomas McKain More McAllane McHenrik, otherwise known as Thomas Cassindonisch, 'suffered the death'. If 'Keonach Ower/Kennoch Owir' had been taken and tried, it is unlikely that, as 'principal enchanter', he would have faced a milder sentence and it is very likely that he was convicted and burned for witchcraft, given that burning was a punishment specifically reserved for those convicted of witchcraft or heresy. Moreover, according to the records, the trial of the witches in 1577–8 took place in the Cathedral Kirk of Ross, which is Fortrose Cathedral, otherwise known as Chanonry; and the burning of Coinneach *Odhar* of tradition is said to have taken place on Chanonry Point.

Regarding the relationship between witchcraft and prophecy, it has been noted that witchcraft occurs in the records as a general term covering a number

*Scotland's Nostradamus*

of occult practices that are specified, and one of these figures prominently in the trial of Hector Munro of Foulis. Among the charges preferred against him is that he entertained witches in his house 'and socht responsis and consultations att them', and that he did this on one occasion when he was ill, anxious presumably to know if he would recover his health. This shows that the standard practises of these exponents of black magic in Easter Ross included those designed to let them see into the future. Matheson also pointed out that as the tradition that built up around Coinneach *Odhar* portrayed him as the archetypal seer, the role of poisoner may well have been reversed in the story that was passed on, with a plot to poison others in the service of a lady (which is what we find in the records of the trials) becoming a plot by a lady to poison him.

There is, therefore, in all of this good reason to believe that, had such a man named Coinneach *Odhar* been burned for witchcraft in such a prominent trial involving the wife of such a prominent landowner and clan chief, he would have been long remembered in the oral culture of the area, especially given the enormous impact that the Scottish 'witch-craze' had on the ordinary people of Easter Ross.

~·~·~

Belief in the power and maleficence of witches seems to have been almost universal in this period throughout Europe. Although the belief in and persecution of witches was nothing new, the late sixteenth century and early seventeenth marked the height of the European 'witch-craze', a time when both the Reformation and Counter Reformation prioritised questions of morality as a matter of public concern and there were more trials and executions of people accused of witchcraft than ever before. Scotland had more than its fair share, thanks initially to King James VI's obsession with the subject, which can be seen in what he wrote about it in his tract *Daemonologie*, which was published in 1597, and in which he described the 'fearefull aboundinge at this time in this countrie, of these detestable slaves of the Devill, the Witches or enchanters'. Written in the form of a dialogue, he set out an argument demonstrating that the existence of witches can be proven and urges their detection and punishment. Although the Scottish Witchcraft Act, which made it punishable by death, had been in force since 1563, no large-scale witch hunts took place until the period during which James was writing.

This all got under way in 1590 when James married Anne of Denmark. On their return from Scandinavia to Scotland, the king's ship was battered by severe storms, and it was suggested that the so-called North Berwick witches had employed their dark arts to prevent the king's safe return to Scotland. After torture, the North Berwick witches confessed. One of the accused, Agnes Sampson, during her confession claimed that she attached parts of a corpse to a cat, sailed to sea in a sieve, then put the cat into the sea to create a storm to shipwreck the king. James personally questioned many of the accused, but initially remained sceptical about the reality of the deeds they confessed to. His view changed, however, when Agnes Sampson said she could prove that she was a witch by recounting to James his conversation with his new bride on their wedding night. Agnes must have convinced James because, from this point on, he appears to have been persuaded of the reality of the threat against him. The notorious North Berwick witch hunt that followed led to the accusation, arrest and torture of a group of about sixty people. Some of the accused were educated and of high status within the community, but, under torture and questioning, many confessed, and, although the records are incomplete, it is likely that many of the accused were executed, probably by burning.

The Scottish historian Professor Louise Yeoman has shown that witch trials in this period have been seen to focus largely on a typical scenario centred on envy and cursing. This is what appears to have driven the great Scottish witch hunts of 1596, 1629, 1649 and 1661–2. The 1563 *Witchcraft Act* resulted in approximately 4,000 people being accused as witches. As with elsewhere in Europe, of those accused, some 85 per cent were women. Of this 4,000, it is estimated that approximately 2,500 innocent Scots were executed. The method of execution was by way of strangulation and then burning at the stake. Professor Julian Goodyear of Edinburgh University has established that there were five times more executions per capita in Scotland than the European average. In 2022 First Minister Nicola Sturgeon issued a Scottish government apology for the wrongdoings of the past, and a member's bill has been introduced at the Scottish Parliament seeking a full pardon.

The last recorded Scottish trial for witchcraft was in 1727 in Dornoch (which is 40 miles north of Chanonry Point), although belief at a popular level survived for many years to come and would have been preserved in the popular memory of folktales for longer still. We know that Colin Mackenzie, the First Earl of Seaforth, was as a Privy Councillor granted a number of commissions to try a group of accused witches from Ross-shire from 1629 to 1631. In particular, he granted a commission to several of his kinsmen to try 'Christian Riach in Stornoway, long bygane suspect' in January 1631. Louise Yeoman has argued that in this particular case the persecution might have been part of the Mackenzies' struggle to control Lewis.

Professor Peter Burke, who I had the good fortune of having as a tutor when I was studying for my degree, has explained that, from about 1650, the number of witch trials began to decline, at least in Western Europe as a whole. This was not because ordinary people had stopped accusing one another of witchcraft: even when Boswell and Johnson visited the Hebrides, there 'the belief of witchcraft, or charms was very common, insomuch that' the local minister 'had many prosecutions before his session ... against women, for having by these means carried off the milk from people's cows' (although the minister disregarded them and preached against it). In fact, by the time of the Third Earl of Seaforth, the learned had for the most part stopped believing in it. If they did not reject

*Scotland's Nostradamus*

the idea of witchcraft altogether, they had become increasingly sceptical about specific accusations.

In Scotland, however, there were two peaks in the so-called 'witch-craze'. The first of these came at the end of 1649, when the country was undergoing civil war and the Covenanters had gained power in pursuit of changing Scotland into a godly state. Following the Reformation in Scotland, many Calvinists believed that they were the new Israelites of the Old Testament. Political, societal and religious upheaval all caused chaos and uncertainty. Worried about the presence of ungodliness at a time when many believed that the 'Last Days' and the Apocalypse were imminent, panic culminated in accusations of witchcraft with a frenzy of paranoia that mirrored the McCarthyism of the twentieth century, resulting in a phenomenon that is comparable with modern conspiracy theories. This craze abated somewhat during Cromwell's occupation, which introduced a different form of Protestantism, but following the Restoration of King Charles II, during 1661 and 1662 there followed the greatest witch hunt in Scottish history, no longer under the Covenanters, but under the restored Stuart monarchy wishing to stamp out the long decades of rebellion and upheaval under the civil wars and the English occupation under Cromwell. It has been suggested that new regimes always want to justify themselves as righteous and this one generated a renewed obsession with ungodliness: the Restoration of the monarchy was justified by the concept of the Divine Right of Kings and one of the Biblical texts that was then quoted was: 'Rebellion is as the sin of witchcraft.'

—·—·—

It is at that precise time, shortly after 1660, that Isobel Mackenzie had married Kenneth *Mor* Mackenzie and become Countess of Seaforth. From having researched the life of our direct ancestor, Murdo McKenzie, who was in 1661 appointed Bishop of Moray, my brother, Kevin, and I became particularly familiar with the contemporary documentation relating to witchcraft in the area. Murdo, who had formerly been a member of the Presbytery of Fortrose Cathedral, residing at a house in the Cathedral Close there, was a cousin of both Countess Isobel and her husband, the Third Earl of Seaforth, and, as a former minister at Contin had effectively acted as chaplain to the Seaforths at Brahan. It is also clear that he was close to Isobel's brother, Sir Georg Mackenzie of Tarbat, since we know from Alexander Brodie of Brodie's diary, for example, that they dined together on their way south in October 1662, presumably to attend Parliament in Edinburgh.

In sixteen months during 1661 and 1662, more than 600 people in Scotland were accused of acts of sorcery and diabolism. One of the most notorious of these was Isobel Gowdie, which took place in Murdo's episcopal see. Isobel confessed to witchcraft at Auldearn, near Nairn in 1662. Her detailed testimony, which we can read in Robert Pitcairn's 1833 *Criminal Trials in Scotland*, was remarkably achieved without the use of violent torture and includes details of charms and rhymes, her claims that she was a member of a coven in the service of the Devil and that she met with the fairy queen and king. Lurid information concerning carnal dealings with the Devil were also provided. In the same year, Bishop Murdo also organised the trial by a jury composed of twenty-four of the principal gentlemen of Elgin and Morayshire of two witches from Elgin, Margaret Kellie and Barbara Innes. While the church courts did the preliminary evidence gathering, they couldn't execute anyone, but had then to turn the accused over to the criminal courts of the Scottish state and one of the commissioners who sought to try them was Thomas Mackenzie of Pluscarden (who was the Third Earl of Seaforth's uncle and had accompanied Murdo to northern Europe on campaign, when he was chaplain in Lord Reay's Regiment).

My brother, Kevin, discovered that as Bishop of Moray, Murdo must in the 1660s have engaged Christian Caddell as a 'witch-pricker', since his seat as Bishop of Moray was at Spynie Palace near Elgin. According to the pamphlet entitled *The Lands and People of Moray Witchcraft Trials in Elgin Morayshire from Kirk Session, Presbytery and other Sources 1560–1734*, published by J & B Bishop in 2001, on 7 May 1662, 'Christian Caddell, now John Dickson, a burgess from Forfar' turned up in Elgin in March 1662. John Innes, the Baillie of Spynie signed her up. 'She conducted her business far and wide and made it as far north as Tain in the Highlands.' This pamphlet tells us that Barbara Innes and Margaret Kellie were tried before a jury for witchcraft and, tragically, 'ordained to be taken outwith the West Port of The Burgh of Elgin on Tuesday next, being the eleventh day of November instant at one o'clock in the afternoon and there first to be strangled to death, and your bodies and burnt to ashes'. This meant that these two women must presumably have been taken to the Knock of Alves, the place where Elgin's witches were executed by being strangled and then burned, and that was also associated with the prophetic witches in Shakespeare's *MacBeth*. Their trial was on 6 November 1662, and their execution was ordered for the following Tuesday.

The reason why they were burned was to deny them any kind of respectful Christian burial, although the standard cause of death for witches would usually have been by strangulation first. The body was then kept propped up at a steak and burned on a pile of wood, also most usually employing peat in the Highlands, along with such combustible materials as dried heather or tar, which would be built into the base of the pyre in barrels. The condemned would thus in reality have been burned *on* a barrel of tar, rather than *in* a barrel of tar, as the story surrounding the Brahan Seer was later conveyed. This would not have taken place in the town square, which would have been a danger to the surrounding buildings, but on the outskirts of the town or city, in a place that is open and where a sizeable crowd could gather to witness the punishment. In Ross-shire, Chanonry Point would have been just such an appropriate location, and, being on the outskirts of Fortrose, also symbolised the nature of this particular crime by placing the condemned outside of the community (in Edinburgh it was often on Castle Hill or in Leith).

*Scotland's Nostradamus*

Also, in August of that year, on the Black Isle, Margaret Simpson and Bessie Watson from Cromarty were accused of witchcraft. A commission was granted to Countess Isobel's brother, Sir George Mackenzie of Tarbat, and several other noblemen. In this commission, it stated that both Margaret Simpson and Bessie Watson had already 'confest themselves to be guiltie of witchcraft'. We do not know the outcome of that trial.

The interesting point here about the case of Barbara Innes and Margaret Kellie is that the pamphlet, in another entry, also states that

apart from a brief notice of a meeting of the Bishop of Elgin with the brethren on 12th November 1662, there is nothing recorded until 22nd April 1663, by which time the mania for persecuting those accused of witchcraft and charmery had ceased throughout most of the country. There was however one more case of witchcraft in Elgin, which although not documented by the Kirk Session, appears in the Register of the Privy Council [this is referring to the same case of November 1662].

Earlier in the same year, James Fraser, the minister of Wardlaw, conveyed the growing scepticism regarding the methods of detecting witchcraft that characterised many of his class by that time when he recorded:

There came to Inverness [March 1662] Mr Paterson, who had run over the kingdom for trial of witches, and was ordinarily called the Pricker, because his way of trial was with a long brasse pin. Stripping them naked, he alleadged that the spell spot was seen and discovered. After rubbing over thew whole body with his palms he slipt in the pin, and, it seemes, with shame and feare being dasht, they felt it not, but he left it in the flesh, deep to the head, and he desired them to find and take it out. Itt is sure some witches were discovered, but many honest men and women were blotted and broak by this trick.

The procedure of 'pricking' witches involved the belief that the body of every witch would have a 'Devils' or 'witches mark'. This mark could be identified because, when pricked on it, the witch could not feel pain. In reality, pricking often took the form of torture, when the accused was pricked multiple times, frequently resulting in a confession.

One Finlay Fraser was a neighbour of and fellow weaver burgess of my ancestor, Daniel McKenzie, who was Bishop Murdo's son, and featured as a witness in a number of my family's baptisms in Inverness at the time. At the direction of the justice depute (that being Sir George Mackenzie of Rosehaugh from 1661 to 1663), and in the presence of the notary, it was Finlay who was tasked with examining those accused of witchcraft in this same year for signs of torture, where he 'did sight and try the hands and feet of the forenamed persons [they being the accused, who were members of the MacLean family] to see if they had any mark of torturing upon any part of their bodies, and if they had to show it

28

to him, which none of them could show'. Nonetheless, it appears that none of the accused were executed, since, on 8 October, Alexander Brodie recorded in his diary, 'At Invernes ther was non of the witches condmnd.' The accusations had, in fact, arisen from a local dispute about land between the MacLeans of Duart and the Chisholms of Comar. Interestingly, local conflicts and rivalries have been highlighted as having been at play, rather than any intrinsic belief in witchcraft, in the notorious Salem witch trials in Massachusetts from February 1692 to May 1693; while the British anthropologist E.E. Evans-Pritchard came up with similar local findings in African tribal societies. Indeed, we have already seen clan rivalry at play, both in the witchcraft trials relating to Katherine Ross's disputes with the Munros over the ownership of Foulis in the 1570s and 1580s; and with the First Earl of Seaforth's commission to try Christian Riach in Stornoway in 1631 in his claim to exert rule over the Isle of Lewis.

Despite this brief surge, whatever its reasons, the frenzy for trying and burning witches by this period was to abate dramatically, thanks to the more rational attitudes of the gentry in this region. As bishop, Murdo would have overseen the Kirk Sessions, or parish committees, which made up the investigators behind the witch hunts. The accused were then tried by Commissioners, presided over by Murdo's kinsman, Sir George Mackenzie of Rosehaugh, as Justice Depute. In April 1662, the Privy Council declared that a lot of innocent people were being unfairly convicted and that there was to be no torture and no witch pricking without order of the Privy Council itself, leading to changes in the laws. Rosehaugh was remarkably influential in all of this.

Bishop Murdo was a close political ally of his kinsman, Rosehaugh, with whom, after 1677, as Lord Advocate (along with his other cousins, the Third Earl of Seaforth and Countess Isobel's brother, George Mackenzie, Viscount Tarbat) he sat in the Scottish House of Lords. Another member of this circle was the minister of Nairn, Hugh Rose, who was part of another prominent local landowning family, and was among the commissioners engaged to try Isobel Gowdie for witchcraft in Auldearn in 1662. Rose had befriended Rosehaugh when the two men were fellow students of law at Leyden in the Netherlands and recent historians have supported J.B. Craven's opinion in his 1908 *History of the Episcopal Church in the Diocese of Moray*, that Rose was 'accomplished and worthy' and considered to be 'a person of great knowledge and integrity'. As Emma Wilby writes in *The Visions of Isobel Gowdie*, 'The fact that Rose's *Meditations* periodically divert – more markedly than the writings of godly contemporaries like Brodie and Katherine Collace – from conventional preoccupations about personal and peer salvation into vivid evocations on the sufferings of the poor and the powerless also suggests that he was a compassionate man.' Rose's bishop, Murdo McKenzie, was also a trained lawyer (a baptism record for one of his younger children described him as 'tutor in law', and when he sat in Parliament he was appointed a Lord of the Articles, which required the ability to draft legislation). The practical outcome of these men's instinctive rationalism was that

*Scotland's Nostradamus*

Sir George Mackenzie of Rosehaugh in particular, as the most senior prosecutor in Scotland, played a central role in the decline of witchcraft prosecutions in Scotland and his obvious leniency in this respect belies the harsher reputation that he is still remembered for in pursuing the Covenanters' rebellion as 'Bluidy Mackenzie'. In *Reason. An Essay*, Sir George wrote: 'It may seem a bold Undertaking in any Man to own right Reason in this Age, it being the declar'd Enemy of our Interests and Inclinations; for it may possibly excite Man to reflect upon what the World and himself does; and so inspire him with Thoughts contrary to those which are generally received.'

The significance of Rosehaugh's thinking was not in the nature of his witch beliefs, which he shared with most educated contemporaries, but in the recommendations that he made regarding the trial and discovery of witches. As justice-depute, Mackenzie became heavily involved in this series of trials staged in the sixteen months during 1661 and 1662. Mackenzie was disturbed by the judicial practices that facilitated the conviction of witches, including their torture, the practice of pricking them for the 'Devil's mark' and their trial by local authorities who had no knowledge of the crime and who allowed the testimony of unqualified witnesses, so that 'poor Innocents die in Multitudes by an unworthy Martyrdom, and Burning comes in fashion'.

Rosehaugh is also known to have examined witchcraft cases in Lothian, where men and women – but mostly women – had been kept in prison in dismal conditions, and often subjected to illegal torture (torture was permitted in law, but only in specific extreme political circumstances). His intervention did something incredibly radical for the time when trying one particular witch: he listened to what she had to say: 'locked up and deserted by everyone, she had despaired of her life and confessed in hopes she would be executed'. Mackenzie thus conveyed the moving plea she made to him 'under secrecie', when she told him that

> she had not confest because she was guilty, but being a poor creature, who wrought for her meat, and being defam'd for a Witch she knew she would starve, for no person thereafter would either give her meat or lodging, and that all men would beat her; and hound Dogs at her, and that thereafter she desired to be out of the World; whereupon she wept most bitterly, and upon her knees call'd to God to witness what she said.

In 1672, Rosehaugh famously defended a woman known by the name of Maevia, who was accused of witchcraft, and published his argument on her behalf in 1672 in his tract, *Pleadings in Remarkable Cases*. After thereafter being appointed in 1677 to the influential position of Lord Advocate (the equivalent of Attorney General, or chief prosecutor of Scotland), he was able to put his teachings into practice on the government's behalf, dismissing charges against four alleged witches in 1680. He recognised that once a good lawyer started evaluating evidence in the way that he should, it became evident that there was no justification for these charges, and therefore for these prosecutions. He was directly responsible, probably more than anyone else, for the decline and eventual end of witchcraft prosecutions. Thus, Mackenzie was instrumental in helping to release innocent suspects, and the scepticism of men like him and his immediate circle helped put an end to the witch-panic.

A year into his role as Lord Advocate, Sir George published his *Lawes and Customes of Scotland in Matters Criminal*, which was the first textbook of criminal law in Scotland and became an influential legal commentary. In the section of the book dealing with witchcraft, Mackenzie made use of the knowledge he had acquired as a judge in witchcraft cases and from reading historical accounts of other witchcraft trials. He said witchcraft did in fact exist – after all, both the Bible and the Scottish criminal code prohibited it – but 'from the horridness of this Crime, I do conclude, that of all Crimes it requires the clearest relevancy, and most convincing probation. And I condemn, next to the witches themselves, these cruel and too forward judges who burn persons by the thousand as guilty of this crime.' Mackenzie deplored abuses such as mass arrests, supervision of the trial process by people without legal training, the illegal torture of suspects and unduly credulous acceptance of confessions potentially produced by torture or despair. Mackenzie censured the 'Prickers' who offered to stick pins into suspects' flesh: the whole thing was a 'meer cheat', said Mackenzie, citing a 'Pricker' who had been arrested for unrelated crimes and admitted that his supposed expertise was bogus.

Mackenzie also called for the rejection of any testimony about witches supposedly changing shape or flying through the air, which he proclaimed impossible (without God's assistance, which, of course, would not be afforded to witches). He declared that many witchcraft suspects 'confess things which all Divines conclude impossible as transmutation of their bodies into beasts, and money into stones, and their going through walls and closed doors, and a thousand other ridiculous things, which have no truth nor existence but in their lunacy.' His insistence on the strictest degrees of judicial rigour and impartiality led to the eventual abandonment of such trials long before Scots and many other Europeans denied the reality or possibility of the crime. This became part of an evidentiary revolution in the practice of law that has had repercussions throughout Europe, and that was in due course to be worked into the codes of judiciaries there. It is likely that the influence of Mackenzie's treatise contributed, not only to a fairer justice system, but in particular to the abatement of the Scottish witch-panics.

All things considered, the likelihood of Coinneach *Odhar's* trial at this time for witchcraft at Chanonry, where this particular circle of magnates was in authority, would therefore appear remote from what we can glean from the historical record. As we shall later see, Sir George Mackenzie of Tarbat corresponded extensively on the subject of second sight and, having been a commissioner directly involved in witchcraft prosecutions on the Black Isle in 1662, he

*Scotland's Nostradamus*

would undoubtedly have mentioned in that correspondence had there been a notorious incident concerning the burning of a man condemned to death by his own sister, Countess Isobel on the Black Isle, at this time.

~·~·~

It is also from researching this same social circle that headed local society at the time of Charles II's Restoration that I first encountered a vivid picture of Countess Isobel's character. The consensus among her peers in the locality was that the Third Earl of Seaforth did not marry well. As we see in the contempt with which the writer of the Wardlaw Manuscript, the Rev. James Fraser, held him and his wife: 'The Earle of Seaforth keeps home, and is matchd with a kinswoman of his own, a daughter of the Laird of Tarbuts; after all mens hops of him debases himselfe mean spirited to marry below himselfe, getting neither beuty, parts, portion, relation.' The mere daughter of a baronet from his own family, it is clearly evident that Countess Isobel was a remarkably unpopular member of Ross-shire society. Another contemporary commentator, Alexander Brodie of Brodie, was as outspoken as Fraser was in his dislike for her. In his diary for 1676, he wrote: 'July 31. My Ladi Seaforth cald; and we being from home, she went to Darnaway' and 'Aug 1. My Ladi Seaforth went by and cald not; I reveranc the Lord's providence.' Seaforth was widely seen as having shocked his contemporaries yet further by then resigning his interests into this woman's hands when he went to Paris: as the 'Person of Quality' (who was the anonymous author of a remarkably comprehensive genealogical account of the Mackenzie family) wrote: 'when the third Earl had set his affairs in order at Brahan, he re-visited Paris, leaving his Countess Isobel, daughter of Sir John Mackenzie of Tarbat, and sister to the first Earl of Cromarty, in charge of his interests in the North.'

I was also to encounter Isobel's unpopularity in the following century, when looking into the life of my ancestor, Bishop Murdo's son, Daniel McKenzie, who was at one point living at Brahan with Frances Herbert, then the widow of Isobel's son, the Fourth Earl of Seaforth. Isobel's brother, Viscount Tarbat (who was famously described by his enemies as 'maggoty', 'chimerical' and 'slippery as an eel') following Queen Anne's appointment of him as her Secretary of State for Scotland, had now been further elevated to the rank of Earl of Cromartie. Under the pretext of preserving the chiefly landholdings within the family, he orchestrated a complex legal manoeuvre whereby his sister, the Dowager Countess Isobel, became the nominal owner of the Seaforth Estates by the time that her grandson, William, had succeeded as Fifth Earl of Seaforth. This was further exacerbated by Isobel's refusal to pay Frances her annuity of £1,000 sterling out of the Seaforth Estate (approximately £70,000 in today's money), which the Third Earl had promised her on their marriage in 1684. Frightened that the Roman Catholic and Jacobite Frances would exert an undue influence on her young son, Isobel did everything in her power to cut her daughter-in-law off. At first Isobel tried to isolate Frances and her two young children financially, so that they were 'neglected and excluded to that degree that they got not above fifteen pound sterling out of the whole Estate'. Ultimately, by 1706 the equally formidable Frances was victorious in the long-running dispute and by May 1708 the Seaforth estate was assigned to the younger Countess, so long as Frances should pay her mother-in-law her yearly annuity. Isobel was obliged to lick her wounds and spend her dying days in a grace-and-favour apartment in the Palace of Holyroodhouse. Countess Frances and her charismatic son William went on to receive considerable affection among what at that time was a largely Jacobite clan, while Countess Isobel was evidently remembered very differently.

~·~·~

From what we can see, second sight in the Highlands was not something that was regarded as being witchcraft and punishable as such, least of all in the latter part of the seventeenth century in this part of Ross-shire. But we have found that it was another formidable and socially powerful woman who was the wife of a local clan chief – Katherine Ross, Lady Foulis – who was associated with a genuine Coinneach *Odhar*, who lived in the sixteenth century, when a genuine witch trial resulted in celebrated executions at Chanonry Point. Like the legend of the seventeenth century Coinneach *Odhar*, who was dubbed the Brahan Seer, the stories about whom have been passed down to us, they were concerned with accusations of consulting with fairies and using poisons in attempts to kill intended victims. From what we know about the true histories of both the sixteenth-century Coinneach *Odhar* and his association with Lady Foulis, coupled with what we know about Countess Isobel's notorious reputation as a powerful woman in a man's world, it should then be no wonder that, such was Countess Isobel's unpopularity in Easter Ross, in particular after she took charge of the Brahan estate when her husband was absent in Paris, that her demonised character was later to be remembered, and as a consequence misremembered and attached to local folklore: in the form of the jealous wife, who sentenced Coinneach *Odhar* to be burned in a spiked barrel of tar at Chanonry Point, for informing her of her husband's infidelity at the French Court.

The Brahan Seer's memorial commemorating his execution at Chanonry Point

The monument to the tragically killed Hon. Caroline Mackenzie, near Brahan

Uig, birthplace of the Brahan Seer, with Uig Lodge, seat of the author's MacAulay ancestors

The ruined Fairburn Tower, where a cow gave birth on the top floor

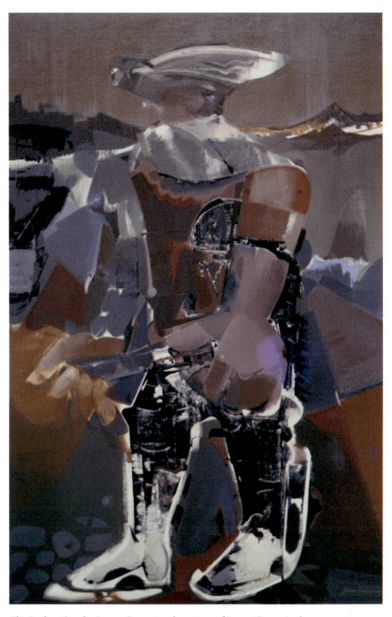

*The Brahan Seer* by James Cumming (courtesy of Laura Cumming)

The Brahan Seer's nemesis, Isobel Mackenzie, Countess of Seaforth, by L. Schüneman, in Fortrose Town Hall

Isobel's husband, Coinneach *Mhor* Mackenzie, Third Earl of Seaforth, by John Michael Wright, in Fortrose Town Hall

Peter Vanderbank's engraving of the owner of 'Right Reason', Sir George Mackenzie of Rosehaugh

George Glover's engraving of the cosmopolitan polymath, Sir Thomas Urquhart of Cromarty

'Glad am I that I will not see that day': David Morier's painting of the Battle of Culloden (courtesy of the Royal Collection Trust)

The Fairies' unfinished causeway, commissioned by Michael Scot, at Chanonry Point

# A Superstitious Highland Backwater?

Some people might see the apparent lengthier endurance of second sight in the Highlands as the result of this part of the world displaying some kind of provincial backwardness that allowed the survival of archaic superstitions. Such an image has arguably been reinforced by some elements of the Scottish tourist industry's tendency to romanticise the country's character, and indeed that of the Scottish Highlands in particular, since it serves their commercial interests to portray this destination as a picturesque escape from modernity, barely touched during the past few centuries by the progress of a more advanced and sophisticated civilisation in the south. Valuing though I emphatically do the Highland's unique history and spectacular beauty, having myself researched my ancestors' stories closely, I have far too much respect for these people to paint the Highlands in such a crude way as a region that was cut off from the rest of European civilisation.

In a number of articles and videos for the Clan Mackenzie Society of Scotland and the UK, I have in recent years been at some pains to challenge the longstanding depiction of the Mackenzies in the seventeenth and eighteenth centuries as 'Highland Savages'. In my book, *May we be Britons? A History of the Mackenzies*, I first challenged in 2012 the pessimistic stance of 'Seaforth's Doom', which depicted a benighted region, whose clan chief and his family were doomed in the face of inevitable historical progress and modernity. Unfortunately, thanks to the huge impact of Diana Gabaldon's *Outlander* series, this picture of the Highlander's tale as one of tragic but noble failure in his struggle against change has, if anything, been further promoted in recent years as a common and popular perception around the world of Highland history today. Yet my continued research into my family's history has shown that, far from being an outmoded remnant of the Dark Ages, the clan system was a remarkably resilient and adaptable phenomenon, which allowed my forebears to make a significant contribution to many of those values that laid the foundations of the modern world. In *May we be Britons?* I concluded: 'It is my view that present day Scottish nationalists might do well to celebrate their ancestors' positive achievements in this respect and resist the tendency to dwell on a perceived resentment of themselves as underdogs.' It is in this wider context that I believe the Brahan Seer's story should also best be understood.

By examining the earliest sources relating to the Mackenzies' roots, my brother, Kevin, and I established that the family first originated as part of a highly cosmopolitan network of kinship (both Gaelic and Norman) that ruled Britain and France in the thirteenth century; and I went on to chart how the

*A Superstitious Highland Backwater?*

family continued to identify in just such outward-looking terms right up until the nineteenth century. Only then did circumstances conspire for them to adopt a more romantic and parochial self-image. Contrary to the perception that most people have of the Highlands as a cultural backwater, the leading lights of the family were among the most advanced thinkers of their time, some of them being major participants in the international movements of the Scientific Revolution and the Enlightenment. By the end of the eighteenth century, the family's leaders were wholly integrated into the elite of the British state system and this course of commitment to a centralised Britain came to be shared by their kinsmen further down the social scale. The building of great canals and railways in Britain, the surveying of oceans and of India, and the exploration of Canada are among the pioneering achievements of this innovative and outward-looking family. The start of the nineteenth century, when 'Seaforth's Doom' was deemed to have been fulfilled, was far from marking the end of a long period of decline. Indeed, it marked the true achievement of this family's ambition. And yet another aspect of the family's achievement – their participation in the Romantic Movement in the nineteenth century – resulted in the very different picture that persists today. It is this gloss that came to mask the reality of the important part such Highlanders shared in forging the modern world.

Remote as the Highlands seem to us today, during a period when most travel was done by sea, rather than road, the region had long reached out in trade to its neighbours on the North Sea and Baltic (as well as to France, to the Mediterranean and beyond) and this had significant cultural repercussions. This was only too evident to me the more I looked into my own family's history. In the seventeenth century, my direct ancestor, Daniel McKenzie, who was a merchant burgess in Inverness, was engaged in maritime trade, dying in Poland; his father, Bishop Murdo, had served abroad as a chaplain in Lord Reay's regiment, fighting on the European continent for Gustavus Adolphus during the Thirty Years' War; and one of Daniel's sons, William, another merchant, was captured by Algerian pirates off the coast of Livorno in the Mediterranean.

Interestingly, one observer of the Highlands who was a contemporary of the historical protagonists in the Seer's legend was the English journalist Daniel Defoe. As gifted in his perceptions and observations on contemporary life as he was a novelist (most famously, of course, for the still much read and celebrated *Robinson Crusoe*), it was characteristic of the man that he could see through the long-standing and deep-rooted prejudice against the Highlander. In his *A Tour Thro' the whole Island of Great Britain*, when he described the territory north of Inverness, Defoe challenged the 'there be dragons' perception of this part of the world:

> Our Geographers seem to be almost as much at a loss in the Description of the North part of Scotland, as the Romans were to conquer it; and they are oblig'd to fill it up with Hills and Mountains, as they do the inner

45

*Scotland's Nostradamus*

> Parts of Africa, with Lyons and Elephants, for want of knowing what else to Place there. Yet this Country is not such difficult Access as to be pass'd undescrib'd, as if it were inpenetrable.

He was perfectly correct, and it is still noticeable that a visitor today could easily mistake the gentle and prosperous rolling fields that make up the Black Isle home of the Brahan Seer, for the English Cotswolds. Defoe continued:

> Nor are the Inhabitants so wild and barbarous as perhaps, they were in those Times, or as our Writers have pretended. We see every Day the Gentlemen born here; such as the Mackenzies, McLeans, Dundonalds, Gordons, McKays, and others who are nam'd among the Clans as if they were Barbarians, appear at Court, and in our Camps and Armies, as polite and finish'd Gentlemen as any other from other Countries, or even among our own in many Things, especially in Arms and Gallantry, as well Abroad as at Home.

In my history of the Mackenzies I showed how the leading lights of the family were truly remarkable as some of the most advanced thinkers of their time. The brother of Countess Isobel, the very lady who was purported to have condemned Coinneach *Odhar* to death, Sir George Mackenzie, Viscount Tarbat and latterly First Earl of Cromartie, was an amateur architect, whose house at Royston showed the influence of Vaux le Vicomte, the French mansion that inspired Versailles. An examination of the books in the surviving inventory of Lord Cromartie's library at Castle Leod, taken on his death in 1714, shows the cosmopolitan, Francophile and heavily European nature of his learning, no doubt acquired during his long years in exile in the 1650s, which included a trip to Italy. His library displayed a remarkable interest for this period in Arabia, India and the Far East: Tavernier's *Les six voyages* (published in Paris in 1676), detailing his travels to the court of the Moghul, Aurungzeb; *The present state of Egypt*; *Baiazet, Prince Ottoman*; *Voyage to Siam*; *Histoire de la religion des Turcs*; *l'histoire Mahometane*; and atlases by Blaeu. And among his furniture at Royston House, as well as the ubiquitous japanned cabinets of this period, were, unusually, Indian and Ottoman pictures and tapestries. These pictures most likely included the forty-eight portraits of Turkish kings that were recorded at Tarbat House during his grandson's time.

As we have already touched on, Isobel's husband, the Third Earl of Seaforth's first cousin, the Lord Advocate, Sir George Mackenzie of Rosehaugh, whose estate on the Black Isle was to be the subject of one of the Brahan Seer's prophecies, which I will discuss later, was also a remarkably cosmopolitan intellectual, well ahead of his time. Quoting Pliny, the title page to my copy of Sir George's *Works* bears witness to the fact that, in addition to holding high public office with a pre-eminent reputation as a jurist, Mackenzie also produced an extensive published output that encompassed jurisprudence, imaginative literature, moral philosophy, and political theory. Mackenzie was the most frequently published Scottish

*A Superstitious Highland Backwater?*

writer of his day, producing at least twenty-one works from 1660 to 1689. Not only did he play a significant part in the decline of witchcraft prosecutions in Scotland, but, in 1660, he published the youthful work, *Aretina, or, The Serious Romance*, now regarded as the first Scottish novel. His poem, 'Caelias' Country House and Closet', reflects the way in which he had been schooled abroad on the Arcadian literature of Mademoiselle de Scudéry and Jean de la Fontaine, and his pastoral vision anticipated the Augustan idyll of John Dryden, Alexander Pope and William Kent. He was admired by the diarist John Evelyn, and respected by the Fellows of Oxford University; and his advice on poetic style was deemed profitable by John Dryden, who remembered 'that Noble Wit of Scotland, Sr George MacKenzy'. It is also no coincidence that Rosehaugh founded the Advocates' Library, which has been described as the 'seedbed of the Edinburgh Enlightenment'. David Hume used it to write his *History of England*, and Adam Ferguson his *Essay on the History of Civil Society*. 'Anthropology, sociology, ethnography,' writes one historian today, 'almost all our modern social sciences got their start from the volumes assembled on the shelves at the Advocates' Library in Edinburgh.' Such was the milieu that surrounded the chief actors in the Brahan Seer's story.

〜･〜･〜

Two stories about Sir George in particular illustrate the way in which tales of Highland superstition in local folk legend could comfortably overlap with accounts about a man whose intellect was unquestionably progressive. According to local lore, on one occasion, it was said, while he was residing at Rosehaugh, a poor widow from a neighbouring estate called to consult Sir George regarding her being repeatedly warned to remove from a small croft which she held under a lease of several years; but as some time had yet to run before its expiry, and being threatened with summary ejection from the croft, she went to solicit his advice. Having examined the tenor of the lease, Sir George informed her that it contained a flaw, which, in case of opposition, would render her success exceedingly doubtful; and although it was certainly an oppressive act to deprive her of her croft, he thought her best plan was to submit. However, seeing the distressed state of mind in which the poor woman was on hearing his opinion, he desired her to call upon him the following day, when he would consider her case more carefully. His clerk, who always slept in the same room as his lordship, was not a little surprised, about midnight, to discover him rising from his bed fast asleep, lighting a candle which stood on his table, drawing in his chair, and commencing to write very busily, as if he had been all the time wide awake.

The story continues:

> Next morning at breakfast, Sir George remarked that he had had a very strange dream about the poor widow's threatened ejectment, which, he could now remember, and he had now no doubt of making out a clear case in her favour. His clerk rose from the table, asked for the key of his desk,

47

*Scotland's Nostradamus*

and brought therefrom several pages of manuscript; and, as he handed them to Sir George, enquired – 'Is that like your dream?' On looking over it for a few seconds, Sir George said, 'Dear me, this is singular; this is my very dream!' He was no less surprised when his clerk informed him of the manner in which he had acted; and, sending for the widow, he told her what steps to adopt to frustrate the efforts of her oppressors. Acting on the counsel thus given, the poor widow was ultimately successful, and, with her young family, was allowed to remain in possession of her 'wee bit croftie' without molestation.

Another story concerning Sir George, which was recorded by the Clach, interestingly makes reference to the supernatural, while at the same time fiercely defending the superiority of the Scots in matters of the legal profession. It explains how, when he was residing in Edinburgh, the King's Advocate invariably walked for half an hour before dinner. One day, while taking his usual exercise along Leith Walk,

he was met by a venerable-looking, grey-headed old gentleman, who accosted him and, without introduction or apology, said – 'There is a very important case to come off in London fourteen days hence, at which your presence will be required. It is a case of heirship to a very extensive estate in the neighbourhood of London, and a pretended claimant is doing his utmost to disinherit the real heir, on the ground of his inability to produce proper titles thereto. It is necessary that you be there on the day mentioned; and in one of the attics of the mansion-house on the estate there is an old oak chest with two bottoms; between these you will find the necessary titles, written on parchment.' Having given this information, the old man disappeared, leaving Sir George quite bewildered; but the latter, resuming his walk, soon recovered his previous equanimity, and thought nothing further of the matter.

At first dismissing the encounter, after subsequently meeting the same old gentleman again on three consecutive days, the latter once more energetically pleaded with Sir George to take up his case, so that he was

induced to give in to his earnest importunities, and accordingly he started next morning on horseback, arriving in London on the day preceding that on which the case was to come on. In a few hours he was pacing in front of the mansion-house described by the old man at Leith Walk, where he met two gentlemen engaged in earnest conversation – one of the claimants to the property, and a celebrated London barrister – to whom he immediately introduced himself as the principal law-officer of the crown for Scotland. The barrister, no doubt supposing that Sir George was coming to take the bread out of his mouth, addressed him in a surly manner, and spoke disrespectfully of his country; to which the latter replied, 'that, lame and ignorant as his learned friend took the Scotch to be, yet in law, as well as in other respects, they would effect what would defy him and all his London clique'. This disagreeable dialogue was put an end to by the other gentleman – the claimant to the property – taking Sir George into the house. After sitting and conversing for some minutes, Sir George expressed a wish to be shown over the house. The drawing-room was hung all round with magnificent pictures and drawings, which Sir George greatly admired; but there was one which particularly attracted his attention; and after examining it very minutely, he, with a surprised expression, inquired of his conductor whose picture it was? and received answer – 'It is my great-great-grandfather's'. 'My goodness!' exclaimed Sir George, 'the very man who spoke to me three times on three successive days in Leith Walk, and at whose urgent request I came here!'

Sir George, at his own request, was then conducted to the attics, and noticed an old trunk lying in a corner.

The Leith Walk gentleman's information recurring to Sir George, he gave the old moth-eaten chest a good hearty kick, such as he could wish to have been received by his 'learned friend' the barrister, who spoke so disrespectfully of his country. The bottom flew out of the trunk, with a quantity of chaff, among which the original titles to the property were discovered.

Next morning, Sir George entered the court just as the case was about to be called and addressed the pretended claimant's counsel – 'Well, sir, what shall I offer you to abandon this action?' 'No sum, or any consideration whatever, would induce me to give it up,' answered his learned opponent. 'Well, sir,' said Sir George, at the same time pulling out his snuff-horn and taking a pinch, 'I will not even hazard a pinch on it.' The case was called.

Sir George, in reply to the claimant's counsel, in an eloquent speech, addressed the bench; exposed most effectually the means which had been adopted to deprive his client of his birthright; concluded by producing the titles found in the old chest; and the case was at once decided in favour of his client. The decision being announced, Sir George took the young heir's arm, and, bowing to his learned friend the barrister, remarked, 'You see now what a Scotsman has done, and let me tell you that I wish a countryman of mine anything but a London barrister.'

Sir George immediately returned to Edinburgh, well paid for his trouble; but he never again, in his favourite walk, encountered the old grey-headed gentleman.

~·~·~

Another of the Black Isle prophecies of the Brahan Seer, which I will also address later, concerns the Urquhart family from Cromarty. The family's most famous son

*Scotland's Nostradamus*

is perhaps the eccentric seventeenth-century clan chief Sir Thomas Urquhart of Cromarty. This remarkable intellectual claimed to have visited sixteen countries, and boasted that his fluency in French, Spanish and Italian allowed him to pass himself off as a native in these countries. His first major publication, in 1645, was his *The trissotetras, or, A most exquisite table for resolving all manner of triangles ... with greater facility than ever hitherto hath been practised*. This wide-ranging tome proclaimed the vast array of his expertise in mathematics, morals and metaphysics. The year 1652 saw the publishing of his family genealogy, *Pantochronochanon, or, A Peculiar Promptuary of Time and Ekskubalauron, or, The Discovery of a most Exquisite Jewel*. This work attempted to vindicate Scottish heroism against the malignancy of Presbyterianism 'by running through all the eminent Scots Urquhart could remember or invent' (according to one historian of Scottish literature). His next publication, *Logopandecteision, or, An Introduction to the Universal Language*, appeared in 1653, which provided a full description of his proposition for a universal language, an early antecedent of Esperanto, which was subsequently created by the Warsaw-based ophthalmologist L.L. Zamenhof in 1887. *The Jewel* might be widely deemed to compete with Rosehaugh's *Aretina* to be regarded as the first extant Scottish prose romance, had it not precociously introduced the Arcadian style in such an eccentric manner that made it quite inimitable. Urquhart's reputation, therefore, is still largely based on his last literary endeavour – his translation of Rabelais. *The first book [and 'The second book'] of the works of Mr. Francis Rabelais, doctor in physick ... now faithfully translated into English by S.T.U.C.* appeared in 1653. Thereafter, two of his letters place him in Middelburg, Zeeland, in September 1655 and again in July 1658 (*Sir Thomas Urquhart ... : the Jewel*, 10). That he died abroad is also likely.

R.D.S. Jack's article on Sir Thomas for the *Oxford Dictionary of National Biography* makes a justifiable claim for greater recognition for this highly original and eclectic (as well as eccentric) thinker, who was purported to have died laughing at hearing of the Restoration of Charles II. Jack concludes with the suggestion that we 'may allow this self-proclaimed universal genius to take his rightful place not only as a worthy successor to Gavin Douglas in that country›s impressive roll of creative translators but as the first herald of a tradition in prose romance which would lead eventually to Walter Scott'.

In 2017, after my employers at Bonhams the auctioneers had sponsored Grantown Museum's exhibition on the eighteenth-century Scottish portrait painter, as part of a conference entitled 'Richard Waitt: New Perspectives on Culture and Context', I gave a talk on artistic patronage in the Highlands, which further challenged this longstanding romantic depiction of the Clan, since nowhere is the Mackenzies' contribution to history more tangible than in their artistic connoisseurship: a field of activity that, as a picture specialist with Bonhams, I could not fail to have appreciated. At that seminar, I also met the distinguished historian

*A Superstitious Highland Backwater?*

of Highlands and Islands culture, Professor Hugh Cheape. I had known Hugh previously from the auction world in which I encountered him when he worked for the Museums of Scotland, and we discussed the National Portrait Gallery's acquisition of Lord Seaforth's commission of Benjamin West's monumental clan painting, *The Death of the Stag*. After discovering that we were of like minds in the way we perceived the Highlands and Islands, we continued to keep in touch and he recently kindly shared with me a paper that he gave in April 2023 to the Royal Society of Edinburgh, in which he argues that we should situate Scotland's past in a wider European and global context. My own findings over the years entirely support Hugh's view that the Highlands and Islands should be seen as less 'remote' than places deep inland, and that the Hebrides in particular have always been connected to a wider European culture. As he writes: 'Of course, places seen conventionally as peripheral might be lined by sea to the rest of the world, known and unknown, and linked to Europe in fact more directly than most parts of Scotland.'

In my own lecture at Grantown Museum, I sought to show how, when the Mackenzie chiefs were elevated, first to the rank of Lord Kintail at the end of the sixteenth century, and then to that of Earl of Seaforth at the beginning of the seventeenth, their newfound illustrious status demanded to be matched by a corresponding outward display. After remodelling the former Bishop's Palace at Chanonry, whereby the First 'Red' Earl of Seaforth improved the 'stately well contrived commodious house', and where he is said to have lived 'in great state and very magnificently', it then became this chief's ambition to build a completely new residence entirely his own. As had been the case with the palace at Chanonry, this was intended as far more than a defensive construction. The site he chose was in the valley of Strathconon, at Brahan, where he created 'one of the most stately houses in Scotland', and established it thenceforth as the foremost seat of the Mackenzies. Before the demolition of Brahan Castle, *Country Life* in 1916 featured an article that recorded the former glory of the house, noting in particular the Fifth Earl (and Second Jacobite Marquis) William's luxurious Tapestry Room, whose Brussels tapestries were designed by Urbanus Leynier. During his exile in France in the first decade of the eighteenth century, William had benefited from an education at the Jacobite court of St-Germain, where he would have had access to what was then considered the most cultivated court in Europe at nearby Versailles. Hence the surviving group of family portraits from the period, which now hang in Fortrose Town Hall, include a number by François de Troy and his studio – de Troy being principal portraitist to the court at St-Germain, as well as being one of the foremost artists employed by the French King Louis XIV and his family.

Later in the eighteenth century, the family's most renowned artistic connoisseur was the Fifth Earl of Seaforth's grandson, Kenneth Mackenzie, the last Earl of Seaforth. It was his long exile on the European Continent that initially encouraged him to become the Grand Tourist par excellence, engendering in him a

*Scotland's Nostradamus*

remarkably cosmopolitan outlook. A friend of Sir William and Emma Hamilton, he took an active role in the first excavations of Herculaneum and Pompeii. A painting the Earl commissioned, that now hangs in the National Portrait Gallery in Edinburgh, depicts his collection of antiquities in his Neapolitan *palazzo*, while the infant protégé Mozart is also shown seated at the harpsichord beside his father. Representing those many Scottish émigrés, who from 1688 onwards settled in France, Spain, Russia and Italy, making a major contribution to the economic, military and, in the last Earl's case, the artistic life of these host countries, he may be regarded, to quote the words of the Jacobite historians Eveline Cruickshanks and Edward Corp, as one of 'the first Europeans'.

~·~·~

So, how then did this perception of two cultures come about?

In Hugh Cheape's paper that he kindly showed to me while I was in the process of writing this book, he traces this perspective of Scottish history in terms of a Highland–Lowland divide all the way back to the second half of the fourteenth century and the bald statements of the frequently quoted chronicler John of Fordoun. Writing in the 1370s, his view has been taken at face value, perpetuating the image of the Highlander and a Highland Line separating two races and repeated with little or no qualification by all his successors with its convenient stereotype of civilised versus barbaric.

Of course, by the eighteenth century, it served the propaganda of the Hanoverian regime to depict the Jacobite rebels from the Highlands as backward and uncivilised remnants of a savage past that they wished to conquer (and following the 'Butcher' Duke of Cumberland's victory at Culloden in 1746, actively and consciously to eradicate). That prejudice is certainly heavily to blame for much of the misconception, even today, especially when some politicians (on both sides of the nationalist argument) attempt crudely to equate present-day nationalism with eighteenth century Jacobitism. But the picture is more nuanced than that, since there were also more intellectual advocates at that time that can explain such a broad generalisation. In the middle of the eighteenth century, in his *Essay Upon Several Subjects Concerning British Antiquities*, the Enlightened Edinburgh economist Lord Kames both reflected and gave momentum to a fundamental attitude that believed that modern commercial society softens and polishes men, uniting people, disposing them to peace, by establishing in every state an order of citizens bound by their common desire of supplying their mutual wants. Ironically, this approach was shared by one contemporary Mackenzie historian with whom I am extremely familiar, because he was a close member of my own particular branch of the family. Dr James Mackenzie was a successful physician who went on to conduct an extremely successful career in England. Among other charitable achievements that earned him the nickname 'Benevolent Mackenzie', he was a, now forgotten, pioneer in the west of inoculation against disease (in his case against the ever-present contemporary curse of smallpox). In fact, Dr James accompanied the last Earl of Seaforth as his tutor on the Grand Tour in Italy in 1753. It should be remembered that many a Highlander participated in the Edinburgh Enlightenment when Edinburgh was dubbed the 'Athens of the North' and Voltaire declared: 'We look to Scotland for all our ideas of civilisation.' Dr James was just such an Enlightened Highlander.

In his *History of Health*, Dr James laid out his structural view of historical development when he wrote how the 'gradual advances made by the human mind in cultivating the sciences' meant that English society represented a standard to which Scotland should aspire, linking commercial society with a more refined existence. In a letter I came across to his cousin, the Edinburgh lawyer John Mackenzie of Delvine, he asserted, 'England indeed gives greater Encouragement to Industry than any other Nation I know.' Thus, while feeling a strong obligation to use his wealth and influence to support those numerous nephews who hailed from the place of Dr James's birth in Sutherland in the far north of the Highlands – which he generously did – his attitude towards them was somewhat ambivalent, frequently referring to them in his correspondence as 'useless blockhead', 'Brutes', 'worthless' and a 'Rabble of Hottentots'. To illustrate how nuanced the culture of these times was, it is also worth noting that Dr James himself was born in Strathnaver where these nephews were still living, and it was in the house there of his grandfather, Alexander Mackenzie, that the incident of second sight that Professor Garden conveyed to the Royal Society occurred.

The great irony of this world view, then was that, by endorsing it, Dr James Mackenzie was a major participant in laying the seeds of a historical perspective that depicted the land of his birth as part of an anachronistic culture. And many other writers on Scotland from the middle of the eighteenth century came to regard the Highlanders as uncouth barbarians, further fuelling the prejudice that came to demonise a stereotype spawned during the Jacobite rebellion of the 'Forty-Five and its aftermath. But, conversely, at this very same time, others began to debate the cultural costs of capitalism. Dr Johnson wondered during his Scottish tour with James Boswell whether any society benefited from becoming entirely 'commercial' in its mentality and attitudes. Adam Smith himself drew attention to the decline of the martial spirit in capitalist society; and Adam Ferguson, comparing the Highlanders to the Homeric warriors and the ancient Spartans and Roman legions, asked whether Scotland was not the poorer for the destruction of its traditional way of life and whether there was a price to be paid for losing the qualities of courage, honour and loyalty in the face of a purely commercial society. His book *Essay on the History of Civil Society* acknowledged that progress involves losses as well as gains, seeing an 'imminent tension between material progress and moral advance'. His 'noble savage' is possessed of 'a penetration, a force of imagination and elocution, an ardour of mind, an affection and courage' beyond that of civilised man.

Also somewhat paradoxically, therefore it was Enlightenment values that sowed the seeds of a Romantic perception of the Highlands that came to most

*Scotland's Nostradamus*

obvious prominence with the extraordinary reception surrounding James MacPherson's *Fingal*, together with his other epic Ossianic poems, and subsequently with the historical novels of Sir Walter Scott, which were to transform later histories (while their precise authenticity has been debated, the Ossianic legends were part of that same oral tradition that will have conveyed the stories surrounding the Brahan Seer through the generations). It was from Scott's immensely influential bestsellers that subsequent popular histories derived the idea of a clash of cultures: Scotsman versus Englishman, Lowlander versus Highlander, Presbyterian versus Episcopalian. As part of a circle that comprised Robert Burns, Henry Mackenzie, John Home and Robert Ferguson, men who were trying to save what they could of their country's Gaelic and Scots heritage, Scott's romantic leanings were part of the cosmopolitan intellectual interest in primitivism that goes back to the Royal Society's scientific concern with Highland curiosities like second sight in the seventeenth century. Marketed as Scotland's answer to Homer, *The Tales of Ossian* were translated into several languages and had phenomenal international success. MacPherson's admirers included Schiller and Goethe; his works were even said to have been among Napoleon's favourite reading.

In *May we be Britons?* I have shown that the interesting point about educated Highlanders such as Dr James and the last Earl of Seaforth is that such people firmly challenge those preconceptions about a simplistic dichotomy between the Highlands and the Enlightenment that began at the time Adam Ferguson and Sir Walter Scott's influential writings were popularised. Indeed, a thorough study of this family can shed considerable light on the complex and nuanced nature of their social circle, which shared its roots with their Episcopalian/Roman Catholic, Jacobite and Freemasonic inclinations. This was a circle that was as at ease with both Highland and Jacobite traditions, as it was with the freshest ideas of the European intellectual elite.

~·~·~

In a zoom lecture for the Clan Mackenzie Society of Scotland and the UK in 2021, I gave a presentation on the social life of the Mackenzies, based on what I had found when delving into the lives of my own direct ancestors (it can now be seen as a YouTube video entitled *Friendship, Wine, Poetry and Music: The Social Life of the Mackenzies in the 17th and 18th Centuries*). What struck me was the remarkably cosmopolitan lives that these people led, even those who were born in some of the remotest regions of the Highlands and Islands. Contrary to a perception that might be common, life at that time in the far north of Scotland was far from being exclusively 'Solitary, poor, nasty, brutish and short' (to quote Thomas Hobbes's depiction of what he saw as 'primitive' societies). I explain how I came to discover that, contrary to the tradition of the Highlander subsisting on illicit whisky and beer, there was a longstanding tradition in my branch of the McKenzie family of importing fine clarets from Bordeaux, thanks to a reciprocal trade in fishing, the lucrative rights to which they owned off Chanonry Point. Billy Kay, in his book, *Knee Deep in Claret*, even argues that claret has a legitimate claim to being Scotland's original national drink, ahead of whisky, describing it as the 'bloodstream of the Auld Alliance': as well as being a military alliance based on a long-standing friendship, a Franco-Scottish deal signed in 1295 gave Scottish merchants privileged access to Bordeaux's finest wines for centuries, much to the annoyance of English wine drinkers, who received an inferior product. At this point I might mention that my studies of family history have also brought me in touch with Aonghas MacCoinnich of Glasgow University, whose own detailed research into the Mackenzies of Seaforth has shown us that Gaelic society before the '45 was not uncommercial, and it was certainly not purely patriarchal. With a family who combined traditional landownership with trade during the seventeenth and eighteenth centuries, that was something I had encountered myself in my own branch of the family, lower down the social ranks.

In my talk on the social life of the Mackenzies, I went on to explain how these Highlanders also shared their sophisticated tastes in music of the highest calibre with the French, owing to a similar reciprocal relationship that began when young Scots often finished their education in France, with their experiences of lute and viol playing, for example, and this was yet further reinforced in the eighteenth century by the presence of exiles at the Jacobite court. I have written elsewhere about the Fifth Earl's widely eclectic tastes. William, along with his twin sister, Lady Mary, who went on to become an intimate friend of the English poet, Alexander Pope, finished his education at the Jacobite court in St-Germain. As clan chief, he continued to employ Murdoch Matheson as his bard and maintained traditional troupes of pipers to entertain him on his progress through his territories in Kintail, Lochalsh and Lewis; but the Seaforth accounts also show him to have remunerated itinerant musicians on an *ad hoc* basis, such as the one-off payment of £1 1s 6d to the classical harper, Daniel Melville in June 1710. Melville is known to have travelled the country as he is also found in Edinburgh in 1709, when he had recently arrived from Ireland with his wife Helen. Such men also entertained the chief and his guests as chroniclers and bearers of news and gossip. William's hybrid nature thus also firmly defies the stereotypical image of the coarse Highland savage that was promoted by both the Lowland Scots and the English well into the eighteenth century. In fact, this prejudice appears to have been so entrenched that it persists even to this day. In 2014, I was invited to take part in the episode entitled 'Battle in the Glens' (concerning the Battle of Glen Shiel in 1719) for the Channel 4 television series, *Walking through History*. After the day's filming, the crew had dinner in the Kintail Lodge Hotel and, during the course of the conversation, Tony Robinson commented on how he loved my idea of William as a mixture of Highland warlord and cultivated European. The two English academic historians present, who were actually quite distinguished and really should have known better, were

*Scotland's Nostradamus*

totally sceptical, being of the opinion that all Highlanders of the period were, without exception, uneducated barbarians.

In this regard one should also remember what has been said of Roderick Morrison, who was dubbed the 'Blind Harper of Dunvegan', who died in 1714. Roderick's brother, the Rev John Morrison, who was sometimes named 'The Bard' and was the minister of Urray, the local parish to Brahan and subsequently of Petty on the Moray Firth, as I will show in due course, was remembered for numerous instances of second sight as the 'Petty Seer'. Roderick, for his part, has been dubbed 'Gaelic Scotland's last minstrel', but recent musicologists recognise that his role as a gentleman musician should also be regarded as representative of the cosmopolitan drawing-room music of the period, cultivated by the upper ranks of society throughout Europe.

The historian David Stevenson has recently shown how political exiles carried Scottish Masonic traditions throughout the 'Jacobite diaspora', where they attracted a startling variety of monarchs, philosophers, scientists and artists to their supposedly defeated creed and culture. It is in this context that the Mackenzies, Jacobite or otherwise, should be placed, alongside Charles Edward Stuart himself (best known today as 'Bonnie Prince Charlie'), who (despite Diana Gabaldon's absurd foppish portrayal) is now being reappraised as an intellectual, owning an extensive library and among whose friends were pre-eminent *philosophes*, such as Voltaire, Montesquieu, Condillac and Helvétius. It is now time to recognise that the social and intellectual circle of those who have been labelled 'Highlanders', and who participated in the Jacobite Rebellions in 1715, 1719 and 1745–6, was also the milieu of Enlightenment. In the light of this family's intellectual affinities over the course of the seventeenth and eighteenth centuries, one might justifiably conclude that, contrary to the widely accepted stereotype, many Highlanders came to identify with Jacobite culture precisely because of their cosmopolitan and cultivated background.

It is thus equally important to remember that Highland culture, whether experienced in the hall of a laird, or in a village *ceilidh* house, derived from a long cosmopolitan tradition that continued to cross many frontiers and reflected the highly sophisticated, diverse and outward-looking nature of the Highlands and Islands during this early modern period. We should recognise that it was in this social and cultural context that the oral folktales surrounding the Brahan Seer were shared as part of that international form of minstrel entertainment, so crucial to life in this region. We should also therefore protest in the strongest terms that the Highlands at this time was far from being a benighted region cut off from civilisation.

# An Occult Laboratory: Part One

From what we have seen of the Highlands from the perspective of the Mackenzies, we now know that they are as well placed in the early modern period in a cosmopolitan European context, rather than being studied with the hindsight of a perspective coloured by prejudices about 'Highland Savages'. In the light of this European cultural context, I think of myself remarkably fortunate in my education at Cambridge University in that, at the same time that I was beginning my studies of Francis, Lord Seaforth, supervised by David (now Professor Sir David) Cannadine, I was also being taught by Peter (now Professor Emeritus Peter) Burke, whose perspective of the entire early modern period was exceptionally European and interdisciplinary. As a consequence of this, I became interested in the wider work of those historians who comprised what is known as the *Annales* school in France, which had been conducted with regard to popular culture in early modern Europe. It was their approach to look at wider, long-term structural changes that affect people's *mentalité*; in other words, their feelings about the wider society and world they live in, and their place within it.

Interestingly, a student of Peter's had remarked to him at some point before he taught me that 'only when intelligent and educated men ceased to take prophecy seriously were the Middle Ages at an end'. In addressing this remark, Peter pointed out the various complexities surrounding this question, since, apart from anything else, much depends on the kind of prophecy one is talking about. Sir Isaac Newton himself tried to put the study of Biblical prophecy on a firmer scholarly basis; while the very subject of second sight in the Highlands can also be shown to have been the subject of serious scientific scrutiny in its own right, both during the seventeenth century and later.

To reinforce this point directly, I should now make clear that, when trying to analyse the historical evidence behind the Brahan Seer, neither Alexander Mackenzie, nor more recently William Matheson and Elizabeth Sutherland, appear to have been aware of the important debate surrounding second sight in seventeenth-century intellectual circles that I have already touched on briefly. It is, in fact, a subject I addressed in my chapter entitled 'Men of Right Reason' in my *History of the Mackenzies*, after discovering how the Mackenzie family played an unexpectedly significant part in what we now regard as a Scientific Revolution in the seventeenth century (as they later did in the Edinburgh Enlightenment). This serious intellectual interest in the phenomenon of second sight was first initiated by Robert Boyle and his colleagues in the Royal Society at precisely the time when the Brahan Seer was purported to have lived, and, crucially, that

*Scotland's Nostradamus*

correspondence was with and about some of the key players in the Brahan Seer's story. Let us therefore examine this evidence more closely.

In fact, the very starting point of this group of intellectuals' interest was the correspondence between Robert Boyle and George Mackenzie, Viscount Tarbat (the future First Earl of Cromartie), who was, as we have seen, none other than the brother of the Brahan Seer's nemesis, Countess Isobel. In this, Boyle had asked Tarbat in October 1678 for information on second sight, and Tarbat gave him an account of two instances of second sight that had occurred while he was in the Highlands during the Interregnum. Tarbat, it seems, had been in touch with the secretary of the Royal Society, Henry Oldenburg, via his Edinburgh contact, Professor James Gregory, in 1675. A letter from the divine, George Hickes, to Samuel Pepys, dated 19 June 1700, records that twenty-two years previously, when Hickes was in Scotland in the entourage of the Duke of Lauderdale, who was then Secretary of State for Scotland, Tarbat had recounted to the Duke and those with him one of the stories concerning his experience of second sight and he subsequently told Boyle, hence stimulating him to seek out Tarbat when he was in London later in the same year.

Before that date only the vaguest awareness of the phenomenon appears to have been known to this English circle, possibly the earliest known reference being that of John Evelyn in a letter, which is now in the British Library dating from about 1670, in which he wrote: 'That some at first view, can tel what events shall happen to any person they see: of these some are very innocent & weake people, especially women; and such as professe they know not how it comes to them.' Subsequently, he added: 'The old Duke of Albermarle told me he knew this to be true, in Scotland; tho at first he much doubted it.'

In his 2002 publication, *The Occult Laboratory: Magic, Science and Second Sight in Late Seventeenth-Century Scotland*, Michael Hunter shows us that Boyle and his colleagues believed that it was quite possible to establish by firsthand, pragmatic observational means the reality of phenomena that appeared to be above the normal course of nature. There was some debate about the very nature of how second sight might have worked – such as that between those thinkers who were influenced by the Platonic tradition, like the Cambridge philosophers, Henry More and Ralph Cudworth, who disagreed with Boyle on the extent to which mechanical principles were adequate to explain the workings of nature; while others offered explanations of the phenomenon in terms of hypotheses of bodily humours, the quality of the air, or the role of fairies or angels. Boyle was aware of the complexity of second sight, writing of it as 'an intermediate region, bounded on the north by psychology'. All were agreed, however, that God might show his activity by intervening in ways that transgressed nature's ordinary course, and that these might be empirically verifiable. Martin Martin, for his part, purposefully refused to offer any explanation of the phenomena of second sight, paying emphasis to the reliability of his informants and the integrity of the information that he purveyed. The important point is that, for all these people, the phenomenon was regularly discussed in a context that took for granted the reality of an active supernatural realm, which seemed as legitimate an object of intellectual speculation as anything purely natural.

Although it might appear 'unscientific' to us today, we should now recognise that the 'supernatural' was at the forefront of intellectual thought in the late seventeenth century and was by no means incompatible with scientific thought any more than alchemy was. As I have touched on, no less a luminary of the Scientific Revolution than Sir Isaac Newton wrote widely on alchemy, as well as producing several treatises on Biblical prophecy: like many of his Protestant contemporaries in England, he was a strong believer in the prophetic interpretation of the Bible.

That is not to say that acceptance of second sight was not met with a parallel current of scepticism, both about second sight and about the presence of supernatural activity in the world of which it formed part, and Hunter describes a 'polarisation between scoffing wits and earnest virtuosi', which is not entirely dissimilar to the kind of 'culture war' and its polarisation that is familiar to us today.

It was in the context of this debate that Lord Reay wrote to Pepys about second sight in the Highlands and Islands. Reay's story related to the servant of his great-grandfather, Donald, First Lord Reay, who was the Third Earl of Seaforth's uncle, and, as a substantial landowner in Sutherland, a close neighbour of his in the Highlands. The First Lord Reay was also a first cousin of my forebears at this time, including Dr James Mackenzie's grandfather, Reay's tenant in Stathnaver, in whose house it was that the incident of second sight took place that Professor Garden had relayed. Reay was a friend of Christian IV of Denmark, for whom he and a number of his close Mackenzie relatives fought in the Thirty Years' War. Christian had a keen interest in alchemy, and his father, Frederick II, was a patron of Tycho Brahe, the astronomer to the Emperor Rudolph II, who also employed Elizabeth I's astrologer, Dr John Dee. Reay himself was known as the 'Wizard of Reay' from the intensive interest in learning that he shared with the Danish king, but he also became the focus of later folklore. During a sojourn in Venice, Donald was supposed to have made the acquaintance of the Devil, becoming one of his best students in philosophy, metaphysics, alchemy, Venetian disguises and carnal pursuits. The most famous story is about how he gets the better of the Devil in Smoo Cave on the north coast of Sutherland after the Devil stole his shadow when Donald was said to have shouted out the proverb: 'De'il tak' the hindmost!'

A story about Donald that has more evidential basis, however, was one that the younger Lord Reay recounts about a footman of the First Lord Reay 'who was mightily concerned on Seeing a dagger in the Lord Reay's breast'. At the time his master simply laughed at his concern, but the footman was apparently vindicated when the doublet Lord Reay was wearing at the time was passed on to a servant, and subsequently 'hee was stabed be another in the breast When that Doublet was one him'. Reay was to write in his letter to Pepys:

> These stories with what is Conntained in my Lord Tarbats Letters are
> the most sufficient to prove the second sight of any ever I heard and The
> people are so much perswaded of the truth of it in the highlands and
> Isles That one would be More Laught at, for not believing it there Than
> affirmeing it elsewhere, for my owne part I Doe not Questione it Tho But a
> small Ground to perswade others to the beliefe of it But I Dare affirm had
> You the same Reasons I have You would be of my opinion.

Hunter points out that Reay's comment was intended to be a challenge to those contemporaries who regarded the likes of Aubrey, following the publication in 1696 of his *Miscellanies*, as a credulous old fool, since it appears that at the time of this first published account of second sight the phenomenon had become a coffee-house joke. 'Second-sighted Highlanders' turn up in burlesques of magical claims in Addison and Steele's *Spectator*, for example, and in pamphlets by Daniel Defoe.

When it comes to Defoe, however, we should remember that, in the 1720s, he wrote three occult treatises: *A Political History of the Devil* (1726), *A System of Magick* (1726) and *An Essay on the History and Reality of Apparitions* (1727). Some people have been rather dismissive of these works, regarding them as pot-boilers, intended, for purely commercial ends, to exploit people's interest in the supernatural and the sensational, or dismissing them at any rate as an anomaly in Defoe's works, which people have long regarded as precursors of 'modernity'. Nevertheless, some recent authorities have taken Defoe's occult treatises seriously, and looked upon them as reliable reflections of this writer's own views on the supernatural, as well as a key to understanding the supernatural elements in his fictional works. Defoe's ideas appear to be founded on those of the Cambridge Neoplatonists and he is certainly known to have investigated the subject at great length in the second sequel to *Robinson Crusoe*, using his celebrated fictional hero to reassert his conviction that 'there is a certain converse between the world of spirits, and the spirits of this world; that is to say, between spirits uncased or unembody'd, and souls of men embody'd or cased up in flesh and blood, as we all are on this side [of] death'.

When we also remember the words of Defoe that we have already seen, which were intentionally respectful and defend the Highlands against accusations of barbarity, those pamphlets of his that mocked second sight should perhaps be seen as part of the ongoing propaganda against the Highlands that I have discussed (and that Defoe was known at one time to have been professionally engaged in as a government spy in Scotland at the time of the Union): that is, the propaganda that reached its zenith in the aftermath of the 'Forty-Five rebellion. In all of this we should therefore be consciously extremely wary of the dangers of anachronism, and we should avoid confusing such writings from the hindsight of what we would today regard as a simple black and white divide between 'superstition' and 'progress', or between 'modern' versus 'backward' ways of thinking.

*An Occult Laboratory: Part One*

The subtle point to be understood here is that those who pioneered a dismissive attitude towards magical phenomena were, in fact, largely atheists, in the sense that they were radical humanists who had little time for the laborious empiricism of the new science; while a scientist like Boyle and those who investigated second sight under his influence, with the goal of employing the rigorous methodology that science demands, were nervous of what they saw as radical ideas, largely because of their fear of the dangerous precedents for religion that such a dismissive attitude towards the supernatural realm might have. One must remember that almost universal Christian belief at that time meant that a belief in the supernatural was the orthodox view among intellectuals, as we can see from the wide-ranging writings of Sir Isaac Newton.

The point therefore to remember, which appears somewhat counter-intuitive to us today, is that Boyle's scientific method sought to provide evidence to challenge the atheists and freethinkers, who were then widely regarded by rational thinkers of the time as being irrational for questioning the very existence of second sight, rather than attempting a sound explanation for it. It genuinely seems as if Boyle and others like him hoped that by offering a well-researched and dispassionate account of a plausible phenomenon like this, they would vindicate the reality of the supernatural realm in a way that extravagant tales of diabolical activity could not. In this there is no doubt that it was confidence in the sober authenticity of reports from reliable witnesses in an area where such practices were common that led Boyle and his like to pursue this topic in the way they did, in the hope that sceptics might be convinced. In the eyes of the modern scientist, they may have been wrong, but the episode is nevertheless a revealing sign of the times. The Restoration spirit of free enquiry allowed many aspects of Gaelic culture to be examined without automatic hostility or condescension. As Michael Hunter has explained, the English members of the Royal Society simply regarded the geographically remote Highlands as a kind of 'Occult Laboratory', which could supply them with empirical evidence for their research.

The result of this debate, which is particularly valuable to those of us who want to understand seventeenth-century thinking in the Highlands today, is that it was to bring to light crucial information about belief systems that might otherwise never have been fully recorded at all. This is especially the case for the very specific light it sheds on the particular case of the Brahan Seer and in that respect, to quote Michael Hunter: 'Boyle and his successors deserve at once our thanks and our sympathy.'

—·—·—

But in all these late seventeenth-century accounts by those who would have been close to the actors in the Brahan Seer's story as relayed to us by Alexander Mackenzie, was there any mention of Coinneach *Odhar* himself or his prophecies? Surely such a celebrated practitioner of second sight would have been central in any account to be conveyed to the Royal Society, since they would have

*Scotland's Nostradamus*

undoubtedly been celebrated and known throughout the Highlands at this time, not least to a man like Tarbat, whose own sister was purported to have played such a central role in his downfall?

Perhaps crucially, we do learn that Countess Isobel's husband, Kenneth Mackenzie, the Third Earl of Seaforth, was himself believed to have claimed the power of foretelling future events. George Hickes, Dean of Worcester, wrote to Pepys in 1700,

> It was commonly reported when I was in Scotland, that the Lord Seaforth then living had the second sight, and thereby foretold a very dreadfull storm to some of his friends who went by sea from London to Scotland, in which they had like to have been cast away. I once heard the Duke of Lauderdale railly about it, but he neithyer did own it, or disown it, according to that maxim of civill law, Qui tacet, ut non negat, sic utique neque fatetur.

In reality, the fact that Lauderdale should have mocked Seaforth for his clairvoyance was most likely motivated by political ends (Lauderdale was a notorious adversary of the Mackenzies: according to the local gossip, the Rev James Fraser or Wardlaw, it was Lauderdale's family, 'the Maitlands' motto to be *mckenio mastix*, the scurge of the Mackenzies; and himselfe was heard to say that to be a Mackenzy was a mortall sin'). In fact, the supposedly worldly Duke himself made investigations into alchemical, as well as architectural and mathematical, lore, and like the Freemason, Sir Robert Moray, who founded the Royal Society and informed his fellow members on Scottish second sight, Lauderdale studied occult writers, acquiring Rosicrucian and Fluddian works for his extensive library. Not only that, but Lauderdale's own wife was herself attributed with the gift of second sight, as well as being learned in the occult sciences, with which she collaborated with Sir Robert.

The crucial point is that an interest at this time in the phenomenon of second sight was a respectable concern for those intellectual luminaries who were responsible for what we now call the Scientific Revolution: far from being backward and benighted, men such as Tarbat, who himself attempted to put forward an environmental explanation for the phenomenon, shared their interest with the most forward-thinking minds of the time. In summary, we are beginning to see that the reasons for the survival of a belief in second sight in Scotland were subtle and complex ones and cannot be accounted for by black and white stereotypes. Keith Thomas concludes his seminal book *Religion and the Decline of Magic* with the observation that the various beliefs that he discusses are not 'intrinsically less worthy of respect than some of those which we ourselves continue to hold. If magic is to be defined as the employment of ineffective techniques to allay anxiety when effective ones are not available, then we must recognise that no society will ever be free from it.'

But whatever the case, now that we have established that the Highlands was far from being an uncivilised backwater, how then can we explain the very specific and widely believed stories about the prophecies of the Brahan Seer from our knowledge of contemporaneous history?

What we do learn from all of this is that there is considerable documentary evidence surrounding the precise circle of the Third Earl of Seaforth available for us to look for the existence of a known factual Brahan Seer, and yet we can be reasonably confident that there was no such contemporary record that relates to such a character, who would undoubtedly have held remarkable prominence at the time. Indeed, I have shown that one of the chief commentators on the subject of second sight was none other than Countess Isobel's brother, Tarbat, whose correspondence with Robert Boyle was central to the whole debate on the subject. Not only that, but, as we have seen, Tarbat was granted a commission in 1662 to try the two witches, Margaret Simpson and Bessie Watson from Cromarty on the Black Isle. He would most certainly have mentioned Coinneach *Odhar* Mackenzie had he been causing such upset as a result of his clairvoyance at the time, resulting in his dramatic execution by Tarbat's own sister. It is, moreover, highly significant that the Rev James Fraser, a contemporary of the Third Earl of Seaforth and his Countess, is both critical of the latter and gives an extensive account of Hugh Lord Lovat's deathbed prophecy regarding the chiefly line of the Frasers in the Wardlaw Manuscript; and yet he makes no mention of the Brahan Seer.

But one observation that is worth making here is a fascinating one that my brother Kevin made in a conversation we once had on the subject. He pointed out that in the person of the Third Earl of Seaforth, we do have a prominent Coinneach *Mhor* Mackenzie, who was described at the time as having second sight, and that *Mhor* (pronounced 'more', meaning 'great', on account of his high social standing, as well as by virtue of his personal physical stature) sounds very similar to *Odhar* (which is pronounced 'or'); Kenneth being the anglicised version of the Third Earl's Christian name in Gaelic, Coinneach. As a seer whose principal seat was Brahan Castle, it would have been perfectly appropriate to have dubbed him 'the Brahan Seer'. Coinneach *Mhor* features prominently in the Brahan Seer's story, as relayed to us by local oral tradition by Alexander Mackenzie, being married to the woman who had the seer executed. Could it be, therefore, that Coinneach *Mhor*, the Third Earl of Seaforth, who was known to have had second sight and lived at Brahan, got confused in the memories of subsequent oral folk traditions with the Coinneach *Odhar* of the previous century, who may well have been burned for witchcraft on Chanonry Point, owing to his earlier entanglement with another formidable local clan chief's wife? Could he be the authentic historical Brahan Seer?

# A Land of Myth and Legend

> On long, dark winter nights it is still the custom in small villages for friends to collect in a house and hold what they call a 'ceilidh'. Young and old are entertained by the reciters of old poems and legendary stories which deal with ancient beliefs, the doings of traditional heroes and heroines, and so on. Some sing old and new songs set to old music or new music composed in the manner of the old.Donald Alexander Mackenzie, *Wonder Tales from Scottish Myth and Legend*, London, 1917, p. 14

The words of Donald Alexander Mackenzie's introduction to his collection of Scottish myths and legends was written shortly after Alexander Mackenzie published his book on the Brahan Seer and I would argue that one important reason why a belief in the Brahan Seer's prophecies survived for so long in this part of the world was that this was an area rich in oral tradition that had a remarkable propensity for preserving the stories of its past. While I have challenged the perception of the Highlands as a backwater of superstition, I have no problem with the Scottish tourist industry celebrating the remarkable richness of the Highlands' folk tradition, a tradition that I would also argue is not in any way the mark of a primitive culture.

We have already seen that Highland folklore was valued at the highest levels of European society in the late eighteenth century and early nineteenth, thanks to some degree to the huge impact of James MacPherson's Ossianic poems. This was inflamed further by the internationally bestselling novels of Sir Walter Scott, who promoted the romantic and heroic nature of the Highlands, and in the middle of the century, one of Scott's biggest fans, Queen Victoria, gave the area the royal seal of approval in the tangible form of Balmoral Castle and her *Highland Journals*, which became, quite literally, a mark of Victorian taste and sensibilities. In fact, the Queen was presented with a copy of Alexander Mackenzie's *The Prophecies of the Brahan Seer* by the Clach himself, when she met him in Inverness.

One of the places the Queen mentioned in her memoirs, when she made an expedition to what she termed 'Mackenzie country', was Loch Maree, where she extended her stay because the scenery and its enchanting atmosphere had such a favourable impact on her. The Queen even made a special visit to the islands on the Loch, where a religious service was held. The Rev Alexander MacGregor, writing in 1901, remarked on how

> In this manner our beloved sovereign, whose eye is always keen to observe, whose taste is exquisite to admire, and whose sensibility is great

*A Land of Myth and Legend*

to appreciate all that is grand and beautiful in Nature's workmanship, has conferred a lasting honour on the true-hearted Highland Chief, Sir Kenneth S. Mackenzie, Baronet; on his loyal and delighted tenantry; as well as on his romantic property in Gairloch.

The Rev Alexander further described the sacred well on Isle Maree, which the Queen visited,

> in which, as in the pool of St Fillan's, lunatics were plunged and healed, and, in short, all manner of diseases cured. Around this sacred spot the usual oblations were made to the tutelary saint, and coins of every descriptions stuck into a tree that grew out of the bank. The sacred water of this well was deemed so effectual in curing the insane, that they were brought to it from the remotest quarters of the north. The treatment they received was no doubt somewhat severe. Before they drank of its waters, it was reckoned indispensable to the permanency of their cure, that they should be dragged at the stern of a boat twice round the Island, pulled by a rope made of horse-hair, fastened under their arms and around their shoulders. They were then dipped in the well, and drank of its water.

The Rev Alexander described the special magic this place held for the romantic Victorians:

> The scene indeed, is so grand, wild, and fantastic, that words are at fault to describe it. Some years ago it was visited by tourists, whose admiration of it cannot be better expressed than in their own words. 'When this majestic scene first burst upon our view, the effect was as surprising and enchanting, as it was unexpected. The lake sparkled bright in the evening sun. The lofty mountains were, at their summits, tinged with his golden rays, while in the hollows, and nearer their base, they were wreathed in mist and light clouds. The effect of this was to increase to a prodigious degree, the apparent height of the mountains, to make every hollow on their rugged sides, seem a deep and inaccessible glen, and to enlarge to an almost immeasurable extent the lake, and the hills which rose at its extreme distance. It was altogether a scene of enchantment never to be forgotten. The white piqued summits of the File-Mountain sparkled like the spires and turrets of an emerald palace, the work of some eastern magician, or of the genii of Arabian romance, and forming a splendid contrast to the dark and rugged Slioch, which rises from the opposite side of the lake!

As MacGregor explained:

> It is by no means surprising that Superstition, in her fantastic freaks, should have, in ages long byegone, selected this weird locality for the manifestation of not a few of her favourite protegés ... This superb sheet

*Scotland's Nostradamus*

of water, from its almost unfathomable depth and other dimensions, furnished a befitting receptacle for brownies, water-horses, uruisgean, kelpies, and such like, while one of the islets of this beautiful lake became the arena of various superstitious practices, and of curing therewith some of the most inveterate diseases.

Having taken a boat myself to Isle Maree, where I saw the famous sacred money tree, I can understand the magic this place has always had. It is no coincidence that Loch Maree was the setting for two legends that can be traced back to the thirteenth century, which might be regarded as something of a golden age of Highland myth and folktale. No lesser a genius than Richard Wagner based most of his greatest works on this period of European legend. Significantly, he regarded the literary content of his *Gesamtkuntsartwerke*, or 'Complete Art Works', as important as their musical accomplishments. One of these two legends that are set on Loch Maree relates the story of a local girl and her lover, who was a Norse prince, whose graves are purported to be the ones that lie side by side, marked with Celtic crosses on the eastern end of the holy island. In short, this tragedy, which included the girl's mistake of displaying a black flag as a signal to the prince's returning ship, instead of a white one, mirrors the more widely known Ancient Greek story of Theseus. The other story, known as the *Legend of the Son of the Goat*, relates how a fleeing prince is suckled by a goat in a cave on the side of Loch Maree (not unlike the story of Romulus and Remus, who, in their case, were suckled by a wolf). The story tells how, after a series of adventures, the 'Son of the Goat' marries the daughter of the Lord of Eilean Donan Castle, ending the local clan rivalries. In *May we be Britons?* Kevin and I analyse how this legend reflected a local folk memory that recorded the alliance between the two major dynasties that founded Clan Mackenzie, before this family went on to dominate the region.

One of the prophecies relayed by A.B. MacLennan recounted how, on the eastern side of Ross-shire,

> In the parish of Avoch is a well of beautiful clear water, out of which the Brahan Seer, upon one occasion, took a refreshing draught. So pleased was he with the water, that he looked at his Blue Stone, and said – 'Whoever he be that drinketh of they water henceforth, if suffering from any disease, shall be placing two pieces of straw or wood on they surface, ascertain whether he will recover or not. If he is to recover, the straws will whirl round in opposite directions; if he is to die soon, they will remain stationary.' The writer knew people who went to the well and made the experiment. He was himself once unwell, and supposed to be at the point of death; he got of the water of the well, and he still lives. Whether it did him good or not, it is impossible to say, but this he does know, that the water pleased him uncommonly well.

*A Land of Myth and Legend*

This prophecy is generally thought to refer to what is now known as the Craigie Well, dedicated to St Benet on the north side of Munlochy Bay in the old estate of Bennetsfield on the Black Isle. It dates from pre-Christian times, and, like the more famous Clootie Well at Munlochy, which is dedicated to Curetán, the Scoto-Pictish bishop saint, can trace its story to a much older pagan past. It is still visited by local people on the first Sunday in May, who, if the ritual is to be correctly observed, should spill a little water three times on the ground, cross themselves and fix a small offering of lace or silk to one of the overhanging trees as a gift to the guardian fairy of the well, before drinking and making a wish. The much better-known Clootie Well at Munlochy draws tourists from all over the world, and generations of rotting rags, can be seen attached to the tree and fence above the spring. The rag or cloot is dipped in the well and tied to a tree in the hope that a sickness or ailment will fade as the rag disintegrates. Here the well was once thought to have had the power to cure sick children who were left there overnight.

The story relating to the Brahan Seer acquiring his 'seeing stone' from the fairies also accords with a longstanding prehistoric belief that associated second sight with the fairy world. Known in the Highlands as *Daoine-sith*, meaning the 'hill-folk', or *Fiosaichin*, ('those that know'), like the spirits in Dante's *Inferno*, they knew the future. What the Highlanders said of the fairies, the Zulus say of the souls of their dead ancestors. Similarly, John Dee sought to contact spirits through the use of a 'scryer', or crystal-gazer, which he thought would act as an intermediary between himself and the angels. This is reflected in both Hugh Miller's account of Coinneach *Odhar* acquiring his gift after falling asleep on a fairy hillock, and in that of Mr Maclennan regarding the Seer's experience of the waking dead at Baile-na-Cille, in the Parish of Uig. Fairies were believed to haunt underground dwellings, cairns or hillocks, where elf arrows are found. Andrew Lang also found a belief in second sight among the Australians, the Tonkaways, the Aztecs, the Incas, the Samoyeds, the Polynesians, the Maories, the Greeks and the Egyptians. Dee's 'speculum', which was subsequently owned by Horace Walpole and is now in the British Museum, was a natural volcanic glass Aztec cult object in the shape of a hand-mirror that was brought to Europe in the late 1520s. Many of the beliefs involved the use of 'divining stones' and being left alone at night at the tombs of brave men, for example. In fact, as we have seen, the nature of second sight in the Highlands as recorded by those who researched it in the seventeenth century (and indeed in later nineteenth century accounts) was of a different order and the suggestion that the Seer used a small pebble with a hole in it, through which he is said to have looked when about to foretell the future, appears to have come from such more longstanding and cosmopolitan folk traditions.

Yet another Wester Ross legend, which could also be regarded as something of a foundation myth of the Mackenzies, is that known as the *Legend of the Birds*. The folklorist William Matheson (who, as we have seen also first identified

*Scotland's Nostradamus*

Coinneach *Odhar* as a genuine historical character), convincingly pointed out the parallels between that story and the crusading links, which the Mackenzies' progenitors were evidently engaged in, in the late thirteenth century. My brother Kevin has further explored the genuine historical context that lies at the origins of this story.

When I was a child of not more than ten years old, I recall being ill with tonsillitis and unable to attend lessons at school. My attentive mother, always keen that her son should not fall behind in his schoolwork, asked my teachers to provide me with homework. The work I was given was a project that looked at the historical origins of nursery rhymes, an example being 'Ring-a-ring-o-roses, a pocket full o-poses, a-tissue, a-tissue, we all fall down!' As many will know, this has been identified as dating back to the Great Plague of the 1660s, the ring of roses being the bubo that was its ominous symptom. While at the time I remember resenting what I deemed to be somewhat superfluous work that wasn't part of my classmates' curriculum, I do recall the subject being one of the most enjoyable ones I can remember from my early schooling, and I have ever since been fascinated by the historical truth behind works of folklore. In retrospect, I am extremely grateful to my mother, having since then always valued myth and legend as having its part in history: the point about 'Ring-a-ring-a-roses' is that it preserves a memory of a particularly momentous historical event that left its mark on people right down through the centuries. That is also one of the most crucial fascinations with the Brahan Seer's story.

~·~·~

It should be seen as no coincidence that one of the best-known prophecies that has been attached to the Brahan Seer's legacy can also be related to a supposedly prophetic figure, who was living in the thirteenth century, known as Thomas the Rhymer of Erceldoune. Thomas purportedly spoke the words: 'The teeth of sheep shall lay the plough on the shelf', which supposedly foresaw the Highland Clearances in the nineteenth century and their devastating displacement of tenant farmers who were replaced by more profitable sheep farming, many of them forced to emigrate overseas. Thomas's words significantly mirror those attributed to the Brahan Seer, in which he is quoted as saying:

> The day will come when the jaw-bone of the big sheep ... will put the plough on the rafters; when sheep shall become so numerous that the bleating of the one shall be heard by the other from Conchra in Lochalsh to Bun-da-Loch in Kintail ... they shall be at their height in price, and henceforth will go back and deteriorate, until they disappear altogether, and be so thoroughly forgotten that a man finding the jaw-bone of a sheep in a cairn, will not recognise it or be able to tell what animal it belonged to.

Coinneach *Odhar* was said to have gone on to describe that people would mass-emigrate from the country and that sheep would once again rule the land until the native peoples' eventual return. 'People will flee from their native country before an army of sheep' and 'The sheep shall eat the men'.

During the Highland Clearances, from 1750 to 1860, families were driven from the lands they had occupied for past centuries by their landowners and the land they had farmed was given over to the grazing of sheep. The harsh impact this had on local communities was devastating. Perhaps the most notorious of these evictions was that conducted in 1814 by Patrick Sellar, who was the Duke of Sutherland's factor, but also a sheep farmer in his own right. He was brought to trial for arson and culpable homicide, after an elderly woman in Strathnaver died when he destroyed the townships by fire so that they could not be reoccupied after eviction. Controversially, he was acquitted.

In Skye, in 1853, Lord MacDonald also conducted some particularly brutal clearances. Suisnish and Boreraig, for example, townships in two fertile, sheltered and beautiful spots on the island, were cleared at the same time when thirty-thre families were evicted in 1853 and their homes burned to make way for more profitable sheep. The ruined houses can still be seen on the hillside. The geologist Sir Archibald Geikie was visiting the area at the time of the clearance, and recalled:

> A strange wailing sound reached my ears ... I could see a long and motley procession winding along the road that led north from Suisnish ... There were old men and women, too feeble to walk, who were placed in carts; the younger members of the community on foot were carrying their bundles of clothes ... while the children, with looks of alarm, walked alongside ... A cry of grief went up to heaven, the long plaintive wail, like a funeral coronach, was resumed ... the sound re-echoed through the wide valley of Strath in one prolonged note of desolation.

And, in 1844, at Greenyards, near Bonar Bridge, 300 locals, mostly women, resisted thirty constables sent to enforce the sheriff's eviction orders and there was a notable skirmish with a number of injuries to the protestors, for example. Alexander Mackenzie's *History of the Highland Clearances*, published in 1883, which rapidly went into several editions, mentions how John Gordon of Cluny, the laird of a kelping estate, spoke of the transporting season when people were dragged down to the ships and sent to Canada.

~·~·~

In 1828, Allan Boyd F.S.A. published his *Prophecies of Thomas the Rhymer: The Ancient Scotch Prophet, Containing the Wonderful fulfilment of many of his Predictions; and those not yet accomplished*. Sir Thomas de Ercildoun, better remembered as Thomas the Rhymer, and also known as Thomas Learmont or True Thomas, was a real historical figure: a thirteenth-century laird from Earlston (which was then called 'Erceldoune') in the Borders of Scotland. In literature, he appears as the protagonist in the tale in which he is carried off by the

*Scotland's Nostradamus*

'Queen of Elfland' and later returned having gained the gift of prophecy, as well as the inability to tell a lie. Boyd claimed how his cryptic heraldic references could be shown to have predicted 'plainly, many things which have come to pass in our days; such as the extirpation of the noble race of the Stewarts, the Revolution, Sheriff-muir', along with 'even every particular of the rebellion in 1745 and 1746'. When speaking of the Battle of Prestonpans, in the year 1745, 'he names the very two neighbouring villages to the spot of ground whereon it was fought, viz. Coyleford-green, and Seton, saying "between Seton and the sea, sorrow should be wrought by the light of the moon" – Which act really came to pass that the morning the battle of Prestonpans was fought'. Like the Brahan Seer, Thomas's prophecies also included ones yet unfulfilled, such as, 'Last of all, a bloody desperate battle in Northumberland, on the river Tyne. Also great havock and slaughter about the broad walls of Berwick. All these things are yet to come to pass; and when the first appears, the rest will soon follow.'

> Who shal rule the ile of Bretaine
> From the North to the South sey?
> A French wife shal beare the Son,
> Shall rule all Bretaine to the sey,
> that of the Bruces blood shall come
> As neere as the nint degree.

Such was perhaps the most celebrated prophecy that has been attached to Thomas the Rhymer, which was printed in a chapbook entitled *The Whole Prophecie* of 1603, published in the aftermath of Queen Elizabeth I's death. The prophecy purported to have presaged the immensely significant historical moment whereby Scottish rule of all of Britain came about under King James I, whose mother Mary Stewart had been raised in her own mother's native France and was briefly the French Queen Consort during her first marriage to King Francis II. It is also worth noting that, as well as being by far the most famous of all of Thomas's prophecies, it has been argued that it was a rehash of an earlier prophecy that was originally meant for John Stewart, Duke of Albany, who died in 1536, and whose mother was Anna de la Tour d'Auvergne, daughter of the Count of Auvergne. Words not substantially different are also given in the same printed book, under the preceding section for the prophecy of John of Bridlington, with the additional date clue there of '1513 & thrise three there after', supposedly facilitating the identification of the 'Duke's son' in question as the Duke of Albany.

Interestingly, Sir Walter Scott attributed the original poem of Tristan and Isolde (or Isolt) to Thomas the Rhymer, although the origins of this legend, which was made particularly famous by Richard Wagner's groundbreaking opera in the mid-nineteenth century, are a matter of scholarly speculation, its geographical source having been placed alternatively in the Celtic domains of Cornwall, Ireland and Wales, as well as in Persia. The legends that were largely first written down in the thirteenth century were ideal sources that provided Wagner with

70

the type of psychological material that was perfect for his dramas. Among such tales that he turned to were those surrounding Parsifal and the Grail Knights, along with his son, the Swan Knight, Lohengrin, whom Kevin and I have identified as part of the network of crusading families who left such a significant mark on those Mackenzie family genealogies and that were, of course, also preserved in the oral tradition of the Clan's *seanachies*, who were the family's professional, often hereditary, bards.

The same prediction of the Highland Clearances, in which tenants were replaced by their landlords with sheep, was also said to have been foretold by the so-called Isla Seer, when he was purported to have prophesied, 'The time is coming when the sheep's tooth will take the coulter out of the ground in Isla.' Another prophecy that was given to the Isla Seer was, 'The day is coming when there will be a bridge on every burn, and a white house on every headland in Isla', which is comparable to the Brahan Seer's prediction that there would one day be 'a ribbon on every hill and a bridge on eery burn' (the ribbons have been presumed to have been roads). This is no coincidence, since Keith Thomas has shown that Thomas the Rhymer's prophecies, as with Merlin's predictions, albeit much adapted and distorted in the telling over the years, can usually be referred back to some specific text. He also suggests that it is often the case that it may be reasonably assumed that the majority of prophecies fell into one of two main genres: they were either genuine utterances of an earlier period, reinterpreted to fit new events in flagrant disregard of their original circumstances of composition (that being much the larger category); or they were spurious inventions by contemporaries, laying fraudulent claims to a sanctified antiquity. In the same way that Thomas the Rhymer was widely quoted in the Borders, as was the Isla Seer in Isla and the Inner Hebrides, in his own homelands of Ross-shire and Lewis, the Brahan Seer was the most celebrated seer and so it was inevitable that many oral tales relating to prophecy (received from the fairies, or the Queen of Elfland) got attached to his name. Each seer had his sphere of influence.

<hr>

In fact, just south of Chanonry Point on the Black Isle, on the southern side of the Moray Firth, the local evictions were supposed to have been predicted by another Highland Seer, the Rev John Morrison, who was minister of the local church of Petty from 1749 to 1774 (in which a number of members of the author's family, who lived in nearby Fisherton, were baptised in the eighteenth century), and thence known as the 'Petty Seer'. One of John's most celebrated predictions, according to A.B. MacLennan (who published a little book called *The Petty Seer*, which went through three editions from 1894 to 1906), concerned the event that occurred 'On the south side of the bay [of Petty, in which] an immense stone, weighing at least eight tons, which marked the boundaries between the estates of Lord Moray and Culloden, was, on the night of Saturday, the 20th February, 1799, removed and carried forward into the sea about 260 yards.' Morrison

*Scotland's Nostradamus*

allegedly cried out during a sermon: 'Ye sinful and stiff-necked people, God will, unless ye turn from your evil ways, sweep you ere long into the place of torment; and as a sign of the truth of what I say, Clach Dubh an Abain, large though it be, will be carried soon without human agency a considerable distance seawards.' MacLennan goes on:

> Some believe that nothing short of an earthquake could have removed such a mass, but the more probable opinion is that a large sheet of ice, which had collected to the thickness of 18 inches round the stone, had been raised by the tide, lifting the stone with it, and that their motion forward was aided and increased by a tremendous hurricane which blew from the land.

Somewhat tellingly, this same story was recounted in Alexander Mackenzie's *The Prophecies of the Brahan Seer*, the first edition of which came out five years later than the first edition of *The Petty Seer*. Mackenzie tells us that it was pretty generally believed at the time that the Devil had a finger in the work, but insists that 'there is no doubt whatever' that the Brahan Seer predicted the moving of the stone.

Given his locality, it comes as no surprise that the Petty Seer was also credited with predicting the Battle of Culloden, which took place close by on Drumossie Moor on 16 April 1746, and was one of the most devastating events in the whole of Highland History, in which the Duke of Cumberland, who led the Hanoverian Government's troops against the Jacobite rebels, was notoriously merciless: Jacobite casualties are estimated to be from 1,500 to 2,000 killed or wounded, with many of them occurring in the pursuit after the battle. 'Oh! Drumossie,' the Brahan Seer was also said to have proclaimed when he visited the site, 'thy bleak moor shall, ere many generations have passed away, be stained with the best blood of the Highlands. Glad am I that I will not see the day, for it will be a fearful period; heads will be lopped off by the score, and no mercy shall be shown or quarter given on either side.'

It may also be no coincidence that the Rev John Morrison happens to have been born in Bragar, on the north-west coast of Lewis, not far from Baile-na-Cille, Uig, which was the Brahan Seer's purported birthplace according to Alexander Mackenzie; although the *Bannatyne manuscript* history of the MacLeods places him as a native of Ness in Lewis and born in the sixteenth century. William Matheson speculated that a number of the tales and prophecies connected with the Seer might have come to originate in Lewis, where many of these tales owe their origin to Norse folklore and other seers from there. After all, the Lewis Chessmen, which were discovered in the Sands at Uig, are believed to have a Norse provenance. Elizabeth Sutherland also pointed out that the mother of George Mackenzie, tacksman of Baile-na-Cille, had a mother who was a Munro of Kaitwell in Easter Ross and suggested that the tales surrounding her cousins, the Munros of Foulis, along with those surrounding Coinneach *Odhar*, may well

*A Land of Myth and Legend*

have been shared around the hearth so that as time passed it must have seemed that both characters and stories originated from Baille-na-Cille.

What is more, a book I own about the Petty Seer's brother, Rory *Dall* Morrison, the 'Blind Harper', who was a relative of my family, quotes many anecdotes that were attached to the wise sayings connected to Rory's father, John Morrison, who was a tenant of the Earl of Seaforth at Bragar on Lewis, and that were passed down in local oral tradition. It could well be that all these stories fused and overlapped with one another in local folk memory, accounting for Alexander Mackenzie's account of the Brahan Seer as a man born on Lord Seaforth's lands on Lewis, who was 'very shrewd and clear-headed, for one in his menial position; was always ready with a smart answer, and if any attempted to raise the laugh at his expense, seldom or ever did he fail to turn it against his tormentors.' These popular and long-remembered stories about John Morrison very much fit such a profile: Martin Martin, who described John as 'a person of unquestionable sincerity, and reputation', recorded how the many stories about his poetry, shrewdness and wit were celebrated in local folk tales.

One such tale is recorded in what is known as the *Morrison manuscript*, by Donald Morrison, a cooper in Stornoway, who died in 1834. It relates how the Third Earl of Seaforth sent for John to come to Stornoway, which served as the Seaforth's capital on the island:

> it was spring time and Morrison was in doubt as to whom he should leave in charge of his farm at Bragar during his absence. In order to fix on the most trustworthy, he took the following plan: – He closed up all the windows and openings that admitted light, and placed a big stone in the passage that led to his room. He then sent to tell all his tenants that he had something to say to them. The tenants arrived, each one stumbling over the stone, till at last an old man, after sprawling across the passage, remarked that that was no place for such a stone, and rolled it out of the way. John Morrison then said to his tenants, 'You may now go away all of you; but while I am absent see you obey the instructions of this old man, who I leave as my substitute, and who appears to be the most careful and willing of you all.'

On another occasion

> John Morrison considered himself overcharged by the factor, and refused to pay his demand. The factor complained to Seaforth, who sent for Morrison to come to Stornoway. Morrison set out at once, putting the rent into one purse and what he considered to be the over- charge in another. When he arrived at Seaforth Lodge a large dog barked furiously at him, on which Morrison struck it a violent blow on the nose with his stick. The dog yelled dismally, and one of Seaforth's servants, on coming to see what was the matter, commenced to abuse Mr Morrison, who punished his insolence by striking him on the jaw. The uproar now was greater than

*Scotland's Nostradamus*

ever, and Seaforth made his appearance. John Morrison explained the origin of the row, and added: –

The boy (menial) and bull-dog (watch-dog) of a laird
Are two that should not be let alone;
Strike the boy on the jaw,
And strike the dog on the nose

Seaforth was amused at Morrison's impromptu verse, and welcomed him cordially. Morrison told him why he had not paid the rent, and presented the bags containing the real rent and what he had been over-charged. On inquiry, it was found that the factor exacted more rent than was just, and he was dismissed, while John Morrison had the honour of paying his rent in future into Seaforth's own hands.

A third story tells of how 'John Morrison had a red-haired wife, who was sometimes in a bad temper, and on whom he occasionally practised his sarcastic humour, as follows: –

The worst of fuel is wet alder;
The worst of weather is soft sleat;
And until the world is at an end
The worst thing in it is a bad wife.

Making a fire in a lake;
Drying a stone in the ocean;
Giving advice to a headstrong wife
Is like the stroke of a hammer on cold iron.

And one more story relates to John's invaluable assistance to Lord Seaforth:

Seaforth having – about 1660 – undertaken the siege of the castle of Ardvreck, belonging to Macleod of Assynt, and finding he made but little progress, sent for John Morrison, who, having gone over the ground, recommended that four hundred raw cow-hides should be made into bags and stuffed with moss. The bags were placed in line and raised to the height of a man, and from the shelter of this rampart the beseigers fired upon their assailants without receiving any damage themselves.

It would seem only too possible that the traditional stories that we know were long remembered in folk memory regarding the much celebrated shrewdness and wit of John Morrison of Bragar, which notably included those about his relationship with the Third Earl of Seaforth and his getting the better of his headstrong wife, became conflated over time with those regarding his supposedly second-sighted son of the same name, John Morrison, the Petty Seer, which in turn became conflated with those concerning Coinneach *Odhar* and the Third Earl's headstrong wife, the Countess Isobel.

# Dante's Scholar Wizard

In my search for the Brahan Seer, I also came across yet two further legends that had their origins in that particularly fertile period of storytelling in thirteenth-century Scotland. In the way in which one of these legends mentions ravens and doves in relation to Heaven and Hell and the other is concerned with Chanonry Point, they should now be added to any comprehensive analysis of the Brahan Seer's legend, and in particular the story that surrounded Coinneach *Odhar's* execution there.

Although he is a little-known figure to most people today, there was a time when the stories of the mediaeval Scottish 'wizard' Michael Scot were told not just in the Highlands but all over the world. Sir Walter Scott gives a lengthy account of his story in his *The Lay of the Last Minstrel: Canto II*. The dealings of this 'white wizard' with kings, witches, fairy folk and the Devil entertained people for hundreds of years. In fact, he was the only Scot to be mentioned by Dante in that great classic of Western literature, *The Divine Comedy*. In the great Italian poet's *Inferno*, Michael is consigned, along with other seers, sorcerers, astrologers and false prophets, to the fourth ditch of the eighth circle of Hell. Although he has only been briefly mentioned by folklorist commentators on the Brahan Seer, he would almost certainly have once been a very familiar character of fable in the ceilidh houses and laird's halls of Ross-shire.

It has been suggested that Scot's interest in the East inspired him to dress up in Arab clothes, which is how his reputation for being a wizard originally came about, going on to colour the legends that surrounded his reputation in the following centuries. Sir Walter Scott also told how Michael was supposed to have gained the knowledge of good and evil, and said that he was 'gifted all the "second sights" that can be acquired' after he dipped his finger in a broth that a witch had made from a snake that he'd killed, recalling the legend of Siegried and Fáfnir in the Old Norse *Poetic Edda*, which can be traced back to the twelfth/thirteenth centuries, in which Fáfnir was able to understand the language of the birds after licking his finger after touching the dragon's heart while it was cooking (as could the hero of the Mackenzie origin *Legend of the Birds*, after drinking from the skull of a raven, which can also be traced back to the thirteenth century). 'The wise-woman was not annoyed in the slightest with Michael for having a taste of the soup, instead she now saw him as a kindred spirit. That night she taught him the rest of her secrets and in the morning he left the lodgings with new insight and the gift of the philosopher's stone in his pocket.' This mirrors Coinneach *Odhar* being gifted his 'seeing stone'. In fact, the use of a magic stone to see into the future was not something ever mentioned in

*Scotland's Nostradamus*

seventeenth-century descriptions of second sight in the Highlands and would not have been considered appropriate, so this would almost certainly have been a later addition remembered from more cosmopolitan folk legends.

Another legend revolves around a witch, known as Long Meg and Her Daughters, and the Bronze Age stone circle that goes by that name at Penrith, near Salkeld, in Cumbria in the North West of England. This is said to consist of fifty-nine stones, set in an oval shape, measuring 340 feet. According to this tale, after Scot was summoned to England to deal with a coven of witches who were congregating in the area, the wizard had a stand-off on the site where the stones now lie, and he is said to have single-handedly defeated them by turning them all to stone. As appears to have been the case with Coinneach *Odhar*, it has been suggested that the witch Long Meg was most likely derived from a genuine historical character, in the person of Margaret Selby, who was born in 1570 and was the mother of Sir William Fenwick of Meldon, near Morpeth in Northumberland, albeit some 70 miles from these stones, and that her name became garbled and intertwined in local folk memory. It was also said that the stones cannot be counted in consecutive order. However, if anyone is able to count them consecutively and then count them consecutively again for a second time after that, the spell that Michael Scot cast would be broken and either the witches would return to our world, or it would bring about very bad luck for the person counting – or for the world itself.

~·~·~

It is, however, two other legends surrounding Michael Scot that link him more directly with those stories that surrounded the Brahan Seer.

The first is related to Chanonry Point, upon which Coinneach *Odhar* was said to have been executed for witchcraft. In his early days, it was told how Michael combined his work as a mason with his magical skills, employing thousands of fairies to help him make buildings, roadworks and bridges. Allegedly, north of the Grampians there are still bridges that were built by him in one night using unseen forces. The fairies it seems were very enthusiastic helpers and on one occasion when work was getting scarce they flocked to Michael's doors, shouting, 'Work! Work! Work!' The wizard had no work for them but didn't want to lose his amazing labour force. He decided therefore to keep them busy with a seemingly impossible task: 'Go and make a dry road from Fortrose to Ardersier, over the Moray Firth.' He supposedly laughed to himself as they set upon this task before he went to bed. I am unaware of exactly how ancient this legend is, but it may be no coincidence that just such an idea of building a road, almost for the sake of it, seems to have prefigured the building of what were dubbed 'Destitution Roads' in the Highlands in the 1840s, when new routes were pioneered in previously remote places, whereby benevolent landowners provided employment for those who were then suffering from the potato blight.

According to this legend, when Michael woke the next day, he took a stroll to the shore to see how the fairies were getting on with their fruitless labour. To

76

*Dante's Scholar Wizard*

his astonishment, he had underestimated their determination and fairy magic; they were only hours away from completing his project. Knowing the damage this would cause to the fishing communities around the Moray Firth, he ordered his workers to stop, but decided to leave the start of the road just at the point of Fortrose to remind travellers of the fairies' handiwork. This is a reference to the apparent geographical anomaly that is Chanonry Point, the site, of course, of the Brahan Seer's execution. The story bears similarities to the legend regarding the Giant's Causeway in County Antrim, with its appearance of an unfinished causeway to an age that didn't understand geography. Indeed, the paramount importance of Chanonry Point in the past consciousnesses of the local fishing community was its crucial economic benefit to the local area and to my own family in particular. A contemporary valuation roll shows that in the first decades of the seventeenth century my ancestor, Bishop Murdo McKenzie's father-in-law, Donald MacAulay, who was a merchant burgess of Fortrose, owned the 'fishings' at Rosemarkie, which was the port of Fortrose. (These fishing rights were inherited by Donald's grandson, Captain James McKenzie, who combined a military career with also being a merchant burgess in Inverness, on the other side of the Moray Firth.) In fact, a later ancestor of mine, Donald McKenzie, who was another Inverness merchant, can in the following century be found in Fisherton, on the southern side of the Moray Firth at this point. The promontories of Chanonry Point, to the north, and that on which Fort George and Ardersier now stand, to the south, create a bottleneck at this point on the Moray Firth, which concentrates the salmon returning to the Rivers Ness and Beauly. This is why it is a popular place for spotting bottlenose dolphins today; and why it would have made a very lucrative place to own the fishing rights. It was already obvious to me that the curiosity that was Chanonry Point would have featured heavily in the consciousness of my McKenzie ancestors, so it came as no surprise for me to further discover that local popular folk legend had invented an occult explanation for this significant geographical phenomenon.

And among the many stories that were recorded about Michael Scot, one other is particularly pertinent for our purposes. It was relayed to us in Sir Walter Scott's *The Lay of the Last Minstrel*. Sir Walter explained how Dante was wrong to identify Michael as one of the seers in the *Inferno*, since he had in fact outwitted the Devil in order to disappoint those of his enemies who threatened him with Hell. According to Sir Walter, Michael said:

> As soon as I die, open my breast and take out my heart. Carry it to a place where people can see what happens. Fix my heart to a long pole and, if Satan wants my soul, he will come in the likeness of a black raven and carry it off; but if my soul is to be saved it will be carried off by a white dove.

Scott continued:

> When the wizard died his friends faithfully obeyed these instructions. A large black raven came flying from the East with great speed, while a white

dove came from the West with equal haste. The raven made a furious dash for the heart, but missed as it was travelling with such force. It couldn't turn back quick enough but the dove, gently reaching the spot at the same time, carried off the heart to the cheers of all the spectators.

This, of course, bears remarkable comparison to the story that was related about the Brahan Seer, which tells us of how, before he was burned to death on Chanonry Point, Coinneach declared to Lady Seaforth that he would go to Heaven, but she would never reach it. As a sign of this, he foretold that when he was burned, a raven and a dove would hasten toward his ashes. If the dove was the first to arrive it would be proved that his hope was well founded, which proved indeed to be the case, allowing him ultimately to outwit his adversary. It seems only too feasible that centuries old oral legends concerning a seer's heart being carried off by a white dove remembered 'the place where people can see what happens' as Chanonry Point, which had also been associated with Michael Scott and that this in turn became a legend about a local man.

~·~·~

A mathematician and scholar of alchemy and the occult, Scot was also a genuine historical character, whose writings are known to us today. In particular, his *De Chiromantia* was a small volume concerned with chiromancy, or fortune-telling by palm-reading. As I shall go on to explain, however, he can also be credited with planting many of the seeds of the scientific developments that preceded the Renaissance.

Sir Walter Scott identified this man with the Sir Michael Scot of Balwearie, who is on record as having been sent in 1290 on a special mission to Norway, although this is rejected by most historians. Born in Scotland around 1175, Michael is thought to have studied at Oxford and very likely both taught and studied at the University of Paris. The earliest certain date in his remarkably cosmopolitan academic career is, however, 1217, when he translated the work of the twelfth-century Andalucian cosmologist, Nur ad-Din al-Bitruji at Toledo.

Michael then went on to translate Averroes, Avicenna and Aristotle, facilitating many of the humanist ideas that influenced the Renaissance. He is, in fact, regarded as one of the greatest intellectuals of his day. His modern biographer, Professor Lynn Thorndike, writes: 'There can be little doubt that Michael Scot was first and foremost an intellectual. He held that every man ought to strive to be sapiens (a sage or "intellectual") in this world.' He flourished under the patronage of the Holy Roman Emperor Frederick II, to whom he served as science adviser and astrologer at his court in Sicily. During his time in Frederick's court, he is said to have predicted the outcome of a war with the Lombard League, a northern Italian alliance, as a result of his astronomical observations. Some sources report that the Emperor used scholars like Michael Scot as messengers to Arab rulers, such as the Egyptian Sultan, Al-Kamil, for diplomatic and scholarly exchanges because of his knowledge of Arabic, and, that he even

*Dante's Scholar Wizard*

took Michael to the Holy Land during the Sixth Crusade in 1228–9. Latin Christendom was intellectually at that time a period of great absorption, synthesis and consequently of originality, largely because of the twelfth-century translation movements in Toledo and Sicily. Within this era, Scot forms an important bridge between the twelfth-century translation movements and the thirteenth-century, university-based scholars. This was a period of intense and accelerated change, culturally and intellectually, as well as socially, termed by historians in the last century the Twelfth Century Renaissance: a rebirth in the sense that the West rediscovered many classical texts, particularly Greek ones, preserved and translated by Muslim scholars.

Frederick is known to have sent Scot to communicate his translations and other scholarly works at prominent European universities, including Oxford, where Scot met a young Roger Bacon (another early advocate of the study of nature and the empirical scientific method, who in the early modern period was also regarded as a wizard). The point here is that Muslim scholarship had retained a better collective memory of the works of the ancient Greeks and other cultures, and Michael Scot played a connecting role in bringing this knowledge into Europe.

Scot's own contributions have been much misunderstood, in part because he lived at a time when science, religion and belief in magic coexisted. Modern-day notions of what are now termed astrology and astronomy were not then differentiated, but simply referred to in one body of thought, simply referred to as 'astrology'. However, Scot employed what would now be considered an approximation to scientific observational techniques. His very meticulous description in Latin, for example, concerning the medical case of 'Mary of Bologna', dismissed as a 'calcified fibroid tumour', was later recognised in the 1970s to be the description of a very rare case of miscarriage or 'spontaneous abortion'; and a recent study in the *International Journal for the Historiography of Science*, from its analysis of a passage written by Michael Scot on multiple rainbows, a phenomenon understood only by modern physics and recent observations, suggests that Michael Scot may have even had contact with the Tuareg people in the Sahara. Scot also explored the Lipari islands, attempting to understand, in alchemical terms, the now recognised connection between volcanic activity and the presence of gold. The California Gold rush of 1849 is now recognised to have been the outcome of just such volcanic activity. Current historians consider alchemy to be an important precursor to the modern science of chemistry. Similarly, John Dee, who was a student of the Renaissance Neo-Platonism of Marsilio Ficino, drew no distinction between his mathematical research and his investigations of Hermetic magic, angel summoning and divination; he was a friend of the influential astronomer Tycho Brahe and familiar with the work of Copernicus. 'Every astrologer is worthy of praise and honour,' Sir Walter Scott wrote, 'since by such a doctrine as astrology he probably knows many secrets of God, and things which few know.'

*Scotland's Nostradamus*

The irony is, therefore, that one of the earliest sources and inspirations for the Brahan Seer's second sight can be traced back to one of the first scholars to introduce to the modern world the writings of the pre-eminent Greek philosopher Aristotle, whom many today regard as the father of science. For Aristotle, the basis of all knowledge was experience. Explanations were only valid if they were induced by observed phenomena. In other words, theories should be formed starting with facts. And this idea is, of course, at the core of the modern scientific method.

~·~·~

By 1228, when Scot was at the Sicilian court of the Emperor Frederick II, he worked on his *Liber Introductorius maior in astrologiam*, (or 'Great Book on the introduction to Astrology'), which he dedicated to Frederick. The work was divided into three books, the last of which was the *Liber Physiognomiae*. This latter section was largely based on Aristotle's *Historia animalium*, in which the Greek philosopher drew a correlation between the length of lines on the palm of the hand and the length of life, and this became a central tenet of the pseudo-science of chiromancy or palmistry, thanks to Scot's translation of Aristotle based on the Arabic.

Similarly, some statements made in earlier chapters of this work by Aristotle contributed to the growth of another pseudo-science, that of physiognomy, which Michael Scot also wrote about, leading to a form of character analysis. We should recognise in this that, prior to 1500, the status of physiognomy was perceived as a learned science, in a way that was fundamentally different from the mystical and almost occult art of physiognomy after that date. It is therefore significant that in the West, it was Michael Scot, who for the first time, around 1230, explicitly called physiognomy a *scientia naturae*, upgrading its pursuit to the status of a scientific branch of natural philosophy. In his poem *Liber Physiognomiae*, Michael advised the Emperor to encourage physiognomic interest and learning at his court as one of the sciences that are beneficial to the ruler in helping him to distinguish between good and evil. His writings appeared in no fewer than twenty editions before 1500.

The second half of Scot's physiognomy is presented in straightforward chapters that are organised by body part, listing signs followed by interpretations. As a whole, these characteristics of Scot's work firmly establish physiognomy as a practice worthy of, and even ideally confined to, the highest intellects of the day. It is noteworthy, however, that Scot chose to place his *Liber Physiognomiae* within a larger work of astrology. This practice seems paradoxical only to modern perception, but would not have been at all strange to mediaeval thinkers. Astrology was the supreme science in the thirteenth century, the fundamental natural law almost to the time of Newton being the subjection of inferior elementary bodies to the rule of the stars.

~·~·~

One of the stories written by Michael himself, that is possibly modelled on his own life story, tells how there was a fatherless boy, whose uncle cared for him as if he had been his own son, and from the love that he had for him, sent him to a university abroad (there were no universities in Scotland until the fifteenth century). He gave him a small amount of money for expenses, saying: 'My son, I know that this money is not enough for you for three months, but go ahead, because, before two months are over, I will come to you, or I will send my own messenger to you with a lot of money.'

The boy then went. But after three months neither uncle nor more money appeared, and he feared that his uncle had died, was ill, or alternatively had become alienated from his nephew through listening to lies about him. The next thing he did was ask an astrologer what he should do and what he should believe. The astrologer told him, 'Note first the hour and fraction of the hour, and to which of the planets the present hour is to be attributed. Then tell him to go into the street and pick up something and bring it to you.' The boy comes back with a piece of glass that is partly covered with mud. The astrologer thereupon affirms that his uncle loves him as much as ever, and has been unavoidably prevented from coming himself or sending money as he had promised, but that he will do so shortly: 'The clarity of the glass signifies love; its solidity constancy; the mud on it, the impediment. But since that glass was part of a broken vase, it signifies that the affair will be quickly expedited, as the glass can be quickly cleaned from mud, and so it will come to him or [the money will be sent].'

It has been suggested that the success of just such an observational method in Michael's own personal experience had served to recommend it to him. Lynn Thorndike also speculated that Michael might have had himself in mind in alluding to the son of a poor woman who remains in poverty throughout his boyhood, but afterwards begins gradually to prosper until he becomes rich in science or attains some dignity of honour. It certainly mirrors Alexander Mackenzie's and Hugh Miller's descriptions of the Brahan Seer as a humble common labourer whose special gift meant he 'was sought after by the gentry throughout the length and breadth of the land'.

A number of chapters in Scot's *Liber Physiognomiae* are concerned with dreams and their significance. Some are true; some are false. Some signify events of the past; some of the present; and some of the future. Some signify nothing but fancy. The age and the food of the dreamer and the stage of the moon should be taken into account. A boy sees dreams in one way; a young man otherwise; an old man still differently; and a woman yet otherwise. A dream before food is digested signifies nothing or concerns the past. A dream while digestion is going on, but is not yet completed, signifies as to present affairs. A dream after complete digestion signifies wholly concerning the future. One is advised to arise immediately and make a note of a dream, which seems of great significance, or not to sleep longer on the side on which one dreams, 'and then he will recall it, when day comes, unless he saw many dreams'. If he has forgotten part

*Scotland's Nostradamus*

of the dream he should rub the back of his head, where the virtue of memory is located. Albeit that scientists believe today that there are three areas of the brain involved in explicit memory (the hippocampus, the neo-cortex and the amygdala), this struck me as a remarkably materialistic explanation for that time, asserting that memory should be stored in a particular part of the brain. There then follow chapters that are concerned with dreams signifying the dominance of each of the four humours (by which medicine in his day was defined) and each of the four qualities – hot, cold, dry and moist.

Subsequent chapters deal with auguries. Although auguries are forbidden by canon law, some are generally accepted, as on meeting a man or animal, or hearing a voice. 'And this sort of augur is he or she who by such a science indicates future events, and by the singular signs if this science knows how to judge in general.' There are also 'some notable events which are properly considered auguries, such as sneezing when kissing, meeting a flock of birds, the song of birds, hearing a voice, or an antecedent dream concerning a proposed affair'.

In all of this I was struck by the similarity with the nature of the stories regarding second sight that were recorded by the members of the Royal Society in the seventeenth century and, later still by the members of the SPR at the end of the ninteenth. Although those auguries were ostensibly visual (as Laura Cumming so beautifully pointed out in her *The Guardian* article and, indeed, by definition that was how a 'seer' functioned, Michael being, of course, widely described as a 'seer') these types of prophecies followed the same sort of mechanism, through observation and experience. It was also noteworthy that Michael employed the term 'science' when describing ways by which the future could be foretold. Even if we do not today agree with his conclusions because science has advanced a great deal since the thirteenth century, we should nonetheless give Michael credit for endeavouring to follow an observational, empirical method.

It was undoubtedly the case that in Michael's own mind there was a difference between such occult forces in nature, which he referred to as 'science', which were good, and what he called the 'magic art', that was bad and diabolical, 'not found or received in philosophy, because it is the mistress of all iniquity and evil, often deceiving and seducing the souls of its practitioners and injuring their bodies'. In the mediaeval universe, demons existed for everyone: they were part of the mental universe of everyone living at that time and, indeed, were to remain so well into what we might regard as a more progressive and properly scientific age.

When I was reading his many thoughts, I was also struck by what a remarkably enquiring intellect Michael had. In one chapter various questions are put, such as why a parent loves a son more than that son loves his parents, and why a brother is not enamoured of his beautiful and delectable sister. The answer in the first case is that the son is flesh and blood of his parents, but not the converse. The answer to the second is that, although the sister is the same flesh and blood, touching one's own hand does not arouse lust. While me may not agree

82

*Dante's Scholar Wizard*

with his conclusions it is notable that in asking such questions (along with his analysis of dreams), he was attempting in the thirteenth century what psychologists, sociologists and anthropologists were to go on to attempt in the nineteenth century and later.

~·~·~

As with the genuine historical events surrounding Coinneach *Odhar* and Katherine Ross, combined with those involving Coinneach *Mhor*, the Third Earl of Seaforth and his Countess, along with the traditions regarding the Isla Seer, Thomas the Rhymer and John Morrison, it would be understandable that all these stories, and those in particular surrounding Michael Scot and Chanonry Point, were confused and conflated in local oral folk tradition over many long centuries, so that they came together to make up one story attached to a person who became known as the Brahan Seer. And to me a particularly interesting point about Michael Scot was that his background as a seer was very far from being backward and insular, but, on the contrary, highly intellectual and cosmopolitan: indeed, as close to being a scientist as his time allowed him to be.

# The Highlands as a Treasury of Wonder Tales

The fundamental message of 'Seaforth's Doom' can be seen to fit a classic pattern of fairy tales, to use the term that would be most familiar when describing such storytelling traditions to an English-speaking audience today. Although one version of the Brahan Seer's story does involve fairies (he is supposed to have received his gift of second sight when sleeping on a fairy mound), some anthropologists prefer the German term *Wundermärchen*, which embraces both folk tales and those stories that include fairy legend. In my heading of this chapter I have chosen Donald Alexander Mackenzie's term 'Wonder Tales', not least because that was the term that he thought appropriate when relaying the type of stories that were being conveyed in the Highlands during the period under discussion here, and that can be considered to include that of the Brahan Seer.

Anthropologists have debated whether the origins of such wonder tales are best seen as reflecting psychological archetypes – that is, collectively inherited, unconscious ideas, or patterns of thought and images that are universally present in individual consciousness. Such archetypes were most famously defined in the writings of the psychologist Carl Jung. Others have suggested that these tales can instead be traced back to known ancient sources. The latter theory, known as Diffusionism, holds that stories are passed on across borders, from distant origins, often Eastern. Marina Warner, the English historian, art critic and novelist, writes:

> Jean de la Fontaine, wandering along the quais in Paris in the 1660s, came across a volume by Bidpai (or Pilpay), a legendary Brahmin sage; he bought it, and the tales he read there became the founding inspirations of his own Fables, commonly assumed to represent the apogee of Gallic urbanity. Motifs and plotlines are nomadic, travelling the world and the millenia, turning up on parchment in mediaval Persia, in an oral form in the Pyranees, in a ballad sung in the Highlands, in a fairy story in the Caribbean.

Indeed, my brother Kevin has established a pedigree for the Mackenzies' origin myth, which is known as the *Legend of the Birds* that can be traced back to the mediaeval tales that we know today as the *One Thousand and One Nights*, which in turn themselves had even earlier origins in the Arab world. Kevin has shown how these were no doubt carried back to the Highlands following the crusades of the thirteenth century. In my previous two chapters, I have also shown how

*The Highlands as a Treasury of Wonder Tales*

many elements of Coinneach *Odhar*'s legend are shared with other tales that originated in Scotland in the thirteenth century, in particular those that relate to Thomas the Rhymer and Michael Scot. It may also be no coincidence that Michael Scot was known to have translated Arabic texts, allowing them to be accessible to Europeans. But it is the very nature of oral tradition that memories overlap and combine, so we should not see the reasons for the origins of these stories as being mutually exclusive, or single out any one source as the primary explanation.

Indeed, there are also obvious traits in the Brahan Seer's story that fit the archetypal motifs that Bruno Bettelheim outlined in his book, *The Uses of Enchantment: The Meaning and Importance of Fairy Tales*. There is a fundamental moral in 'Seaforth's Doom', which is the victory of the underdog, a humble labourer on the Seaforth estate, who uses his skills to outwit an oppressive social superior, in the person of the haughty Countess Isobel. Ultimately, the Seer is the victor, because he goes to Heaven, while she goes to Hell. His story begins with an inspirational tale of rags to riches, when Coinneach's gift was 'acquired while he was engaged in the humble occupation of cutting peats or divots, which were in his day, and still are in many places, used as fuel throughout the Highlands of Scotland'. And in both Hugh Miller's and Alexander Mackenzie's stories, 'He was very shrewd and clear-headed, for one in his menial position; was always ready with a smart answer, and if any attempted to raise the laugh at his expense, seldom or ever did he fail to turn it against his tormentors.' In fact, the fundamental story that came to surround the Brahan Seer was very much at odds with what we know about the way in which second sight was perceived in the Highlands and Islands in the seventeenth century from examining contemporary accounts. As can be seen from seventeenth-, as well as from twentieth-century accounts, second sight was invariably represented as an involuntary gift, even an affliction, and never something to be sought after for personal gain and advancement (Robert Kirk, in his *The Secret Commonwealth of Elves, Fauns and Fairies*, wrote that seers 'find such horrour and trouble by the entercourse' with visions and precognitions granted by fairies 'that they would often full gladly be as free from them, as other men'). While such a description may have been a distant memory of the reputation that came to surround Michael Scot (and perhaps also John Morrison), this common labourer who made good will also have been eminently relatable to a commonplace audience in the local ceilidh house. It is in precisely this way that the fairy tale brings reassurance to those who might feel powerless and disadvantaged and for whom life otherwise holds no meaning.

As Bettelheim explained, 'This is one of the manifold truths revealed by fairy tales, which can guide our lives; it is a truth as valid today as it was once upon a time.' As he explained, throughout man's history his intellectual life, apart from immediate experience with family, depended on mythical and religious stories and tales.

*Scotland's Nostradamus*

Some fairy and folk stories evolved out of myths; others were incorporated into them. Both forms embodied the cumulative experience of a society as men wished to recall past wisdom for themselves and transmit it to future generations. These tales are the purveyors of deep insights that have sustained mankind through the long vicissitudes of its existence, a heritage that is not revealed in any other form as simply and directly, or as accessibly, to children.

Although Bettelheim's theory was primarily concerned with the effect such tales had on the minds of children during their formative years, at which point they were struggling to make sense of a strange world, as Donald Alexander Mackenzie explained, these stories were recited to both young and old, and they would have been equally reassuring to all age groups. Thus, 'Seaforth's Doom' includes the universal lessons surrounding greed, jealousy, lust and cruelty, which fairy tales give us. Such tales often attack received ideas, championing lost causes, opening up a brave new world, where different rules may apply. 'Seaforth's Doom' can also be seen as following a longstanding tradition of misogyny in fairy tales, the classic archetype being the wicked stepmother: or, in Countess Isobel's case, the wicked wife and mother-in-law.

~·~·~

This storytelling tradition should not be seen as a symptom of a primitive and remote 'low' culture, any more than a belief in second sight should. In fact, there are parallels in all of this with the 'high' culture that was at the height of fashion in continental Europe in the early modern period. We have already seen how Sir George Mackenzie's schooling in the literature of Jean de la Fontaine was a mark of his cosmopolitan sophistication; and, in 1714, the court tutor, the Abbé Fénelon, writing to a friend, said that the most serious men today enjoy 'fables – even those that are like fairy tales ... We willingly become children again.' As well as highlighting that Jean de la Fontaine's fables were the 'apogee of Gallic urbanity', Marina Warner has outlined how the seventeenth and eighteenth centuries were the heyday of the folktale as a literary form, describing

'the magic entertainment [that] helps the story look like a mere bubble of nonsense from the superstitious mind of ordinary, negligible folk. The enchantments also universalize the narrative setting, encipher concerns, beliefs and desires in brilliant, seductive images that are themselves a form of camouflage, making it possible to utter harsh truths, to say what you dare. The disregard for logic, all those fairytale non-sequiturs and improbable reversals, rarely encompass the emotional conflicts themselves: hatred, jealousy, kindness, cherishing retain an intense integrity throughout. The double vision of the tales, on the one hand charting perennial drives and terrors, both conscious and unconscious, and on the other mapping actual, volatile experience, gives the genre its fascination and power to satisfy.'

It is thus important to recognise that folktales, just like popular songs, appealed to some intellectuals in seventeenth-century France, which we have seen to have had crucial links with Highland culture, especially following the Jacobite diaspora that had such an impact on the Seaforth family. At the court of Louis XIV, fairy stories were very much in fashion, some writers even publishing their own versions, including Madame d'Aulnoy, Mademoiselle l'Héritier and, most famously, the senior government official Charles Perrault (although he did not put his name on the title page of the first edition of his publication). Peter Burke writes:

> Perrault and the others did not take folktales altogether seriously, or at least they did not want to admit that they did; yet they found the stories fascinating. It is as if educated people were beginning to feel they needed an escape from the disenchanted world, the Cartesian intellectual universe they now inhabited. It was precisely the unscientific, the marvellous, which attracted them in folktales, as it attracted the historians of 'superstition'.

The same was true in the nineteenth century of the 'high' art of Wagner, who turned to mediaeval folk tradition, which made up in fantasy for what is missing in reality. For the early German Romantics, fairy tales were 'universal poetry': in the words of the philosopher and mystic Georg Philipp Friedrich Freiherr von Hardenberg, known as Novalis, 'Everything poetic must be like fairy tale.' For Wagner, life was empty and lacking in purpose, while art, he believed, gave it a purpose. The psychological function of art was to serve that need, regardless of social class or geography. And myth and the folk tradition above all responded to those psychological needs.

Nor was the concept of the telling of oral folktales around the fireside unique to the rural Highlands, whether in the laird's hall, or the humbler ceilidh house. Even at a much later date, the *veillée* – or evening gathering for gossip, news and stories – were part of artisan, working life, in cities, as well as in agricultural life in the country in France, at least as late as 1900, when Donald Alexander Mackenzie was describing the same tradition further north. We should also remember that Oscar Wilde's father, an ophthalmic surgeon in Dublin's Merion Square in the mid-nineteenth century, used to ask for stories as his fee from his poorer patients (his wife, under the pen name Speranza, then published them and they went on to influence their son's acclaimed and moving literary masterpieces, such as *The Selfish Giant* and *The Happy Prince*).

Peter Burke has also explained how, after about 1650, it is possible to find scholars in Britain, France and Italy who distinguish between learned culture and popular culture, reject popular beliefs, but at the same time found them, like second sight, to be a fascinating object of study. John Aubrey, whom we have already encountered in the context of scientific study and the Royal Society, is also an obvious example in this respect. His attitude was that 'old customs and

*Scotland's Nostradamus*

old wives-fables are gross things: but yet ought not to be quite rejected: there may be some truth and usefulness be elicited out of them'. The scholar-clergy of the late seventeenth century and early eighteenth saw popular culture in a similar perspective: they collected information about customs and 'superstitions', disapproved of much of what they collected, but continued to collect it all the same.

According to Alexander Mackenzie, the folk stories relating to the Brahan Seer that he recorded were conveyed in the native Gaelic tongue. In the Scottish Highlands, in Adam Ferguson's day, Gaelic became, as he put it, 'a language spoken in the cottage, but not in the parlour, or at the table of any gentleman'. This was, in fact, a widespread phenomenon in Europe in the early modern period. Similarly, in Languedoc, for example, the nobility and bourgeoisie adopted French, which distinguished them from the craftsmen and peasants who spoke only Occitan; in eighteenth-century Norway, educated people spoke Danish, the language of the court in Copenhagen; in Bohemia the nobles were mainly Germans; while in Finland educated people spoke Swedish. It is tempting to see the two languages as representing two entirely different cultures. But in the Highlands, where the stories relating to the Brahan Seer were passed down in Gaelic, were these stories really a part of an entirely separate culture? The reality is more complicated, since, as I have shown with the phenomenal high-brow cult that surrounded the poems of Ossian at the end of the eighteenth century and beginning of the nineteenth, that were purported to be direct translations from oral Gaelic, 'As the gap between the two cultures gradually widened, so some educated men began to see popular songs, beliefs and festivals as exotic, quaint, fascinating, worthy of collection and record.'

The earlier collectors of folk tale thus had what Peter describes as a 'pre-split mentality'. They thought of the ballads and proverbs that they transcribed and published as a tradition that belonged to everyone, not just the common people. While, by around 1800, 'the educated classes had ceased to participate spontaneously in popular culture, they were in the process of rediscovering it as something exotic and therefore interesting. They were even beginning to admire "the people", from whom this alien culture had sprung.' Today it might be described as 'authenticity'.

In all of this, I might also stress how the clan system allowed the survival of a more egalitarian class system in the Highlands, whereby interest and identities were shared, and this was more evident than ever during the Napoleonic Wars, when regiments such as Seaforth's Highlanders were raised by the Clan Chief, sharing an identity by wearing, in their case, a form of the Black Watch's regimental tartan, a tartan design that was to go on to become 'Mackenzie' as much as it had been 'Seaforth Highlanders'. Of course, it was appropriate that one of the great themes of the Brahan Seer's prophecies was the demise of the Mackenzies' chiefly and officer classes – and subsequently the dispersal of their wider clansmen, culminating in the passing of the clan system in general – so it occurs to me that it is no wonder that this part of Europe was such a crucible for the dying embers of such popular culture.

But, once again, it is important also to place this phenomenon in a wider European context. It was in the late eighteenth century and early nineteenth, when traditional popular culture was just beginning to disappear, that the 'people' or the 'Volk' became a subject of interest to European intellectuals. The Grimm brothers regarded the authorship of folktales as communal, belonging to the whole people: like trees, they were not made, but simply grew organically. The aesthetic appeal of the wild, unclassical and 'primitive' can be seen at its most vivid in the vogue for 'Ossian' that I described, but Rousseau, for example, also valued folksongs because they were simple, naïve and archaic and he was an advocate of cultural primitivism. Johnson and Boswell, as we have seen, went to the Hebrides to witness a pastoral society. This was a reaction to the Enlightenment. The Grimms prized tradition above reason; the instincts of the people over the arguments of intellectuals. Although their arguments were made then in a more subtle and sophisticated way, there are noticeable parallels with the so-called 'culture wars' that we hear of today, which promote the 'voice of the people' above the supposedly exclusive perspective of a 'metropolitan elite'.

This theme of a vanishing culture, which must be recorded before it is too late, recurs in the writings of nineteenth-century folklorists. Sir Walter Scott declared that he collected Border ballads in order to 'contribute somewhat to the history of my native country; the peculiar features of whose manner and character are daily melting and dissolving into those of her sister and ally'. He believed that his contemporaries really were hearing the lay of the last minstrel, describing one singer as 'perhaps the last of our professed ballad reciters', and another as 'probably the very last instance of the proper minstrel craft'. Peter Burke draws comparison with Norway, where, a few years later, one collector compared the country to a 'burning house' from which there was just time to snatch the ballads before it was too late.

This is precisely the spirit in which the fossil hunter, Hugh Miller, and the crofter's champion, Alexander Mackenzie recorded the oral folk traditions surrounding the Brahan Seer in Ross-shire. 'Old greyheaded men, and especially old women became my books' wrote Miller. He further remarked:

> It has often been a subject of regret to me, that this oral knowledge of
> the past, which I deem so interesting, should be thus suffered to be lost.
> The meteor says my motto, if it once fall, cannot be rekindled ... The
> Sibyline tomes of tradition are disappearing in this part of the country
> one by one; and I find, like Selkirk [Alexander Selkirk was the model for
> Defoe's *Robinson Crusoe*] in his island when the rich fruits of autumn
> were dropping around him, that if I myself do not preserve them they
> must perish. I therefore set myself to the task of storing them up as I best
> may, and urge as my only apology the emergency of the case. Not merely

*Scotland's Nostradamus*

do I regard them as the produce of centuries, and like the blossoms of the Aloe, interesting on this count alone, but also as a species of produce which the harvests of future centuries may fail to supply.

It should thus be seen as no coincidence that many of Coinneach *Odhar*'s prophecies foretold a doomed and disappearing world. Somewhat counter-intuitively, I would argue, therefore that, in some of their aspects at least, the prophecies of the Brahan Seer were as much a reflection of a high European literary culture as they were of a 'primitive' Highland tradition.

~·~·~

And let us not forget that some of the major sentiments of the prophecies of the Brahan Seer – those of displacement and exile, in particular – were powerfully conveyed in Robert Burns's famous poem of 1789, *My Heart is in the Highlands*:

Wherever I wander, wherever I rove
The hills of the Highlands for ever I love.

And this sentiment was given yet further currency by Sir Walter Scott, when he quoted it in his bestselling 1812 novel, *Waverley*:

Farewell to the mountains high cover'd in snow
Farewell to the straths and green valleys below.

The same theme of displacement was expressed in two masterpieces of Scottish painting, which depict the moment of the Highlanders' departure from the lands their ancestors had occupied for centuries: Thomas Faed's *The Last of the Clan*, painted in 1865; and John Watson Nicol's *Lochaber No More*, of 1883. In both these sentimental images of the Scottish emigrant experience, the landscape is depicted as a place that had a shared sense of former belonging, a place that was once lived in and now desolate: an emotion that is strongly conveyed in many of the Seer's most repeated predictions. Yet, all these depictions, both literary and artistic, are not those of a Highland backwater; they are those of a Lowland cultural elite, which established the parameters of nineteenth-century Scots identity, based on themes of loss, nostalgia and the empty landscape of a lost past.

Thomas Faed's *The Last of the Clan* (courtesy of Kelvingrove Art Gallery and Museum)

John Watson Nichol's *Lochaber No More* (courtesy of the Fleming Collection)

William Dyce's portrait of the 'Last of the Seaforths', Francis Humberston Mackenzie in The Highlanders' Museum, Fort George

Romantic symbols of the demise of the old order in the Highlands: the castle ruins of (from top to bottom) Kilcoy, Brahan and Eilean Donan

The ruined township of Suisnish in the shadow of the Cuillin mountains on the Isle of Skye

A poster advertising Strathpeffer Spa, where 'crowds of pleasure and health seekers shall be seen'

Sheep on the otherwise depopulated Isle of Lewis

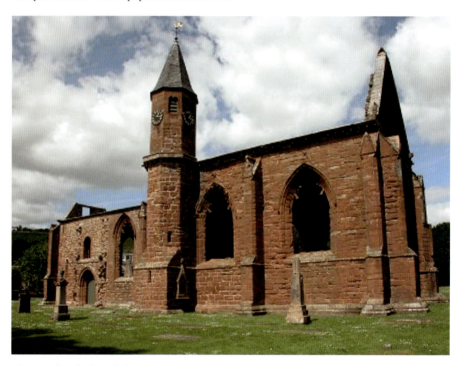

The ruined Cathedral of Chanonry in Fortrose

Knockfarrel, site of Fingal's fortress

The grounds of Castle Leod after the River Peffery burst its banks in October 2023 (courtesy of John, Earl of Cromartie)

The Eagle Stone, Clach an Tiompain, Strathpeffer

# An Occult Laboratory: Part Two

I have already shown how seeking an empirical, observational – indeed 'scientific' – explanation for prophecy was what Michael Scot was attempting to do in the thirteenth century. I have also shown how similar attempts were made by the learned members of the Royal Society by means of their correspondence with Highlanders, such as Viscount Tarbat and Lord Reay. Fascinatingly, this was also exactly what a group of people were trying to do at the end of the nineteenth century, at a time when Alexander Mackenzie's book about the Brahan Seer was proving so popular (it went through five editions from 1877 to 1907).

The occult and the supernatural dominated the bestselling literature at the end of the nineteenth century, including Bram Stoker's *Dracula*, Arthur Conan Doyle's *The Hound of the Baskervilles* and the Occult Tales of Marie Corelli, such as *The Sorrows of Satan*, blending mysticism, religion and psychic phenomena. To quote from Conan Doyle's *Memoirs*, 'The unknown and the marvellous press upon us from all sides.'

It was during this same period that the infamous occultist and member of the esoteric Hermetic Order of the Golden Dawn Aleister Crowley met Rose Edith Kelly, whom he married in 1904, on Strathpeffer Golf Course, just up the hill from Castle Leod. The Hermetic Order taught its own version of scrying, not dissimilar to that of John Dee in the sixteenth century, with an emphasis on 'inner seeing', by focusing on a symbol or mirror. Later retiring to a guesthouse in Hastings, Crowley put a curse on the town. Crowley's curse said that if you have lived in Hastings you can never leave and if you try you will always come back. The only way to truly leave is to take with you a stone with a hole from the beach. This stone sounds very similar to the Brahan Seer's 'seeing stone', although there are also many other folklores pertaining to stones with natural holes in them, called 'Hag Stones', which were often hung outside the front door of a house to deter witches.

Since our very first visit to Earl Rorie at Castle Leod in the 1980s, Kevin and I have become good friends with his son, John Cromartie, and his Countess, Eve. At the first opportunity following the lockdown during the 2020–21 COVID-19 pandemic, we made a short trip, first to the Isle of Lewis, where we paid a visit to Uig, where our MacAulay ancestors came from in the sixteenth century, and also the Brahan Seer's purported birthplace. Following this, we stayed with John, the current Mackenzie Clan Chief, or *Cabarfèidh*, at Castle Leod. One evening John, who has inherited both his father's warm hospitality and his love of local history, told us how his grandmother, Countess Sybil, regularly saw a ghost, known as the Night Watchman in the Great Hall of the Castle. John was clearly very fond of his Grannie, who was a remarkable woman and an interesting representative

*Scotland's Nostradamus*

of two particular movements that have been termed the 'Occult Revival' and the 'Celtic Renaissance'. One of my favourite short stories by the Countess of Cromartie is entitled *The End of the Song* and reflects her interest in both these groups, since it is about a Scottish couple who are reunited having been reincarnated from their earlier heroic ancient Celtic personas, thus combining its writer's fascination with the paranormal with the Highland folklore tradition. Countess Sybil was a friend of the collector and translator of Irish myths and legends, Augusta, Lady Gregory, who introduced her to William Butler Yeats, the great Irish poet and author of *The Wanderings of Oisin*, which is based on the very same Fenian Cycle of Irish mythology that lay behind James Macpherson's writings in the eighteenth century. Yeats was also heavily involved with theosophy and with hermeticism, particularly with the eclectic Rosicrucianism of the Hermetic Order of the Golden Dawn, with which Aleister Crowley had ties.

An article entitled 'Swedenborg, Yeats and Jacobite Freemasonry', by Marsha Keith Schuchard, that my brother Kevin came across around the time of that stay at Castle Leod, tells how 'the beautiful and romantic Sybil Blunt-Mackenzie, Countess of Cromartie' in 1905 'made a special visit to Galway to consult Yeats on some psychic problems. Staying with Lady Gregory at Coole Park, she shared her hostess's interest in Jacobite poetry, which Lady Gregory was translating from the Gaelic. We do not know if the Countess also shared stories of her ancestors' Jacobite and Masonic activities, but if so, she had quite a tale to tell – one which stretched from the Highlands of Scotland to the forests of Sweden, from the eighteenth to the twentieth century.' Sybil's Scottish friend and fellow mystic, Violet Tweedale, observed of her: 'from childhood, her psychic powers have always been extraordinary'. When she sought out Yeats in 1905, she wanted his spiritual help in liberating her from her previous incarnation as a slave and lover of an Irish king. Through his 'evocations', Yeats was able to cure her, 'not of her vision, but of her longing to get out of life', and he remained intrigued by her psychic gifts and esoteric interests. Lady Gregory described Sybil Cromartie as 'gentle, fragile, beautiful', while she sought from Yeats 'some mystic knowledge'. She certainly had an intriguing Christian name, given both the prophetic subject matter of the present book and her psychic disposition. Yeats's friend, the journalist Henry Nevinson, described her as 'a young witch ... who looked very wicked & sorceress'.

Subsequently, Yeats was invited to stay at Castle Leod, which impressed him immensely (as it always has Kevin and me). He was especially intrigued that ravens still roosted on Raven's Rock (a local name, along with the Blackwater, that had always sounded to me as if they belonged on a map of J.R.R. Tolkien's Middle-earth), 'where according to folklore Gaelic warriors found physical prowess, victory in battle, second sight and the gift of prophecy'.

It was this story and Countess Sybil's links with the Society of Psychical Research that then got me looking into that organisation's particular interest in second sight in the Highlands at this time.

—·~·~

*An Occult Laboratory: Part Two*

I mentioned earlier the report that appeared in August 1894 in the columns of the *Oban Times*, the leading local paper of the Western Highlands and Islands of Scotland, under the title '"Second Sight" in the Highlands', which began: 'We understand that several members of the Society for Psychical Research are at present on a tour of the West Highlands and Islands collecting information from the natives in regard to that peculiar faculty said to be possessed by many people, especially in the Highlands, and popularly known as "second sight", as well as kindred subjects.' The Society for Psychical Research (or SPR) had been founded by a number of persons, mostly Cambridge intellectuals, in 1882, 'for the purpose of making an organized and systematic attempt to investigate various sorts of debatable phenomenon which are *prima facie* inexplicable on any generally recognized hypothesis'. Its stated purpose was 'to approach these varied problems without prejudice or prepossession of any kind, and in the same spirit of exact and unimpassioned enquiry which has enabled science to solve so many problems, once not less obscure nor less hotly debated'. Early members of the Society included the physicists William F. Barret and Sir Oliver Lodge; the Cambridge Professor of Philosophy, Henry Sidgwick; the renowned chemist Sir William Crookes; the Nobel laureate Charles Richet; and the psychologist William James. Given the earlier scientific attention it had received from the Royal Society in the seventeenth century, it was natural that the SPR would want to include Highland second sight in its research.

Nearly 2,000 copies of their circular letter were sent out. While the first series of letters received a poor response, following a second more personally addressed follow-up in February, along with circulars to 200 newspaper editors throughout Scotland and a circular of Andrew Lang's article published in the *Glasgow Evening News*, the enquiry assumed 'a more hopeful character' as replies started to come, 'some of them of a very interesting character – one particularly so from the parish priest of Beauly [the Rev Canon John Cameron]'.

As the next stage of the investigation in the middle of 1894, a Miss Ada Goodrich Freer was engaged with the financial backing of the Marquis of Bute and sent to the Highlands to investigate matters on the spot in order to interview persons who had replied to the schedule and anyone else who was interested, particularly the alleged seers, if possible. But it was another member of the Society, the Rev Peter Dewar, who discovered Father Allan McDonald and his folklore collection. From November 1895 to June 1897, the Rev Father Allan McDonald, parish priest of the island of Eriskay in the Outer Hebrides, made a manuscript collection of second sight and ghost stories on behalf of the SPR, which he entitled 'Strange Things'. It was only in 1968 that this information became known to the wider world, when it was published in 1968 by John L. Campbell and Trevor H. Hall in a book of that same title.

After staying under his 'hospitable roof' on Eriskay, Dewar's report to Lord Bute described the cases there of

101

*Scotland's Nostradamus*

lights of a supernatural character – foreshadowing deaths; phantasmal funeral processions, seen in many instances months before the deaths they seem to presage; processions of the dead by which the Seers sometimes are met and carried in an unconscious state, for considerable distances: phantasmal writings or the hum of phantasmal voices engaged in conversation heard some days or even weeks before a death; a chest containing grave clothes (kept by the people in view of any emergency that might occur) being seen to open and shut with a loud noise a few days before neighbours begged the loan of a winding sheet or shroud; phantom ships seen by fishermen on a certain part of the coast where subsequently – (in some cases a considerable period of time thereafter) vessels of an exactly similar description were wrecked and the lives of the crew lost; of living maidens to whom they were previously engaged or with whom they had at one time 'kept company', but whom they subsequently deserted in favour of a more attractive rival.

Despite the evident awe with which Highlanders supposedly regarded second sight, the most fundamental difficulty the Enquiry was met with was the deeply rooted disinclination of Highlanders to answer leading questions put to them by strangers, particularly in writing. The *Oban Times* on 26 September 1896 reported regarding Miss Freer:

while the orally transmitted folklore of the West is still common at evening Ceilidhs or gossip parties from Arisaig on the mainland to Barra, the stranger who would benefit from these quaint recitals must be possessed of winning ways and a knowledge of the language spoken in Eden [that is, Gaelic], for the natives, garrulous enough among themselves, filling up the long winter evenings round the peat with the most ingenious history, sgeul [folk-tales] and song, close like oysters and become as taciturn in the presence of a stranger, who by race, training and prejudice cannot be expected to have the right sort of sympathy with old romance and fancy.

It went on to mention the presence of water horses in the Highlands and how 'Loch Ness is full of water-bulls. But none of these manifestations is, we fear, for a lady interviewer with a kodak. To them must be brought the eye of faith and an hereditary nose for the uncanny gifts that stenography and the snapshot lens are a poor substitute.' It transpired that Miss Freer, a monoglot English speaker with no previous knowledge of the Highlands, had in fact no particular qualifications for taking charge of such an enquiry apart from her claim to be a clairvoyant herself and her claim that she could win the confidence of the Highland seers. Ultimately, the islanders' suspicious instincts later proved to be perfectly well-founded when Miss Freer turned out to be a hoaxer. Freer was later investigated by the SPR and, under strong suspicion of fraud, she was disowned

*An Occult Laboratory: Part Two*

from the Society. She was later caught cheating at a séance and subsequently emigrated to Jerusalem

The conclusion of John L. Campbell and Trevor H. Hall in their later account of all this, *Strange Things*, was:

> What was wanted for the Enquiry, apart from the absence of newspaper publicity, was a trained psychical researcher with a knowledge of Gaelic, of psychology and of the values of evidence. To the Highlanders themselves, Miss Freer must have appeared as just another Sassenach busybody. Indeed, it is doubtful if it would have been possible for anyone to have obtained the kind of substantiation in the form of dates, signed statements, and personal witnesses, from a people of whom at that time many knew little or no English and whose only timepiece was the cockerel crowing in the morning.

In the end the SPR's Enquiry cannot be said to have added anything to what was already known of the subject from the older literature, apart from evidence that in the 1890s second sight was still widely believed in certain districts (mostly in the islands).

This emphasis for a need for a knowledge of psychology was also reflected in what Norman Macrae wrote in his 1908 study, *Highland Second Sight with Prophecies of Coinneach Odhar and the Seer of Perth*. In this he concluded,

> Prophecies then of the Second-Sight order are not altogether illusions – though their accompaniments of vision are – but the lines of probable judgments may converge to a focus, and this focus thrown upon the scree of our imagination so withdraws the attention by the vividness of the vision that consciousness is diverted from a belief in its inwardness of the picture to a belief in its outwardness in the world of space and time as is the manner of dreams. If the conjecture fall out to be true, we mark it, and if not the dream passes into oblivion to give place to others as evanescent, unless some fix and transmute the form and colour of the dream into a seeming reality. To summaries then what we have said as to the probable origin or nature of Second-Sight, we recognise that in the physical proves where sight and sound are most engaged the effects of past experience are the most enduring in consciousness. The retention by the brain of the changes impressed upon it by impact through the nerves of the world of sense forms, as it were, the store-house of memory. By the law of association no imagery ever comes to the front in consciousness unless it has been somehow connected with our previous experience. The law of association has been by psychologists recognised as of several types, viz., association by contiguity, association by similarity, contrast, etc. In the phenomenon of Second-Sight the mode of operation is less that of the 'productive' than it is of the 're-productive' imagination, and this

latter under the sub-conscious influence of the emotions of hope, fear, etc., as the case may be. The elements which go to the formation of the image so formed are, as has been remarked, drawn from our experiences of the past. In ordinary everyday life this procedure is the means by which we ordinarily forecast the future. By it we are enabled so to focalise our experiences of the past as to have them as a guide or pole-star to our line of action in the future. This analysis of Second-Sight is suggested by all the observed facts of this peculiar phenomenon. Some facts connected with it, however, lack vividness in form and colour, and in our twilight of dubiety regarding their full significance we are tempted to take refuge in the all-embracing truth that 'There are more things in heaven and earth than are dreamt of in our philosophy.'

~·~·~

Another interesting point to be gleaned from Father Allan's notebooks for the purposes of this study is how the stories reported have close parallels with those stories traditionally associated with the Brahan Seer. One prophecy, which predicted the end of the MacDonald of Boisdale family, mirrors Countess Isobel's encounter with Coinneach *Odhar*, who was at first reluctant to tell her an uncomfortable truth in the story of 'Seaforth's Doom', along with the prophecy that predicted the demise of the Mackenzies and their return to Ireland in a single fishing boat. Father Allan told of how Colin MacDonald of Boisdale was at a funeral in Hallin. There was a man who had the reputation of being a seer, called Angus MacInnes. Boisdale sent for him and asked him to tell him the future about himself and his family, to which the *fiosaiche* (or seer) replied: 'I'd sooner not, as you may not care to hear it.' 'Come,' said Boisdale, 'it can't be very bad, and I insist on hearing it.' Angus then said: 'You will be very well off all your days. Your son will be very well off after you, but your grandson will be worth little. And at the end a Norwegian skiff would be able to carry every one of your descendants past the point of Ardnamurchan.' "'Och, you old fool," said Colin, "my estate will never be like that." "But wasn't it," says Angus MacInnes quietly.'

Indeed, the Brahan Seer was believed to have predicted the downfall of another prominent family in the Outer Hebrides. 'The day will come when the old wife with the footless stocking (*Cailleach nam mogan*) will drive the Lady of Clan Ranald from Nunton House, in Benbecula.' The Clach believed this to have been fulfilled when the MacDonalds took the farm of Nunton, locally known as 'Baile na Caillich'. Lady Clan Ranald was in the habit of wearing just such stockings so that she was generally known locally as *Cailleach nam Mogan*. 'Clan Ranald and his lady, like many more of our Highland chiefs, ultimately went to the wall, and the descendants of the "old wife with the footless stocking" occupied, and, for anything we know, still occupies the ancient residence of the long-distinguished race of Clan Ranald of the Isles.'

104

*An Occult Laboratory: Part Two*

Another prophecy recorded at this time was attributed to the Barra Seer: the *fiosaiche* or 'Wizard' was purported to have said that the old MacNeils of Barra had predicted that 'Barra will yet be under rats and grey geese'. The prophecy was regarded to be true as to Eoligarry, from which its people were evicted. Although Eoligarry was resettled after the First World War, at the time it was proverbial for its rats.

However limited its conclusions may have been in terms of its own scientific intentions, and however uncritical the SPR's acceptance of Miss Freer's reports may have at first been, the Society deserves the credit of having been the first learned body outside the Highlands since the Royal Society 200 years earlier to see that there was something unusually interesting surviving in the Gaelic oral tradition, and to make some kind of systematic attempt to investigate and record it.

# 'Seaforth's Doom'

In my history of the Mackenzies, *May we be Britons?*, in the chapter entitled 'The Making of a Myth', I explained how, before my book, Alexander Mackenzie's interpretation of the family's history, which was a tale of inevitable decline, had been established in the most widely popular of all his writings, *The Prophecies of the Brahan Seer*. Some of the best-known predictions quoted in it related to the demise of the Mackenzies: how the extensive Mackenzie lands would pass into the hands of strangers; and how their noble castles of Fairburn, Kilcoy and Redcastle would in time fall into dereliction, so that even a cow would give birth on the upper storey of the once stately Fairburn Tower. The lines that follow relate how Sir George Mackenzie's estate at Rosehaugh would pass into the ownership of the son of a fisherman from nearby Avoch, the proud Mackenzie heraldic emblem of a stag being superseded by that of the goat, the heraldic emblem of the Fletchers, who subsequently acquired ownership of Rosehaugh (thus mirroring the heraldic symbolism employed in Thomas the Rhymer's prophecies):

> But foolish pride without sense
> will put in place of the seed of the deer the seed of the goat;
> and the beautiful Black Isle will fall
> under the management of the fishermen of Avoch.

The story of the Clan's chiefs, the Mackenzies of Seaforth, is above all pervaded with the same general narrative in Alexander Mackenzie's portrayal: one of an inescapable progression of decline and ruin, largely put down to the family's romantic attachment to the House of Stuart. 'But their downfall came at last, and the failure of the male line of this great historical family, was attended with circumstances as singular as they were painful.' The closing years of 'the Last Seaforth' were, in the Clach's words, 'darkened by calamities of the severest kind'. He was compelled to dispose of a part of his Kintail estates – the 'giftland' of the family, as it was termed, and about the same time his only surviving son, 'a young man of talent and eloquence', suddenly died. 'The broken-hearted father lingered on for a few months, his fine intellect enfeebled by paralysis, and yet, as his friend, Sir Walter Scott, said, "not so entirely obscured but that he perceived his deprivation as in a glass, darkly."' This 'last *Cabarfèidh*' followed his son to the grave in January 1815, and then,

> Of the line of Fitzgerald remained not a male,
> To bear the proud name of the Chiefs of Kintail.

The truth that belay such a catastrophe as Seaforth's sons predeceasing him is thus revealed in the lines of Sir Walter Scott's poem, 'The Lament for the Last Seaforth':

Thy sons rose around thee in light and in love,
All a father could hope, all a friend could approve;
What vails it the tale of thy sorrows to tell,
In the spring-time of youth and of promise they fell!

Regarding his close friend Lady Hood, who was Seaforth's daughter and who inherited the mantle of chief following his death in 1815, Scott continued:

And thou gentle Dame, who must bear to thy grief,
For thy clan and thy country the cares of a Chief,
Whom brief rolling moons in six changes have left,
Of thy husband and father and brethren bereft;
To thine ear of affection, how sad is the hail
That salutes thee – the heir of the line of Kintail!

The demographic crisis relating to the Mackenzie chiefship caused a great stir among the poet's circle at the time. In the same year, Scott wrote to a friend (in the somewhat misogynistic terms of his time) that 'there are few situations in which the cleverest women are so apt to be imposed upon as in the management of landed property, more especially of an Highland estate. I do fear the accomplishment of the prophecy, that when there should be a deaf Caberfae, the house was to fail.'

The prophecy he was alluding to connected the fall of the Seaforth family with the appearance of a deaf chief. Known as 'Seaforth's Doom', it was ascribed to the subject of this book, Coinneach *Odhar*, of whose prophecies, as we have already seen, Alexander Mackenzie wrote: 'Sir Walter Scott, Sir Humphrey Davy, Mr. Morritt, Lockhart and other eminent contemporaries of the "Last of the Seaforths" firmly believed in them. Many of them were well known, and recited from generation to generation, centuries before they were fulfilled in our own day, and many are still unfulfilled.'

Although the prophecy was indeed well known, the circumstances that were supposed to announce its fulfilment, concerning the disabilities of four great lairds, in fact fitted a much-repeated formula that could be readily adapted in one form or another, to suit the times. Evidence for the fulfilment of the prophecy is generally given as coinciding with the leading lairds of the region, Seaforth, Gairloch, Chisholm, Grant and Raasay, being in turn deaf, buck-toothed, hare-lipped, half-witted and a stammerer. An alternative form was also given by Alexander Mackenzie: 'Another prediction of some alteration upon the families when black-kneed Seaforth, black-spotted Lord Lovat, squint-eyed Mackintosh and a Chisholm blind of an eye.'

Yet, an incredibly similar prediction was also said to have been repeated to James Fraser, minister of Wardlaw and Tutor of Lovat, at a much earlier date, in

*Scotland's Nostradamus*

1648, which was then widely believed to have been confirmed by the birth of the 'Blackspotted Lovat' in 1666:

> Now is our old predictions confirmed of 4 considerable chieftains in the North born with signall marks of which the Master of Lovat is one ... 1. M'khinnich Glundow; 2. M'khimmi Baldow; 3. Mackintoshich Cline; 4. Shissolach Came: that is Blackneed M'Kenzie; Blackspotted Lovat; Squint Mackintosh; and Shiesholm blind of an eye. All four are so, and whither for good or evil, to raise or ruin their families, they are signally marked and remarked. I shall not ominat; let future continguinces verify the truth of it.

Indeed, the way in which the prophecy was manipulated to fit the facts is again revealed in Elizabeth Grant of Rothiemurchus's *Memoirs of a Highland Lady*, writing of a meeting in 1815, in which she said that the presence of the new member for Ross-shire, in the person of the buck-toothed Mr Mackenzie of Applecross, was soon the only topic of conversation, 'for an old prophecy ran that whenever a mad Lovat, a childless ---, and an Applecross with a buck-tooth met, there would be an end of Seaforth'.

And the Clach recorded yet another such prophecy that was current in the Island of Raasay:

> When we shall have a fair-haired Lochiel; a red-haired Lovat; a squint-eyed, fair-haired Chisholm, a big deaf Mackenzie; and a bow-crooked-legged Mac-Gillechallum, who shall be great-grandson of John Beg, or Little John, of Ruiga: that Mac-Gille-challum will be the worst that ever came or ever will come; I shall not be in existence in his day, and I have no desire that I should.

As Alexander Mackenzie explained,

> When the last Macleod of Raasay was born, an old sage in the district called upon his neighbour, and told him, with an expression of great sorrow, that Mac-Gille-challum of Raasay now had an heir, and his birth was a certain forerunner of the extinction of the house. Such an event as the birth of an heir had been hitherto, in this as in all Highland families, universally considered an occasion for great rejoicing among the retainers. The other man was amazed, and asked the sage what he meant by such unusual and disloyal remarks. 'Oh!' answered he, 'do you not know that this is the grand-grandson of John Beg of Ruiga whom Coinneach Odhar predicted would be the worst of his race.' And so he undoubtedly proved himself to be, for he lost for ever the ancient inheritance of his house, and acted generally in such a manner as to fully justify the Seer's prediction; and what is still more remarkable, the Highland lairds, with the peculiar characteristics and malformations foretold by Kenneth, preceded or were the contemporaries of the last Mac-Gille-challum of Raasay.

108

The Clach quoted how comparable prophecies related the following similar patterns in fragments of Gaelic oral tradition: that '*Mhac Shimidh ball-dubh, a dh'fhagus an oigreachd gun an t-oighre dligheah*' ('Mac Shimidh, which is the Gaelic designation for Lord Lovat, the black-spotted who will leave the Estate without rightful heir'); that '*An Sisealach claon ruadh, a dh'fhagus gun an t-oighre dligheach*' ('Chisholm, the squint-eyed, who will leave the estate without the rightful heir'); and that '*An tighearna storach a dh'fhagus oighreachd Ghearrloch gun an t-oighre dligheach*' ('The buck-toothed laird who will leave the estate of Gairloch without rightful heir'). Alexander Mackenzie noted,

> We do not know whether there has been any Lovat or Chisholm with the peculiar personal characteristic mentioned by the Seer, and shall be glad to receive information on the point, as well as a fuller and more particular version of the prophecy. We are aware, however, that Sir Hector Mackenzie of Gairloch was buck-toothed, and that he was always known among his tenants in the west, as An tighearna storach. We hold old people maintaining that Coinneach was correct even in this instance, and that his prediction has actually been fulfilled; but at present we abstain from going into that part of the family history which would throw light on the subject. A gentleman is trying to assert rights over the Lovat estates at the present moment.

The latter comment was a reference to the following fragment regarding the Lovat Estates:

> A claimant will come from the South
> Like a bird from a bush;
> He will grow like an herb;
> He will spread like seed,
> And set fire to Ardross.

Interestingly, although not a claimant to the Lovat Estate, on 1 May 1984, by decree of the Court of the Lord Lyon, the Twenty-first Lady Saltoun was made '*Chief of the name and arms of the whole Clan Fraser*', arising to some confusion. The Frasers of Saltoun are 'from the South', being the elder, Lowland branch of Clan Fraser, but Lady Saltoun is not a descendant of the *Shimidh*, the Simon from whom the Frasers of Lovat trace their lineage, being descended from the *Shimidh*'s older brother. So, although the Lord Lovat is still the Chieftain of Clan Fraser of Lovat (the *MacShimidh*) the Lord Lyon has made official the seniority of the Lady Saltoun's line: the line, that is, of the 'claimant from the south'.

~·~·~

Each of these variations foretold fundamental changes in the succession of the leading families in their respective regions. The prophecy of 'Seaforth's Doom',

*Scotland's Nostradamus*

moreover, should also be placed firmly in the context of the profound psychological impact of the most momentous period of social change in the Highlands for centuries, when the entire clan system was disappearing as huge numbers of people were first cleared off the land their ancestors had lived on for centuries. This coincided with mass emigration and in many cases the traditional patriarchal landowners being replaced with commercial owners, often from the south. All these major changes and upheavals were profoundly reflected in other prophecies of the Brahan Seer.

From the end of the eighteenth century to the middle of the nineteenth, landlords were increasingly clearing their estates to make room for sheep farming, demolishing the old inland townships and moving the people to the coast, where they were needed to fish, to weave, to farm or to harvest kelp for the estate. This came at a time when the landowning elites, such as Lord Seaforth, who wished to restore his family's fortunes following the major political and economic upheavals of the Jacobite period, were further indebted because of the expensive lifestyle that integration demanded if they wished to compete socially with their southern counterparts.

One consequence of this desire for integration with the British state system was the removal of people from the lands they had occupied for centuries. Herring prices, as well as the value of kelp, the seaweed that was used in the manufacture of chemicals, soap and glass, in particular, were artificially inflated as a result of the Napoleonic Wars, when imported alternatives were not available. Because the kelping industry was labour-intensive, one factor in the initial stage of the Highland Clearances involved uprooting people to the shorelines from the inland straths, where they were replaced by sheep. When forced to the coast, they were given small crofts, which were insufficient to subsist on, the intention being to encourage them to take part in herring fishing and kelping, which were by then more lucrative for the landlords. People were moved perhaps forty or fifty miles from where their families had lived for three or four hundred years. This had an obvious psychological impact on those who had wanted simply to be left to pursue their traditional way of life, unhindered in a way they had been accustomed to do for centuries.

At the same time, with the demilitarisation that followed Culloden, the tacksmen (the gentry tenants who sublet the land, often cousins, or cadets of the clan chief) were considered uneconomical because they had until then paid a peppercorn rent in return largely for their military support and political loyalty; but, after Culloden, those military activities were now proscribed, so these middlemen were often seen as surplus to requirements. A number of these tacksmen served as officers in America in the Seven Years' War and the American War of Independence, where they were rewarded with land for which they needed labourers to mirror the old system they had known in Scotland, but that was no longer economically sustainable there; so it was in their interest to attract clansmen to emigrate to North America in particular.

110

Another major change then came after the end of the Napoleonic Wars in 1815, when what had been an age of relative economic optimism ended in the Highlands. Further technical advances then totally destroyed the recent burgeoning kelp market in the 1820s. A more marked increase of sheep farming was then introduced towards the middle of the nineteenth century. With all of this, there came forced evictions, when landlords would cancel rent arrears only if their tenants agreed to migrate to Canada, Australia or New Zealand.

All of this was further exacerbated by the rise in population, which by this time had become exponential and was unsustainable. The population shift during this period was immense: according to Webster's Census in 1755, which is still largely accepted, 51 per cent of the Scottish population lived north of the Tay, with one-third of the Scottish population living in what might be broadly defined as the Highlands; this fell to a low of about 4 per cent in the twentieth century. This major demographic shift from the Highlands was centrally important to the life of Scotland in terms of the way in which population and institutions were being marginalised and must have had an enormous impact on the way the Highland Clearances were perceived in the popular psyche.

In all of this it is important to recognise that from the 1760s onwards there had been no concerted attempt to expel people forcefully: on the contrary landlords wanted to retain the labour force and were very much against immigration during this early period. Emigration was at that stage anathema to the landlords, loss of population denoting a loss of wealth to the estate. Recruitment for the wars also valued a high population, since it entailed 'harvesting sons': in the words of one MacDonald document, land in Skye was given in exchange for sons. Thus, when that bond between patriarchal landowner and people was later betrayed, this had an immense psychological impact. In this subsistence-based society, in which survival was entirely dependent on access to land, the ties between the people, the land and the landowning elites were reflected in the term *dùthchas*, a Gaelic word that had a variety of meanings, including a sense of belonging, and the belief among clan members that the landowning elites had a duty to give them protection, the clearances being the greatest possible violation of that bond, creating deep feelings of anxiety and confusion. Since the clan system was bound together by kinship (both real and mythical) and landownership, when those ties ceased, it will have had the most profound psychological impact on people's lives.

This was my experience of the motivation behind the actions of the 'Last Seaforth', of whom I made a close study when I was writing my university degree dissertation in 1986 and later in my history of the Mackenzies, *May we be Britons?* And such eminent historians of the Highland Clearances as Tom Devine and Murray Pittock have since emphasised the difference between this earlier period of the Highland Clearances and the post-Napoleonic period of forced evictions. In the earlier period, landlords would often cut their losses by paying for their tenants to emigrate. It was only after the collapse of military recruitment and the

*Scotland's Nostradamus*

kelping and fishing industries during the post-Napoleonic war period that large-scale evictions, sometimes accompanied by forced expulsions, reached a crescendo in the 1840s and 1850s, when the dreaded potato blight resulted in either voluntary or cleared emigration and about a quarter to a third of the population of the Inner and Outer Hebrides left, as can be seen by comparing the censuses of 1841 and 1861. Prior to that, the local inhabitants had looked to their landowners as their protectors, their way of seeing their place in the world having long been imbued with a sense of loyalties and traditions, whereby a strong bond had built up between chieftains and clansmen in northern and western Scotland. Clan magnates and gentry having fulfilled an almost monarchical role in such communities, after the period that followed the Napoleonic Wars, a lot of estates were beginning to pass out of the hands of their hereditary landlords.

~·~·~

I believe that the importance of these prophecies to history should be seen in their function as palliatives against the major traumas these families were undergoing. As I have already touched on, according to Sir Keith Thomas, prophecies would often appear at times of crisis, invented to soften the impact of uncomfortable change by bestowing on them the sanction of inevitability. They were particularly common in earlier genealogical histories, which maintained the fiction of an unbroken continuity of rules, since 'the first action of the parvenu is to invent himself a past'. It would now seem that the ancient patrimony of Kintail was to pass from the male line for the first time since its acquisition by the Mackenzies five centuries earlier, when its very origins had been legitimised by means of a prophecy.

The origin of the clan's dominance in the north-west Highlands was traditionally linked with the legend of the Mackenzies' ancestor heroically rescuing King Alexander III from a stag. Thus, the Chief was purported to have received the right to display the *Cabarfèidh*, or deer's antlers, a heraldic emblem borne ever afterwards by his descendants. And thus, we are told, began the tradition of the family's romantic attachment to the Scottish Royal House, that was further reflected in the clan motto, *Cuidich an Righ*, or 'Serve the King', and their subsequent struggle for the Jacobite Cause. This is the epic story that is depicted in Benjamin West's painting that now hangs in Edinburgh's National Gallery. Such an ideal depiction of the staunchly loyal Highlander has entered the popular perception of Scottish history, and this striking image might even be seen as a symbol of the quintessential clansman, as emblematic of Scottishness as Sir Edwin Landseer's noble *Monarch of the Glen*, which now hangs on the other side of the gallery.

The *Legend of the Birds*, which also relates to the origins of the Mackenzies, was a story that was still very current in nineteenth-century oral tradition. This tale tells how the 'only son' of a Kintail Chief 'of the same race as the Mathesons' was imbued by his father with supernatural powers by giving him his first drink from the skull of a raven, which enabled him to understand the language of the birds. Thus, he was able to report the conversation of a flock of starlings that had landed on the roof of the Chief's stronghold at Eilean Donan in Kintail. He recounted to his father the birds' prophecy that one day the Chief would find himself in the position of servitor to his son, while still residing in his own castle. This and the youth's arrogance rankled with the old man, so that shortly afterwards the son took himself off to France, where his powers greatly impressed the King, whose court he rid of a plague of sparrows. For this service he was presented with a fully equipped galley in which he visited many lands, including one in which he gained merit by ridding the court of a plague of rats. Finally, he returned to Kintail and was met by his father, who failed to recognise him. Treating him with marks of great respect inappropriate between a father and son, and waiting on him at table, the birds' prediction was thus fulfilled.

Kevin and I showed in *May we be Britons?* how, like other oral folklore, the story is a tapestry of interwoven threads of fact and fiction. Although it obeys one of the patterns widely found in Aryan culture that anthropologists have termed the 'expulsion-and-return-formula', as I have already discussed, certain details within the legend may be alluded to in order to shed light on a historical reality that underlies them, relating in particular to the participation of the Mackenzie progenitor, Kenneth MacMathan (or Matheson) in the thirteenth-century crusade of Saint Louis; while Kevin has also found a link to a similar story that can be found in the Arabian literature of that time, known to us in the West as *One Thousand and One Nights*, which also influenced the well-known story of *Dick Whittington and his Cat*. Other elements that tie in with Michael Scot, one of the men whose translations first introduced Arab literature to the West, when he most likely returned from the thirteenth-century crusades, have also struck me here. In one folktale Michael Scot obtained his prophetic abilities by accidentally drinking a potion from a dead animal; while Michael Scot also placed particular emphasis on meeting a flock of birds and the songs of birds as significant auguries.

Another prophetic origin legend for the family, the *Legend of Loch Maree*, tells how a powerful Chief is murdered by a rival and the Chief's only son is taken by his sister to Loch Maree, near Gairloch, where he is suckled by a goat, as a result of which he comes to be known as *MacGabhan*, or the 'Son of the Goat'. Hearing of the boy's name, the Lord of Eilean Donan seeks him out, fearing that he will be supplanted in fulfilment of an old prophecy:

The son of the goat shall triumphantly bear
the mountain in flame; and the horns of the deer
from the forest of Loyne to the hill of Ben-Croshen
from mountain to vale, and from ocean to ocean.

After further adventures in which *MacGabhan* takes part in a raid on the neighbouring territory, which turns out to be his ancestral domain, his identity becomes apparent to his mother by means of a sword and cloak he was given

*Scotland's Nostradamus*

as a child and he is thus acclaimed by the people as '*MacCoinneach Mhor*', or 'Great Son of Kenneth', chief of his clan. Subsequently he marries Mary, the only daughter of the Lord of Castle Donan, and by her inherits a considerable estate. This marriage not only ended the feud between the neighbouring clans (bestowing a happy ending on the timeless archetype of *Romeo and Juliet*) but also fulfilled the prophecy that had caused so much uneasiness to his father-in-law and that, of course, alludes to the Mackenzie crest and arms and the family's subsequent predominance across the whole of Ross-shire (yet another heraldry-based prophecy, like those of Thomas the Rhymer).

In the early nineteenth century, it would appear that the sanction of the past was called upon once more by this proud and historically conscious family. In *May we be Britons?* I showed how 'Seaforth's Doom,' and indeed the whole preoccupation of people like Mrs Stewart-Mackenzie (the former Lady Hood, or 'white coiffed lassie from the east' of the prophecy) with everything Scottish, fits into a trend that historians have detected, in which British landowners invested their rule with myths of antiquity and inevitability. This, I believe, began the whole misreading of the Mackenzies' experience of inevitable decline that can be found in subsequent histories, including, and possibly starting with, Alexander Mackenzie's history.

Seaforth's daughter was at pains to re-invent and re-legitimise herself as a Highland chief at precisely the time when Scott and his contemporaries had not only removed the perceived threat of Jacobitism by portraying it as utterly futile, but also made it positively chic in the guise of the original Lost Cause. And it was in that most widespread best-seller of the day, his most celebrated novel, *Waverley*, published in 1814, that Scott first promulgated the idea of the Mackenzies as pre-eminent Jacobites at the time of the 'Forty-Five. After invoking the loyal traditions of Clan Ranald, Glengarry, Sleat, Lochiel and Keppoch, Scott went on to celebrate the chivalrous spirit of Clan Kenneth:

> Stern son of Lord Kenneth, high chief of Kintail,
> let the stag in thy standard bound wild in the gale!

As I have shown, it was, moreover, from Scott himself that subsequent popular histories derived the idea of a clash of cultures: Scotsman versus Englishman, Lowlander versus Highlander, Presbyterian versus Episcopalian. This, as we have seen, was the movement that found its full flowering in the cult of Ossian, surrounding James MacPherson's epic poems that were of such prominence at the time that 'Seaforth's Doom' was being discussed by the likes of Sir Walter Scott, Sir Humphrey Davy, Mr Morritt, Lockhart, and other eminent contemporaries of the 'Last of the Seaforths'. Lord Seaforth's son-in-law and Scott's friend, Henry Mackenzie, was subsequently the editor of the famous *Ossian Report* of 1805, which was commissioned to examine the authenticity of the poems; as well as being the biographer of the writer, John Home, another enthusiast for old Gaelic poetry who was fascinated by Highland culture.

## 'Seaforth's Doom'

In fact, the idea of 'Seaforth's Doom' is entirely in line with the romantic spirit of James MacPherson's wistful harping back to a lost heroic past: 'Where are our chiefs of old? Where are our kings of mighty name? The fields of their battles are silent. Scarce their mossy tombs remain. We shall also be forgot. The lofty house shall fall. Our sons shall not behold the ruins on grass. They shall ask of the aged, "Where stood the walls of our fathers?"' (from James McPherson's *Fingal*, first published in 1762, the influence of which was felt throughout Europe in the coming decades).

—·~·~

I would also argue that another and lesser-known prophecy regarding the Seaforth Mackenzies can also be placed into this same pattern of providing the reassurance of a significant and unexpected occurrence with the sanction of being prophesied. This particular prediction stated: 'The day will come when the Lewsmen shall go forth with their hosts to battle, but they will be turned back by the jaw-bone of an animal smaller than an ass.'

It was said by Alexander Mackenzie that 'this was a prediction accounted ridiculous and quite incomprehensible until it was fulfilled in a remarkable but very simple manner'. The Clach then recounts the background to the prediction surrounding the story of the Lewismen being turned back by the jawbone of an animal smaller than an ass as follows.

The Rev Colin Mackenzie, a brother of the Mackenzie Laird of Hilton, minister of Fodderty and Laird of Glack, in Aberdeenshire,

> was the first in the neighborhood of Brahan who received information of Prince Charlie's landing in 1745. Seaforth had still a warm feeling for the Prince. His reverend friend, though a thorough Jacobite himself, was an intimate friend of Lord President Forbes, with whom he kept up a regular correspondence. He decided, no doubt mainly through his influence, to remain neutral himself; and fearing that his friend of Brahan might be led to join the Prince, he instantly, on receipt of the news, started for Brahan Castle. Although it was very late at night when he received the information, he crossed Knockfarrel, entered Seaforth's bedroom by the window – for he had already gone to rest for the night – and without awakening his lady, informed him of the landing of Charles. They decided upon getting out of the way, and both immediately disappeared. Seaforth was well known to have had previous correspondence with the Prince, and to have sent private orders to the Lews to have his men there in readiness; and Fodderty impressed upon him the prudence of getting out of sight altogether in the meantime. They started through the mountains in the direction of Poolewe, and some time afterwards, when there together in concealment near the shore, they saw two ships entering the bay, having on board a large number of armed men, whom they at once recognised as Seaforth's followers from the Lews, raised and commanded by Captain

*Scotland's Nostradamus*

Colin Mackenzie, the great-grandfather of Major Thomas Mackenzie of the 78th Highlanders. Lord Seaforth had just been making a repast of a sheep's head, when he espied his retainers, and approaching the ships with the sheep's jaw-bone in his hand, he waved it towards them, and ordered them to return to their homes at once, which command they obeyed by making at once for Stornoway; and thus was fulfilled Coinneach Odhar's apparently ludicrous prediction, that the brave Lewsmen would be turned back from the battle with the jaw-bone of an animal smaller than an ass.

William *Dubh* Mackenzie the Fifth Earl and Second Jacobite Marquis of Seaforth, along with the leading cadets of the Clan, were famously 'out' in the Jacobite risings of the 'Fifteen and the 'Nineteen. Indeed, William's part in the latter rising, which culminated in the Battle of Glen Shiel in Kintail, and the blowing up of Eilean Donan Castle, was little short of heroic, when he was wounded in the shoulder and carried over the mountains and into exile. When it comes to the 'Forty-Five Rebellion, most histories of the Mackenzies have highlighted the family's Jacobite credentials and draw attention to how George, Third Earl of Cromartie, raised the clan in support of the Stuart cause. The Seaforth family's allegiance, however, by that point was more nuanced. It was only a few years before the 'Forty-Five uprising that the Seaforth estates had been restored. There seems to be no question that William's son, Lord Fortrose, was sympathetic to Prince Charlie, and his wife was known to have entertained the Prince at Brahan Castle on the eve of Culloden. In Lady Mackintosh's Jacobite regiment was a number of men whom Lady Fortrose detached from the regiment that her husband had raised for the Government. Of the Mackenzie Chief's wife, the French envoy, the Marquis d'Eguilles, informed his Government: 'It is assured that her zeal is equal to that of the other two [Lady Mackintosh and Mrs Mackenzie of Fairburn], although she appears less lively and less courageous.' Given the influence that was no doubt exerted by Fortrose's early life in exile, it seems more than likely that he turned a blind eye to his wife's Jacobite activity. Active Jacobitism, however, was not representative of the clan as a whole by that time. The numbers that Cromartie raised during 1745 and 1746 were quite irrelevant compared to the Government regiment of Fencibles raised by the actual Chief of the clan; while the great houses of Gairloch, Scatwell and Coul, which had played a major part in the 'Fifteen, now kept aloof from the fighting.

Of course, the mention of a jawbone of a sheep in this particular prophecy is familiar in other predictions, particularly those that relate to the Highland Clearances that were popular throughout the Highlands and Lowlands and that were also attributed to seers other than Coinneach *Odhar*. What is interesting here is that the mention of a jawbone appears to have been conflated in oral tradition with the genuine and dramatic historical events of the mid-eighteenth century, when the once staunchly Jacobite Mackenzie chiefs broke with tradition and held back from rebellion, an action that itself might by many a clansman who sympathised with the Jacobite cause be 'accounted ridiculous and quite incomprehensible until it was fulfilled'.

Indeed, the unlikelihood of Fortrose's actions in 1745 can be gleaned from Prince Charlie's own reaction. In the later account of Lord MacLeod (the Third Earl of Cromartie's heir) when he met with the Prince and recalled

> that nothing surprised the Prince so much as to hear that the Earl of Seaforth [that is, Fortrose] had declared against him, for he heard without emotion the names of the other people who had joined the Earl of Loudon at Inverness; but when I told him that Seaforth had likewise sent two hundred men to Inverness for the service of the Government, and that he had likewise hindered many gentlemen of his clan from joining my father for the service of the Stuarts, he turned to the French Minister and said to him, with some warmth, 'He! mon Dieu! et Seaforth est aussi contre moi!'

Once more, it would appear, we have an unlikely event that is given the reassuring sanction of prophecy to render it acceptable to those many Mackenzie clansmen who still held Jacobite sympathies.

—·—·—

And I believe the same psychology is also involved in those prophecies that were concerned with more parochial and personal occurrences. One such example was repeated in Gaelic as follows: '*Beirear nighean mhaol dubh air cùl Eaglais Ghearrloch*'. This foretold that 'a bald black girl will be born at the back of the Church of Gairloch'. It seems that during one of the usual large gatherings at the Sacramental Communion a well-known young woman was taken in labour, and before she could be removed, she gave birth to the 'nighean mhaol dubh', whose descendants are well known and pointed out in the district to this day as the fulfilment of Coinneach's prophecy. Others recorded such predictions as that 'a white cow will give birth to a calf in the garden behind Gairloch House'; and that in Flowerdale (the west coast seat of the Mackenzies of Gairloch), 'a black hornless cow (*Bo mhaol dubh*) will give birth to a calf with two heads', which prophecies were said to be well known to people before they came to pass. Once again, to view such aberrations and unusual events as having been foretold would no doubt have comforted the local community.

Similarly, according to Hugh Miller, the Seer predicted with regard to Fortrose Cathedral that 'the ancient Chanonry of Ross, which is still standing, would fall "full of Mackenzies"'. Miller made the observation that 'as the floor of this building has been used, for time immemorial, as a burying-place by several powerful families of this name, it is supposed that the prophecy cannot fail, in this way, of meeting its accomplishment'. However, it also strikes me that could also have been a memory of past events that had a powerful impact on the local community. The Cathedral has long been a prominently visible ruin. After it lost its status as a cathedral at the Reformation in 1560, although it remained in

*Scotland's Nostradamus*

use for local services, its decline was inevitable. Lord Ruthven was granted the lead from the roof to sell in June 1572, and thereafter the building began to fall apart in the later sixteenth century and early seventeenth. Tradition has it that Cromwell's men removed most of the masonry from the Cathedral for his citadel at Inverness, when the stone from the now roofless nave was taken away in the 1650s. None of the pier bases or vestigial walls, which do remain at places like St Andrew's Cathedral, survive here.

~.~.~

Ravens will drink their fill three times of the blood of the Mackenzies off the Clach Mhor.

This ominous prediction was said to have come from the lips of the Brahan Seer, and he was also widely reported to have foretold that the Mackenzies one day would be so reduced in numbers that women will fight over a pock-marked, squint-eyed tailor and the sole surviving members of the family will finally return to Ireland, from whence they came, in an open fishing boat.

A major element in these powerfully evocative local legends was the prediction that the demise of the Mackenzies meant that their lands were to pass into the hands of strangers. This reflected the major crisis for the entire clan system in the half-century following Lord Seaforth's death in 1815, when the ownership of Highland soil was to undergo enormous upheaval. James Mackenzie of Findon, writing on the Clan Mackenzie in 1879, described this change as a complete revolution: 'Forty or fifty years ago the greater part of the old Mackenzie possession in Ross-shire remained in the hands of their ancient lairds, or the relatives of these; but now it is a fact, that where one such holds ten acres the stranger has a thousand.' Given the way this one family had for so long held sway in this part of the world it is no wonder that such a huge upheaval found its way into local oral tradition. 'Seaforth's Doom' in particular reflected the way in which the chiefly system was becoming removed from people's lives, which was a momentous change in Highland society.

The true reckoning had come for the Seaforths when agricultural prices, and consequently rents, began to fall after 1815. Thus, the debts, which Lord Seaforth had built up as a necessary part of his strategy for integration into the wider British elite, could no longer be sustained by the landed estate. No longer able to support the interest of debts on her diminished disposable income, the twice-widowed Mrs Stewart-Mackenzie was compelled to sell one section after another of her inheritance: the remaining portion of Kintail, the fertile braes of Ross, the church lands of Chanonry, the barony of Pluscarden and the great principality of Lewis were each disposed of one after the other until by 1879 the *Edinburgh Daily Review* could write that 'nothing remains of the vast estates except Brahan Castle and a mere remnant of the ancient patrimony (and that in the hands of trustees), which the non-resident, nominal owner has just been prevented from alienating. *Sic transit.*'

*'Seaforth's Doom'*

How much more poignant was the loss of Kintail – Seaforth's 'giftland' – when viewed with the nineteenth century's profound appreciation for the picturesque? To a man such as Alexander Mackenzie contemplating the Atlantic seaboard in this part of the Highlands, 'how glorious is the scene which presents itself from the summit of the hills when the great ocean is seen glowing with the last splendour of the setting sun, and the lofty hills of the farther isles rear their giant heads amid the purple blaze on the extreme verge of the horizon'. It was under the shadow of the loss of these lands that Alexander wrote the first romantic précis of the clan's history in his *The Prophecies of the Brahan Seer*. It is from this time, when the family had already dispossessed themselves of the majority of their ancestral lands and were threatening to sell more, that date the subsequent popular commentaries on the clan that give the same pessimistic emphasis on what was seen as the predicted and inevitable decline of the family.

And there could be no more prominent symbol of the decline of this family's former powerful presence in the region than the all-too visible ruins of their once formidable strongholds in the local landscape. Coinneach *Odhar* predicted, 'No future chief of the Mackenzies shall bear rule at Brahan or Kintail.' Brahan Castle itself was demolished in 1951; while Eilean Donan in Kintail was blown up by gunpowder during the Jacobite Rising led by the Second Marquis of Seaforth in 1719. The 16,000-hectare estate of Kintail was eventually to be entirely relinquished by the successors of the 'Last Seaforth' in the nineteenth century. Now designated a National Scenic Area, most of it is owned by the National Trust for Scotland.

Not far south of Brahan, standing high on a ridge between the Conon and Orrin river valleys, could be seen until recently the ruins of Fairburn Tower. The Landmark Trust has only within the last two years done a wonderful job in restoring some of the refined Renaissance details that were incorporated into the original building for my own direct ancestor, John Mackenzie of Fairburn, who was a Master of the Bedchamber to King James V. 'The day will come when the Mackenzies of Fairburn shall lose their entire possessions; their castle will become uninhabited and a cow shall give birth to a calf in the uppermost chamber of the tower.' Fairburn Tower did become a ruin, and in 1851, a cow calved in the garret that was being used by a farmer to store hay. The prophecy was so well known that people came via railway to Strathpeffer or Muir of Ord and then by coach to see the cow. She had gone up the tower following a trail of hay, had a good feed at the top and became stuck. She gave birth to a fine calf, and both were taken down some five days later, allowing enough time for the incredulous to come and see the prophecy fulfilled for themselves. While sceptics say that the Brahan Seer could have second guessed such innovations as the Caledonian Canal, this prediction stood out as remarkable for its implausibility.

Another prediction pertaining to Fairburn Tower foretold that a rowan, or mountain-ash tree will grow out of its walls, and when it becomes large enough to form a cart axle, then Seaforth would return. This prophecy was thought to

*Scotland's Nostradamus*

have been fulfilled when the grandson of the 'white coiffed lassie', James Alexander Francis Humberston Stewart-Mackenzie, was given a new peerage, as Baron Seaforth in 1921, which in the status-obsessed society of that time would have given great cause for pride in the vicinity.

Just to the south-east on the Black Isle stood Kilcoy Castle, which had belonged to the Mackenzies for nearly 300 years until 1813. The Seer predicted:

When the girls of Kilcoy house cry out,
'The shell (cup) of our murders is flowing over.'
A fox from Croy will come
Who shall be like a wolf among the people
During forty years and more,
And in his coat shall be many curses;
He shall then be thrown empty and sorrowful,
Like an old besom behind the door;
The large farmers will be like sportful birds,
And the lairds as poor as the sparrows –
There's a blessing in handsome honey
And curses in the shedding of blood.

When the stern Castle of Kilcoy
Shall stand cold and empty,
And the jackdaws and the rooks
Are artfully flying past it,
A loathsome man shall then dwell
Beside it, indecent and filthy,
Who will not keep the vow of the marriage coif,
Listen neither to cleric nor friend;
But from Creag-a-Chow to Ferrintosh
The dirty fellow will be after every girl –
Ochan! Ochan! woe's me,
The cunning dog will swallow up much land.

The 'stern Castle of Kilcoy' did 'stand cold and empty' after the last of the line of Kilcoy to live there died in 1813, falling into a ruinous state until its restoration after 1891. A.B. MacLennan suggested that the second and last line of the first stanza of the Seer's prophecy about Kilcoy referred to the following story:

Towards the latter end of the seventeenth century a large number of cattle, in the Black isle, were attacked with a strange malady, which invariably ended in madness and in death. The disease was particularly destructive on the Kilcoy and Redcastle estates, and the proprietors offered a large sum of money as a reward to any who should find a remedy. An old warlock belonging to the parish agreed to protect the cattle from the

120

*'Seaforth's Doom'*

ravages of this unknown disease, for the sum offered, if they provided
him with a human sacrifice. To this ghastly proposal the laird agreed.
A large barn at Parkton was, from its secluded position, selected as a
suitable place for the horrid crime, where a poor friendless man, who
lived at Linwood, close to the present Free Church manse, was requested,
under some pretence, to appear on a certain day. The unsuspecting
creature obeyed the summons of his superiors; he was instantly bound,
and disembowelled alive by the horrid wizard, who dried the heart, liver,
kidneys, pancreas, and reduced them to powder, of which he ordered a
little to be given to the diseased animals in water. Before the unfortunate
victim breathed his last, he ejaculated the following imprecaution: *Gum
b'ann nach tig an latha 'bhitheas teaghlach a Chaisteil Ruaidh gun oinseach
, na teaglach Chulchallaidh gun amadin.* (Let the day never come when
the family of Redcatle shall be without a female idiot, or the family of
Kilcoy without a fool.) It appears, not only that this wild imprecaution
was to some extent realized, but also that the Brahan Seer, years before,
knew and predicted that it would be made, and that its prayer would be
ultimately granted.

In Wester Ross, where Mackenzie lairds had once been equally predominant, it
was foretold that a 'dun, hornless cow' will appear in the Minch and blow down
the six chimneys of Gairloch House. This was presumably a reference to Mackenzie of Gairloch's west coast seat, Flowerdale House. Following the Battle of
Culloden, Sir Alexander Mackenzie of Gairloch was concealing the Jacobite rebel
Fraser of Foyers there when one of the Government's men o'war was cruising in
the bay and the captain sent word to Sir Alexander to come on board. The latter
sent his compliments to the captain, regretting that he could not accept his invi-
tation. The response was a broadside against the house as the ship sailed off, the
canon-ball lodging close to the recess where the fugitive was hidden, together
with a stash of swords and guns.

~·~·~

It is perhaps apt that, in the very same way that the Brahan Seer was purported
to have foretold the end of the Seaforths in the early nineteenth century, he was
also said to have foreseen their initial usurpation of the MacLeods in Lewis when
Colin Mackenzie, Lord Kintail took possession of the island principality from
them two centuries earlier, adopting the title of First Earl of Seaforth, after the
island's great sea loch of that name. The *Bannatyne manuscript* history of the
MacLeods, which dates from around 1832, in which he was said to predict the
downfall of the MacLeods, places the Brahan Seer as a native of Ness in the Isle
of Lewis, where he was purported to have been born in the sixteenth century.
    Even as late as the 1890s, as we have seen, Father Allan reported to the SPR
how the Brahan Seer was believed to have predicted the end of the MacDonald of Boisdale family; and, around the same time, it was reported that the old

*Scotland's Nostradamus*

MacNeils of Barra had predicted that 'Barra will yet be under rats and grey geese'. In all of this I have detected a pattern in local legends of prophecies concerned with the end of those prominent landowning families that had dominated the region for centuries and were now suddenly disappearing. The emphasis of these legends was on the prediction that their lands were to pass into the hands of strangers. Perplexed by debts, racked by competing demands for scarce funds as the capital value and consequently the financial security of land came into doubt, Mackenzie laird after Mackenzie laird in particular in this part of the world was to sell his patrimony. The disposal of lands came first in the Outer Hebrides; those on the western seaboard followed and then, as the century progressed, even the relatively prosperous Low Country estates of Easter Ross were sold. This dispersal by the historic aristocracy of the clan's lands broke down what remained of kinship ties between former close neighbours, while in the meantime the exponential growth in population, coupled with the extensive geographical diaspora of the younger cadets of the family, finally broke what was left of the old clan system. The impact on the psyche of the local community would have been immense and unprecedented.

In fact, the rarity of finding a Mackenzie today in what was once their 'Giftland' and in which this clan had for centuries held sway as the dominant presence, was illustrated when my parents first took my brothers and me as children to Kintail. When the landlady of our accommodation in the village of Dornie, which is close to Eilean Donan Castle, was interrupted while she was engaged in conversation with my father, she turned impatiently to the other guest and said, 'Do you mind? I'm talking to Mr McKenzie!', the strong emphasis being on our surname. The very name had left a profound impression, even if it no longer retained a physical human presence in the neighbourhood.

# A Highland Conspiracy Theory

'Seaforth's Doom' thus came in the wake of extreme trauma for his immediate family, but, as he was the leading landlord and chief of a clan, also for much of the community of Ross-shire. The decline and disappearance of the Mackenzie lairds in the area was then followed by the Highland Clearances, mass emigration and widespread social change resulting from industrialisation, all of which were even more impactful to the region and amounted to by far the most overwhelming change to its people's way of life for centuries.

It was an earlier devastating change in the region that formed the subject of another famous prophecy, in which the Brahan Seer was said to have proclaimed: 'Oh! Drumossie, thy bleak moor shall, ere many generations have passed away, be stained with the best blood of the Highlands. Glad am I that I will not see the day, for it will be a fearful period; heads will be lopped off by the score, and no mercy shall be shown or quarter given on either side.' The Battle of Culloden in 1746 was one of the most shattering and infamous events in the whole of the Highlands' history, in which the 'Butcher' Duke of Cumberland was notoriously brutal, while the draconian reprisals that followed were to change the nature of Highland society for good.

In the following century, the Highlands were to be devastated once more by the Highland Clearances. In the words of the Brahan Seer's prophecy, 'Sheep shall eat men', and 'The day will come when the jaw-bone of the big sheep ... will put the plough on the rafters; when sheep shall become so numerous that the bleating of the one shall be heard by the other from Conchra in Lochalsh to Bun-da-Loch in Kintail.' He went on to predict that the people would emigrate en masse from the country and that sheep would rule the land. 'People will flee from their native country before an army of sheep.' The Highland Clearances, from 1750 to 1860, when tenant families were driven out by their landowners and the land they farmed was given over to the more profitable grazing of sheep, had an impact throughout the Highlands and Islands, and indeed in parts of the Scottish Lowlands too. Thus, as we have already seen, similar prophecies were recounted elsewhere: the Isla Seer saying, 'The time is coming when the sheep's tooth will take the coulter out of the ground in Isla'; while the so-called 'Lowland Seer' and purveyor of folktales, Thomas the Rhymer, declared: 'The teeth shall lay the plough on the shelf.'

The consequence was confusion, resentment and guilt. Confusion because of a belief in *dùthchas* – the sense of belonging and a common purpose in the land with the landowner as protector. To a degree, a concomitant sense of loyalty to the landowner survived, which meant that resistance was piecemeal and limited,

*Scotland's Nostradamus*

compared, for example, to the resistance that occurred in Ireland. The landlord was still seen as 'one of us', and this is reflected very much in the Seer's prophecies. Indeed, a sense of guilt accompanying the Clearances has been detected in recent research into the statements of those who emigrated to Canada, in which the emigrants explained how, although they were cleared from the land, they recognised that they had left voluntarily. Such guilt was a characteristic of Presbyterianism, which survived the move to the Free Church in the 1840s, whereby people believed that their misfortune was a consequence of their sins. Collective punishment to their townships and to their crofts was seen as having been brought upon them owing to their short fallings, thus further increasing the levels of confusion that was already endemic, owing to the shattering of the assumptions that came with the concept of *dùthchas*. The psychology of the Highland Clearances was thus far more complex than has later been portrayed. Professor Tom Devine has pointed out that the politicisation of resentment against the Clearances was a later phenomenon that only really came into play after the 1960s, coinciding with the rise of Scottish nationalism in the later part of the twentieth century. The polemical literature about the Clearances only becomes intensified, exaggerated and to some degree mythologised in the language of the Crofting Commission, after the late 1870s and 1880s with the great potato blight of 1846/7, enduring for another eight or nine years, killing the main subsistence source for the people, but saved to a large degree by the relief organisations mounted by landlords in the first two years.

That is not to say that many people were not aggrieved; but owing to their centuries-old ties to the landed elites, more than anything else the Highlanders were psychologically disorientated, and it was very difficult for them to respond collectively in terms of a full-scale regional assault, so that any protests were fragmentary and ineffectual. The overriding response was one of confusion and powerlessness.

~·~·~

Another prophecy attributed to the Brahan Seer put it differently when he foretold 'That the people will degenerate as their country improves. That the clans will become so effeminate as to flee from their native country as their native country improves.' The latter prediction was a reference to the significant events that were to have an impact on local communities which followed the introduction of industrialisation to the area, as they had throughout Britain at this time of rapid and overreaching progress. A prediction that 'Ships will one day sail round the Tomnahurich Hill near Inverness', and that the lochs in the Great Glen will be joined, were believed to have been accomplished by the construction of the Caledonian Canal by Thomas Telford, which was begun in 1803. A similar prophecy was 'That the day will come when there will be a road through the hills of Ross-shire from sea to sea, and a bridge over every stream.' It was also said that Coinneach *Odhar* talked of 'great black, bridleless horses, belching fire and

*A Highland Conspiracy Theory*

steam, drawing lines of carriages through the glens.' The full prediction of what has been interpreted as the coming of the railways to the Highlands, more than 200 years after this prophet was said to have been executed on Chanonry Point, was handed down in the following stanza:

> When there shall be two churches in the Parish of Ferrintosh,
> And a hand with two thumbs in *I-Stiana*,
> Two bridges at *Sguideal* (Conon) of the gormandizers,
> And a man with two navels at Dunean,
> Soldiers will come from *Cam a Chlarsair* (Tarradale)
> On a chariot without horse or bridle,
> When will leave the *Blar-dubh* (Muir of Ord) a wilderness,
> Spilling blood with many knives;
> And the raven shall drink his three fills
> Of the blood of the Gael from the Stone of Fionn.

According to the Clach,

> We already have two churches in the Parish of Ferrintosh, two bridges at Conon, and we are told by an eye-witness that there is actually at this very time a man with two thumbs on each hand in *I-Stiana*, in the Black isle, and a man in the neighbourhood of Dunean who has two navels. The 'chariot without a horse or bridle' is undoubtedly the 'iron horse'. What particular event the latter part of the prediction refers to, is impossible to say; but if we are to have any faith in the Seer, something serious is looming not very remotely in the future.

Elizabeth Sutherland further pointed out that a local tradition held that this prediction was already believed to have been fulfilled, before the days of the railway in the north, when the Duke of Portland travelled by a road car driven by steam; and also that *'Fearchair a Ghunna* ('Farquhar of the Gun, an idiot simpleton who lived during the latter part of his extraordinary life on the Muir of Tarradale) seems, in his own quaint way, to have entered into the spirit of this prophecy, when he compared the train, as it first passed through the district, to the funeral of 'Old Nick'.

A yet further version tells: 'after four successive dry summers, a fiery chariot shall pass through the *Blar-dubh*'; and Coinneach *Odhar* was not the only person who foresaw the coming of the railways, since it was also commonly reported that a man residing in the neighbourhood of Beauly, who was gifted with second sight, had a vision of the train, travelling at speed, when he was on his way home one dark autumn night, several years before a railway was ever contemplated in the area.

The ceremony of cutting the first sod of the railway from Inverness to Dingwall, known as the 'Inverness and Ross-shire Line', took place on 19 September 1860, and it was opened two years later. It was extended to Strome in 1879 and

*Scotland's Nostradamus*

to Kyle of Lochalsh in 1897, and is now known as the Highland Line. In all of this, the Brahan Seer offers us a very nineteenth-century fairy tale – modern and embracing technological change, but at the same time rooted in myths that are anchored in the human psyche.

In fact, at much the same time that the chiefly line was undergoing dramatic change, my own three-times great-grandfather William McKenzie also underwent economic misfortune when the family's cosmopolitan mercantile business, which operated from the Moray Firth, for 200 years, collapsed and he was obliged to work as a labourer on Telford's canal, before moving south, first to Liverpool, where his cousin, another William Mackenzie, was pioneering the building of railways, and then to Birmingham, where he participated in the manufacturing boom of the Industrial Revolution, establishing himself as a pewterer there. I believe it was very much this background of dramatic and sometimes traumatic social upheaval that explains much of the phenomenon that we know as the Brahan Seer.

And then yet more predictions are attached to the Brahan Seer's name going into the twentieth century, when his concerns also appear to have surrounded certain influential events that impacted the local community. The Seer was told to have said of Strathpeffer (the present-day settlement that is just up the road from Castle Leod and that wasn't even a small village in Coinneach *Odhar's* lifetime) that '[u]ninviting and disagreeable as it now is, with its thick crusted surface and unpleasant smell, the day will come when it shall be under lock and key and crowds of pleasure and health seekers shall be seen thronging its portals in their eagerness to get a draught of its waters'. The popularity of Strathpeffer's sulphurous waters promoted it to the status of a fashionable Spa resort that reached its height in the Victorian era; while in the 1960s when The Beatles played in the Strathpeffer Pavilion, with people coming from as far as Elgin, the *Ross-shire Journal* recorded Strathpeffer as being 'a boom-town with the shops open until 11.00 p.m.!' As I mentioned in my Preface, another prediction pertaining to Strathpeffer claimed that the Seer once said when pointing to a field far from any seashore, loch or river, that a ship would anchor there one day: 'A village with four churches will get another spire,' said Coinneach, 'and a ship will come from the sky and moor at it.' In 1932, an airship made an emergency landing in the town and was tied up to the spire of the new church.

The Seer was widely believed to have announced that when there were five bridges built over the River Ness then there would be 'worldwide chaos'. In August of 1939, a fifth bridge was constructed and shortly afterwards Hitler invaded Poland and the Second World War commenced. Elizabeth Sutherland explained how this prophecy was first brought to light by Mr Ian C. Young of Ipswich as follows:

> The suspension bridge which stood at the foot of Bridge Street in
> Inverness was condemned in 1937, and it was agreed that a temporary

## A Highland Conspiracy Theory

traffic bridge be placed alongside to relieve the strain on the old bridge and also as an alternative crossing while the old bridge was being dismantled. A letter printed in the Inverness Courier pointed out that the Seer had said that when it would be possible to cross the River Ness dryshod in five places, a frightful disaster would strike the entire world. If the temporary bridge was put into use *before* the suspension bridge was closed to foot traffic, the forecast would be proved, for there would then be five bridges. The construction went ahead, the temporary bridge was opened for traffic during the last days of August 1939, and Hitler marched his troops into Poland on 1 September. There are few people who were living in Inverness during those months who do not believe that World War II was forecast by the Seer.

Similarly, the Brahan Seer declared that when a ninth bridge would be constructed over the River Ness then 'fire, blood and calamity' would ensue. This ninth bridge was finished in 1987 and the following year the Piper Alpha oil platform, in the North Sea off the Ross-shire coast, exploded and sank, killing 165 of the men on board, thirty of whose bodies were never recovered.

Another much discussed prediction was, 'A black rain will bring riches to Aberdeen.' During the mid-twentieth century many significant oil deposits scattered across the North Sea were discovered that saw the creation of the petroleum industry in Aberdeen. He also supposedly predicted, 'Streams of fire and water would run beneath the streets of Inverness and into every house.' Inverness was one of the first towns in Scotland to have its own gas works, opened in 1826 by the Inverness Gas and Water Company, with gas street lighting.

Most recently, as I also mentioned in my Preface, Coinneach *Odhar* was said to have spoken of the day when Scotland would once again have its own Parliament. This would only come, he said, when men could walk dry shod from England to France. The completion of the Channel Tunnel in 1994 was followed a few years later by the opening of the first Scottish Parliament since 1707, a political event of enormous moment for Scottish nationalism.

As you can see, I have detected a pattern in these prophecies, all of which concern some of the most impactful events that affected the people who resided in Coinneach *Odhar*'s homeland. My explanation would be that the common theme to most of these predictions reflects the way that people attempted to come to terms with major changes, particularly those they perceived as disasters. As Keith Thomas explained regarding the prophecies that were widespread in the sixteenth and seventeenth centuries, prophecies give sanction and act as a panacea for otherwise inexplicable and traumatic changes. That was the conclusion that I drew in my Epilogue to *May we be Britons?* with regard to 'Seaforth's Doom', and I would suggest the same can be said of most of his predictions concerning other major events in the area from the eighteenth century almost up to the present day. In fact, I can show that this type of psychological explanation

*Scotland's Nostradamus*

can be detected in the contemporary world we live in, and in nations that are deemed to be perfectly rational, progressive and civilised.

—·—·—

Owing to the oral nature of Highland culture during the period we are looking at, with the Brahan Seer's predictions we have few indications of there being records of any prophecies that were written down prior to the events that they supposedly predicted, although it may well have been that such prophecies as the earlier demise of the MacLeods on Lewis, or the coincidence of the leading lairds of the region all at one time being deaf, buck-toothed and hare-lipped, for example, fitted archetypal patterns in folklore, which then struck a chord in people's minds when very similar events occurred in their own time, allowing them to believe with perfect conviction that they had heard the prophecy before the event. This probably explains Sir Walter Scott's statement that many of the Brahan Seer's prophecies 'were well known, and recited from generation to generation, centuries before they were fulfilled'.

There is another comparable seer, whose prophecies were recorded and written down before the events that people believed they were foretelling actually happened. He may lend a clue to at least some of what was going on in the Brahan Seer's case. My attention was drawn to this man when discussing my project on Scotland's Nostradamus with a former work colleague and friend of mine, Julian Roup, who is also a fellow amateur writer (he writes beautifully). Julian, who is from South Africa, told me about a man from his homeland, Siener van Rensburg, who is considered by some to be a 'prophet of the Boers' ('Siener' is Afrikaans for 'seer'). As a toddler, this man's mother commented on his visual hallucinations, and said that these seemed to disturb him. General Hertzog described him as someone continuously distracted by a maze of imagery and symbolism. Seven hundred of his visions have been documented. Van Rensburg himself interpreted his hallucinations as visions that were usually connected to the welfare of the Boere, the Netherlands and Germany. Van Rensburg's visions have also been described as both predictions of local events, such as the death of General Koos de la Rey, and as being connected to major international events, such as the start of the Second World War, the rise of Communism and the political transition of South Africa.

A Boer soldier, named Deneys Reitz gave a vivid account of one of this seer's predictions as follows:

> a prophet, a strange character, with long flowing beard and wild fanatical eyes, who dreamed dreams and pretended to possess occult powers. I personally witnessed one of the lucky hits while we were congregated around the General's cart. Van Rensburg was expounding his latest vision to a hushed audience. It ran of a black bull and a red bull fighting, until at length the red bull sank defeated to its knees, referring to the British. Arms outstretched and eyes ablaze, he suddenly called out: 'See, who comes?';

128

*A Highland Conspiracy Theory*

and, looking up, we made out a distant horseman spurring towards us. When he came up, he produced a letter from General Botha, hundreds of miles away. General de la Rey opened it and said: 'Men, believe me, the proud enemy is humbled'. The letter contained news that the English had proposed a peace conference. Coming immediately upon the prophecy, it was a dramatic moment and I was impressed, even though I suspected that van Rensburg had stage-managed the scene. Of the general's sincerity there could be no doubt as he firmly believed in the seer's predictions.'

Siener's visions were first written down by C.P. Nieuwenhuizen, a cellmate of his, during their time in prison, and subsequently by his daughter, Anna Badenhorst in 1916. They were later interpreted by several persons. Just to give one example, his Vision number 372 tells, 'The maize stand green on the fields about two feet tall, but thin, and the maize disappears until there is nothing left. In Europe there is a rough blue stone which changes into a wheel and when the wheel starts rolling the wheel falls apart.' Two interpreters, named Boy Mussmann and Nellie van Syl, both saw this as predicting the Second World War, which saw the Germans first undertake a large offensive that then fails. An alternative interpretation by Adam van Snyman saw this as predicting the collapse of the Wall Street Stock Exchange, which followed shortly after the closure of major financial institutions in Europe.

Still today the Suidlanders, an ethnonationalist Afrikaner survivalist group, are heavily influenced by Siener van Rensburg's prophecies, and I came across the following recent comment to a YouTube video about his visions, which is both critical of them, but also takes them seriously by attempting to analyse them:

> The Siener Nicolaas Van Rendsburg was wrong when he predicted that the queen would lose her throne because of Germany. He also pointed out that there would probably be no successor. We all know that Charles became the new king. Let's see how long he stays as King. In another vision Siener spoke about the beheading of a prominent British leader (King Charles?). A prominent Englishman will brutally be killed while in Europe on a charity mission. Nobles and other distinguished persons will attend his burial.

I would suggest that it is possible that something very similar went on in the Highlands with the Brahan Seer.

～·～·～

Earlier on in this book, I quoted certain predictions attributed to Nostradamus that did the rounds in emails at the time of the 9/11 attack on the Twin Towers in New York and were widely circulated in the United States. One such quote included the lines:

> In the City of God there will be a great thunder,
> Two Brothers torn apart by Chaos
> While the fortress endures, the great leader will succumb ...

*Scotland's Nostradamus*

It has since been shown that these three lines were taken, not from Nostradamus, but from an essay, written in 1977 by Neil Marshall, then a student at Brock University in Canada. Marshall included the made-up lines in an essay to demonstrate how easy it was to take vague imagery and use it as 'proof' that a certain event had been foretold long ago. It would appear that someone picked up the verses, added another line and distributed the quatrain over the Internet. Others then added more lines to it, supposedly from Nostradamus, as the message made its way round the Internet.

Another widespread message at the time included these lines:

> In the year of the new century and nine months,
> From the sky will come a great King of Terror.
> The sky will burn at forty-five degrees.
> Fire approaches the great new city.

While this quatrain as it was presented in this form was not the work of Nostradamus, it does include some of his verses. It is an adaptation of two different quatrains of his.

Century 10, Quatrain 72 said the following:

> The year 1999, seventh month,
> From the sky will come a great King of Terror:
> To bring back to life the great King of the Mongols,
> Before and after Mars to reign by good luck.

And Century 6, Quatrain 97 said:

> At forty-five degrees the sky will burn,
> Fire to approach the great new city:
> In an instant a great scattered flame will leap up,
> When one will want to demand proof of the Normans.

Sceptics suggest that believers are paying attention only to the pieces that fit, discarding the parts that do not (such as 'the great King of the Mongols', for example). Additionally, they have argued that the 'great new city' is a misleading translation of Nostradamus's lines. In the original French, Nostradamus referred to 'Villeneuve', which literally means 'new city', but is also the name of a town outside Paris, which is indeed near 45 degrees latitude. Critics have further credited the similarity of 'Mabus' and Osama bin Laden, which was also widely circulated at the time of 9/11, to coincidence, drawing attention to the fact that up until then many Nostradamus followers had claimed that Saddam Hussein was 'Mabus' ('Mabus' spelled backwards is 'Subam').

This selective approach, which is similar to the game of Chinese whispers, is precisely the way that oral folktale works, as we have seen with the tales relating to Michael Scot, Thomas the Rhymer, Coinneach *Odhar*, Katherine Ross, the Third Earl of Seaforth, his Countess and the two John Morrisons. Since all the

*A Highland Conspiracy Theory*

various traditions surrounding the Brahan Seer were created over such a long period of time, they would have been able to add ever more complex layers of both fact and fiction.

~·~·~

Not long after I completed my interviews about the Brahan Seer with Jared Smart for the *Clan Mackenzie Podcast*, I happened to listen to some other fascinating podcasts and radio programmes that attempted to explain why conspiracy theories had become so prevalent recently. One series in particular was especially enlightening on the subject: the historian Phil Tinline's BBC Radio 4 Series *Conspiracies: The Secret Knowledge* followed on from his academic research interest into how to distinguish between fictional stories and stories of fact. He made the point that this might at first appear obvious, but recent history and even our very own times show us how easily fact and fiction become blurred.

In another BBC Radio 4 broadcast, the writer and comedian David Baddiel pointed out how life doesn't really have narrative; narrative is an illusion and life is just a series of random events: here's something that's gone wrong, he explained, which then gives satisfaction if a way is found to explain it, to crack the code and make sense of the world. Thus, the crisis of the COVID-19 pandemic was fertile ground for irrational conspiracy theories, which arise in situations of uncertainty, when people feel that they are helpless, that they don't have any power over the things that are happening to them. It's all about the feeling of being at the mercy of unseen forces. This has been nothing new, but in times of crisis we see much more of this way of thinking as people are trying to make sense of a very complex situation that they are really struggling with. The Brahan Seer can be perceived as addressing just such times in his various prophecies.

In modern forms of conspiracy theory, other commentators have said how noticeable it is that, in such events as the assassination of J.F. Kennedy, in the aftermath of the 9/11 attack on the World Trade Center and most recently in the light of the COVID-19 pandemic of 2020–21, these were all times when people felt that things were out of control and events were occurring over which they felt powerless. Such occurrences are always fertile ground for irrational conspiracy theories to come into play. The world by its very nature is full of random events and it is reassuring and comforting to follow any sort of explanation that appears to put an unpredictable world into some kind of order. Uncertainty and fear lead people to cling on to something that explains what is otherwise incomprehensible, since satisfaction is always derived from finding a way of explaining things.

A considerable amount of authoritative academic research has been conducted on this subject in both the United Kingdom and the United States, in particular, since conspiracy theories have become embedded in our culture so much. The American political scientist Michael Barkun in his 2003 book *A Culture of Conspiracy: Apocalyptic Visions in Contemporary America* has claimed that

*Scotland's Nostradamus*

conspiracy theories all make three major assumptions: first, nothing happens by accident; second, everything is connected; and third, nothing is as it seems. As Richard Evans, the author of *The Hitler Conspiracies*, who ran a project at Cambridge to research conspiracy theories, says:

> One of the common features of conspiracy theories is that they have as a premise that nothing happens without someone having intended it to happen ... what conspiracy theories don't accept is that things can happen by chance. In a fictional drama, a plot in which everything is connected and nothing is coincidence is highly satisfying, but that's not how the world really works. Reality can be strange and bizarre with lots of dead ends. Narrative isn't real and that's what's so alluring about conspiracy theories: they are narratives. A good writer will go back and rewrite reality in order to make his [*sic*] plot make sense and that's exactly what conspiracy theorists do.

And that's precisely how oral folktales work. Both the tellers of folktales and modern-day conspiracy theorists construct their narratives, not with the logic of a journalist or historian, but of a screenwriter, or novelist, connecting everything they are concerned about back to the machinations of a single, all-powerful force. In our case, that force is the Brahan Seer's curses and predictions.

In Phil Tinline's BBC Radio 4 series he showed how the fiction of writers such as G.K. Chesterton, John Buchan and Graham Greene created templates on which the public's paranoia fed and a number of conspiracy theories grew in the twentieth century, which were easily believed because they confirmed a pattern that people had already read about in fiction of a small circle of powerful men or a single evil mastermind conspiring to shape the world in smoke-filled backrooms. This is something we see again and again in the history of such conspiracy theories as those about the Protocols of the Elders of Zion Conspiracy Theory, which came out of a mixture of separate nineteenth- and twentieth-century stories of both fact and fiction that were cobbled together to produce one single coherent story. A conspiracy theory works like a piece of folklore, starting from certainty and imaginatively connecting apparently unconnected domains to give an all-round explanation of how the world works, which tells a story of good and evil. Not only did all of this strike a chord in me, recalling both Keith Thomas's explanation for belief in prophecies in history as a panacea in times of great upheaval, but it also reminded me of the way that fact and fiction appeared to be intertwined within the Brahan Seer's story.

The particular mention of smoke-filled rooms also reminded me of a school of history that was still prevalent at Cambridge when I was there in the mid-1980s, and in the light of which, in a paper I gave at the time, I contrasted to the *Annales* school of history, whose approach it was to look at wider, long-term structural changes that affect the way people view their place in the world. It now strikes me that the so-called High Political, or Peterhouse School of History

*A Highland Conspiracy Theory*

(named after the Cambridge college that at that time comprised a group of like-minded right-wing thinkers) mirrored the conspiracy theory promulgated by Enoch Powell, which argued that history was conducted by what would now be termed a centrist 'metropolitan elite' of civil servants. Over the twentieth century it can be shown that conspiracy theories have come from both the left and the right of politics, when people feel that they are losing control. After the unexpected upheavals of Brexit, there have even been centrist conspiracy theories that sought an explanation for the world that moderate thinkers had hitherto thought they had understood. But the important point I am making is that these conspiracy theories were not promulgated, as one might have expected, by the uneducated masses, but even by a highly educated group of Cambridge dons.

Of course, the narrative in the Brahan Seer's story is different, modern conspiracy theories from the last century onwards often claiming that there is literally a conspiracy of powerful men producing misinformation in order to manipulate the world for their own ends; but the psychological mechanism is very similar, providing comfort for people's helplessness by giving narrative explanations for huge upheavals that seem to be otherwise inexplicable. Such recent ideas thus mirror Keith Thomas's more historical observation when discussing early modern belief systems in *Religion and the Decline of Magic*: that the various beliefs that he discusses are not 'intrinsically less worthy of respect than some of those which we ourselves continue to hold. If magic is to be defined as the employment of ineffective techniques to allay anxiety when effective ones are not available, then we must recognise that no society will ever be free from it.'

The Highlander's longstanding preoccupation with knowing the nearness of death, be it that of a humble crofter's loved one, or that of a mighty clan chief that impacted on an entire community, should also be understood in the context of those who lived in a world where for most people life expectancy was relatively brief and death was frequent, indiscriminate and often disconcertingly sudden. The desire to know the nearness and manner of the event thus assumed what would appear to have been a disproportionate importance in the minds of those of us today who can hope for an average life expectancy that exceeds seventy years. In the pre-Industrial European mentality, neither status, youth nor virtue was a defence against mortality's ever-present threat.

All of this has made it evident to me that the beliefs surrounding the Brahan Seer, which are concerned with major calamities and upheavals, and indeed those numerous stories that have been told in the Highlands and Islands for centuries about how the deaths of loved ones were foreseen by those gifted with second sight, have nothing to do with a primitive and superstitious society. Rather, it appears quite simply to be part of the human condition: when you have civilisation, you have conspiracy theories. It's all about the feeling of being at the mercy of unseen forces.

# 'I see into the far future ...'
# Prophecies Believed to Have Been as Yet Unfulfilled

Writing in 1877, the Clach listed a number of prophecies that he had recorded from current local folklore that he deemed yet to have been fulfilled. One such prophecy concerned the Isle of Lewis, as follows:

> however unlikely it may now appear, the Island of Lews will be laid waste by a destructive war, which will continue till the contending armies, slaughtering each other as they proceed, shall reach Tarbert in Harris. In the Caws of Tarbert, the retreating host will suddenly halt; an onslaught led by a left-handed Macleod, called Donald, son of Donald, son of Donald, will then be made upon by pursuers. The only weapon in the champion's hand will be a black sooty *cabar*, taken off a neighbouring hut; but this intrepidity and courage will overpower their pursuers. The Lews will then enjoy a long period of repose. It has not hitherto been suggested that this prophecy has been fulfilled, and we here stake the reputation of our prophet upon its fulfilment, and that of the following predictions, which are still current through the Northern Counties of Scotland.

He then went on to list a number of other prophecies that he deemed to have been unfulfilled at that time.

Any reader's first reaction to this account of events in Lewis thus described is that they have very much the air of an unruly clannish skirmish of the type that was a regular occurrence in the Hebridean island's more distant past, rather than anything likely to be seen in the future history of modern-day Lewis, unless society should regress markedly. And indeed, in an article for the *Transactions of the Gaelic Society* (Vol. 46, 1968) entitled 'The Historical Coinneach Odhar and Some Prophecies Attributed to Him', the Rev William Matheson suggested that there is evidence to suppose that this prediction has already been fulfilled. The place referred to in Harris is on the south side of East Loch Tarbert and in the *Celtic Magazine* there is an account of a feud between the Morrisons of Ness in Lewis and the MacLeods of Harris. These events occurred around 1544 to 1545, when Donald *Dubh* MacDonald was contesting the Lordship of the Isles, making this 'prophecy' older than the times in which the Brahan Seer was purported to have lived, be he the Coinneach *Odhar* of the late sixteenth century, or the Coinneach *Odhar* of the seventeenth century. Unless it was a folk memory

134

*'I see into the far future ...' Prophecies Believed to Have Been as Yet Unfulfilled*

of a yet earlier prophecy, it seems most likely that this account of a skirmish in Lewis was simply a folk memory of an actual historical event that took place in the sixteenth century.

Another such battle that, according to the Clach, has not yet occurred

> will be fought at Ault-nan-Torcan, in the Lewis, which will be a bloody one indeed. It will truly take place, though the time may be hence, but woe to the mothers of sucklings that day. The defeated host will continue to be cut down till it reaches Ard-a-chaolais (a place about seven miles from Ault-nan-Torcan), and the swords will make terrible havoc.

Once again, such a battle conducted with swords would seem unlikely to be yet to take place in the modern world and in the same paper Matheson quotes the prophecy more fully and explains how it might in fact describe a battle in which the MacAulays were massacred at a place called Allt nan Torcan, between Stornoway and Uig. Matheson quotes the prophecy more fully as follows:

> It is on the day of Allt nan Torcan
> that injury will be done to the women of Lewis;
> between Eidseal and Aird a Chaolais
> the sword edges will be struck.
> They'll come, they'll come, 'tis not long till there
> will come ashore at Portmaguran
> those who will reduce the country to a sorry state:
> alas for the woman with a little child –
> everyone of the Clan MacAulay
> will have his head dashed against a stone,
> and she herself will be slain along with him.

As a descendant of Margaret and Donald MacAulay, whose family from Lewis he has researched, the author is well aware of the importance of this event and the place it will have had in the collective memory of the people of Lewis. His ancestor's cousin and namesake Donald *Cam* MacAulay (who was living between about 1560 and around 1640) was the MacAulay chief and a notorious rebel who resided in various fortifications around Uig (the purported birthplace of the Brahan Seer). Early in his career, Donald *Cam* fought in the Irish wars as a mercenary, probably in the service of Hugh O'Neill, Earl of Tyrone, along with the Lewis MacLeods. The MacAulay chief then returned to Lewis and lived a violent life, battling with the Morrisons and the Mackenzies, taking part in the siege of Stornoway Castle in 1605, and attracting the attention of the authorities, leading to their attempt to expel all MacAulays from their lands in Uig. Donald *Cam* had a reputation for being 'fierce with the sword and quick to anger'. He is the subject of many stories told over the centuries since. His by-name, *Cam* ('squint-eyed') is said to originate from a quarrel with the smith at Kneep, named an Gobha Ban, when the smith put out one of Donald's eyes with a red-hot poker. Earlier in the

*Scotland's Nostradamus*

sixteenth century the MacAulays were practically exterminated in a single battle, the only survivor being the chief's youngest son, Iain *Ruadh*, and his illegitimate half-brother. Iain was Donald *Cam*'s grandfather. The massacre supposedly described by the Brahan Seer would thus appear to be that of the MacAulays in the early sixteenth century: one that was notorious and still spoken of in Uig up until recent times. This was when an army under the command of the Earl of Huntly invaded Lewis in 1506 to quell a rebellion by Donald *Dubh* MacDonald, who had been under the protection of Torquil MacLeod of Lewis. The MacLeods were closely allied to the MacAulays and both clans seem to have sided together (which both clans did again when the Mackenzies invaded and conquered Lewis just over 100 years later). Their defeat and the near extinction of the MacAulays will have had an immense impact on the local community, and by explaining these sensational events by way of a prophecy, this would appear once more to endorse Keith Thomas's account of prophecies as providing a panacea against extreme upheaval and trauma.

～·～·～

Putting his MacAulay ancestry to one side, a more ominous prophecy for the author is the one that predicts, 'The day will come when the ravens will drink their full of the Mackenzies' blood three times off the top of the Clach Mhor, and glad am I' continues the Seer, who was, of course, a fellow Mackenzie, 'that I will not live to see that day, for a bloody and destructive battle will be fought on the Muir of Ord. A cam [squint-eyed], pox-pitted tailor will originate the battle; for men will become so scarce in those days that each of seven women will strive hard for the squint-eyed tailor's heart and hand, and out of strife the conflict will originate.' Donald Macintyre, a schoolmaster of Arpafeelie in the Black Isle, who assisted the Clach in collecting and writing down as many tales and prophecies connected with Coinneach *Odhar* that he could find, wrote of those related predictions that he came across:

> The prophecies that 'the raven will drink from the top of Clach an t-Seasaidh [an angular stone that once stood upright near Muir of Ord], its full of the blood of the Mackenzies for three successive days', and 'that the Mackenzies would be so reduced in numbers, that they would all be taken in an open fishing boat (scuta dubh) back to Ireland from whence they originally came', remain still unfulfilled.

In the versions of these predictions that were current in Kintail, similar prophecies foretold that the MacRaes were to get so scarce that

> a crippled tailor of the name is to be in such request among the ladies as to cause a desperate battle in the district between themselves and the MacLennans, the result of which will be that a black fishing wherry, or *scuta dubh* will carry back to Ireland all that remains of the clan Macrae, but no sooner do they arrive than they again return to Kintail. Before this

*'I see into the far future ...' Prophecies Believed to Have Been as Yet Unfulfilled*

was to take place, nine men of the name of Macmillan would arrive at manhood (assume their bonnets) in the district; assemble at a funeral at Cnoc-a-Clachain in Kilduich, and originate a quarrel.

The MacRaes have indeed lost their predominance in Kintail since the eighteenth and nineteenth centuries, while the MacMillans were believed to have met in this spot and originated a quarrel. In the Seer's day there was not a single man of the name MacMillan, and the MacRaes were at the height of their prosperity in Kintail, so nothing could have seemed more unlikely than this prediction. Its passing down at the time that the Clach and Macintyre were writing no doubt reflects the unprecedented way in which locals regarded times to have changed and the impact those changes had on their lives.

Indeed, such prophecies were current regarding almost all old families in the Highlands. According to the Rev Donald MacLeod in the appendix to his *Life of the late Dr Norman MacLeod*, 'the Argyll family were of the number; and there is a prophecy regarding the Breadalbane family as yet unfulfilled which I hope may remain so. The present Marquis of Breadalbane is fully aware of it, as are many of the connections of the family.' Of the MacLeods, he recounted a prophecy that was purported to have been made at least a hundred years prior to the events he related:

> it was foretold that when Norman, the third Norman (*Tormad nan 'tri Tormaid*), the son of the hard-boned English lady (*Mac na mnatha caoile cruaidhe Shassunaich*) would perish by an accidental death; that when the 'Maidens' of Macleod (certain well-known rocks on the coast of Macleod's country) became the property of a Campbell; when a fox had young ones in one of the turrets of the Castle, and particularly when the Fairy enchanted banner should be for the last time exhibited, then the glory of the Macleod family should depart; a great part of the estate should be sold to others; so that a small 'curragh', a boat, would carry all gentlemen of the name of Macleod across Loch Dunvegan; but in times far distant another John Breac should arise, who should redeem those estates, and raise the power and honours of the house to a higher pitch than ever.

The Rev MacLeod went on to explain the events that followed the discovery of the Fairy Flag in a chest in a chamber in the East Turret of Dunvegan Castle (this celebrated heirloom is an ancient piece of cloth that is now believed to date back to between the fourth and seventh centuries AD, made of silk from Syria or Rhodes, but traditionally said to have been gifted by the fairies).

> On this occasion, the melancholy news of the death of the young and promising heir of Macleod reached the Castle. 'Norman, the third Norman', was a lieutenant of HMS *Queen Charlotte*, which was blown up at sea, and he and the rest perished. At the same time, the rocks called 'Macleod's Maidens' were sold, in the course of that very week, to Angus

*Scotland's Nostradamus*

> Campbell of Ensay, and they are still in possession of his grandson. A
> fox in possession of a Lieutenant Maclean, residing in the West Turret of
> the Castle had young ones, which I handled, and thus all that was said
> in the prophecy alluded to was fulfilled, although I am glad the family of
> my chief still enjoy their ancestral possessions, and the worst part of the
> prophecy accordingly remains unverified.

The original John Breac, incidentally, was John *Breac* Macleod of Dunvegan, who
was a great patron of Highland traditional culture and the subject of Roderick
Morrison's *Òran do Iain Breac MacLeod*, which laments the Blind Harper's sep-
aration form the chief, and praises him as a soldier and warrior who would lead
his men in France.

A comparable prophecy concerned the 'land-grasping Urquharts of Cromarty', predicting 'that, extensive though their possessions in the Black Isle
now are, the day will come – and it is close at hand – when they will not own
twenty acres in the district'. During the time of the seventeenth century chief,
Sir Thomas Urquhart (who, as we have seen, was an illustrious scholar and something of an eccentric genius), his family owned vast tracts of land on the Black
Isle. They had also been hereditary Sheriffs of Cromarty since the days of Robert
the Bruce (Walter Urquhart is named as Sheriff in both writs calling for the arrest
of the historical Coinneach *Odhar* in 1577 and 1578). Yet, by the second half of
the eighteenth century, practically all their possessions had been disposed of.
The great castle of Cromarty was razed to the ground, a mansion being built
nearby by a new owner. After Major Beauchamp Urquhart was killed in 1898 at
the Battle of Atbara in Sudan, the chiefship passed to a collateral branch of the
clan, the Urquharts of Braelangswell, who had emigrated to the United States in
the eighteenth century. All that Colonel Wilins Fisk Urquhart of Urquhart, who
became the twenty-eighth chief of the clan in 2012, now owns on the Black Isle
is the ruin of Castle Craig on the shore of the Cromarty Firth.

The present writer, however, from his knowledge of his own ancestors' Black
Isle Leslie cousins and Dunbar in-laws in this period could not help detecting
that this 'prophecy' may also have been a folk memory of the difficulties the
Urquhart family were already facing in the seventeenth century. Sir Thomas's
father fell into debt, and in the mid-1630s his son's name appears regularly in
documents outlining claims made by creditors. Although the *Annals of Banff*
confirm that Sir Thomas senior had received his lands unburdened by any debts,
by 1632 he was borrowing £20,000 from one of his neighbours, William Rig of
Adernie. On 29 June 1636 he even sold to Rig £2,000 worth of annual rent from
the Cromarty estates in order to delay full repayment. On t25 January 1637, when
Alexander Dunbar of Westfield and Katherine Dunbar, widow of David Brodie,
raised a case against Urquhart senior for non-payment of a debt of 5,000 merks,
he was outlawed by the Privy Council. Lands as well as money were under threat.
In July 1637 Patrick Smith of Braco seized part of the Cromarty estates in lieu of

*'I see into the far future ...' Prophecies Believed to Have Been as Yet Unfulfilled*

financial recompense. While Sir Thomas later had some success in holding off his creditors, that success was short-lived. Led by Leslie of Findrassie, Urqhart's creditors made claims on him at a time when his Episcopalian beliefs were also bringing him into conflict with the local Presbyterian clergy. On 31 March 1647, Sir Robert Farquhar of Mounie apprised the title and estate of Cromarty. He also replaced him as Sheriff of Cromarty.

But it was ultimately national, rather than local, politics that led to the nadir in Urquhart's fortunes. In 1650, Sir Thomas marched with Charles II and fought in the Battle of Worcester, where the Royalist forces were decisively defeated and Urquhart was taken prisoner, first at the Tower of London and later at Windsor, losing all his cherished manuscripts, which he had brought with him for safekeeping, and he was obliged to forfeit all his property. Perhaps these seventeenth-century misfortunes, rather than the future demise of the family, are what accounts for the folk legend regarding the loss of land in the district that was 'close at hand', by the 'land-grasping Urquharts of Cromarty'?

With regard to the prediction that Clan Mackenzie will be reduced to such small dimensions that they would return to Ireland in a *scuta dubh*, while that would seem today inherently unlikely given that the surname Mackenzie/ McKenzie is the fifteenth most popular in Scotland, not to mention the tens of thousands that are living in not only their Scottish homeland, but also in England, Canada and the United States, as well as elsewhere throughout the globe, the very similar variant of this prophecy relating to the MacRaes may well have conflated such a concern surrounding the depopulation of these families in their Highland homelands where they had once been such a powerful presence. Alternatively, as Elizabeth Sutherland wrote: 'If the prediction, however, be confined in its application to the Mackenzies of Seaforth, it may be said to have been already almost fulfilled.'

—·—·—

In the Clach's words, another unfulfilled prophecy,

> by which the faith of future generations may be tested, is the one in which he predicted 'that a Loch above Beauly will burst through its banks and destroy in its rush a village in its vicinity'. We are not aware that such a calamity as is here foretold has yet occurred, nor are we aware of the locality of the loch or village.

But Elizabeth Sutherland in her 1977 edition of *The Prophecies of the Brahan Seer* pointed out, 'In 1967, heavy rain caused the Hydro-Electric dam at Torachilty to overflow, thus forcing the river Conon to burst its banks. The subsequent flooding destroyed buildings, cattle and crops, and created havoc in the village of Conon Bridge, five miles north of Beauly.'

Today, it seems inevitable that the even more recent impact of climate change in the present century renders such natural disasters all the more likely, enabling

*Scotland's Nostradamus*

the almost certain fulfilment of yet more unfulfilled prophecies of Coinneach *Odhar*.

A further unfulfilled legend tells how the Brahan Seer said that, if the Eagle Stone fell down three times, Loch Ussie would flood the valley below so that ships could sail to Strathpeffer. A little way up the hill from Castle Leod, on the right-hand side of the road, just before you come into Strathpeffer, is an ancient monument known as Clach an Tiompain (strictly known more correctly as Clach an Tuindain, the 'Stone of the Turning', or, more commonly, as the Eagle Stone), that has attracted a host of legends through the centuries. It was once said to have been put up in memory of the slain by the Munros after a battle with the Mackenzies. The standing stone, which is inscribed with Pictish symbols, is now known to be of far greater antiquity, dating from around 500 to 700 AD. It was originally located further down the valley, in the old churchyard of Fodderty, before it was moved to Strathpeffer. The reason why it was moved was probably in order to mark the graves of those Munros who were killed during a victory by the clan over the MacDonalds, in a skirmish that preceded the Battle of Harlaw in 1411, presumably because the ancient eagle symbol that is carved on it is also the heraldic device of the Munros.

In reality, in ancient times ships probably did come all the way up the valley, so perhaps the story preserves part of a very ancient oral memory that dates all the way back to those days. This is an area steeped in ancient legend. In the tenth and eleventh centuries this locality was in the possession of Leod, Jarl of Orkney and then his great-nephew, Jarl Thorfinn II Sigurdsson. Thorfinn was the half-brother of MacBeth, who was believed to have been killed at the Battle of Torfness, which is now widely thought to have been fought in the vicinity of Castle Leod, certainly near Dingwall and most likely below Knockfarrel, at a time when the waters of the Cromarty Firth extended further up the valley. The vitrified fort at the top of the steep slopes of Knockfarrel that overlooks Castle Leod was described in the eighteenth and nineteenthh centuries as a 'Fingalian Fortress', reflecting those Ossianic legends that James MacPherson made internationally popular, 'which was originally constructed, says tradition, by a gigantic tribe of Fions' according to Hugh Miller, 'for the protection of their wives and children, when they were themselves engaged in hunting'.

According to one legend, while they were hunting on the slopes of the Cromarty Firth, their womenfolk decided to play a trick on the unpopular Conon who was left in charge. Finding him asleep outside the fort, they staked his seven braids of hair to the ground, ran off and rang the alarm bell. Conon, leaping up, left half his scalp behind. Mad with rage and pain, he drove the women into the fort, set fire to it and destroyed them all. It is possible this legend may have been conflated with memories of the notorious story that will have been grafted on local memory surrounding the chapel at Kilchrist, near Urray on the south side of Knockfarrel. The legend is now deemed to be apocryphal but was long part of popular Ross-shire folklore. This now ruined church was supposedly the

140

*'I see into the far future ...' Prophecies Believed to Have Been as Yet Unfulfilled*

scene in 1603 of the merciless burning of the whole congregation of Mackenzies by the MacDonells of Glengarry, whose piper was said to have marched round the building, mocking the shrieks of its desperate inmates with the pibroch that came to be known under the name of *Kilchrist*, as the family tune of the Clanranald of Glengarry. On the southern slopes of Knockfarrel is also Loch Ussie, in which the Brahan Seer is believed to have thrown his 'seeing stone' before he died.

Regarding Knockfarrel, the Clach describes how 'Having found our way to the top of this magnificent and perfect specimen of a vitrified fort, we were so struck with its great size.' He goes on to explain how

> On the summit of the hill we met two boys herding cows, and as our previous experience taught us that boys, as a rule – especially herd boys – are acquainted with the traditions and places of interest in the localities they frequent, we were curious enough to ask them if they ever heard of Coinneach Odhar in the district, and if he ever said anything regarding the fort of Knockfarrel. They directed us to what they called 'Fingal's Well', in the interior of the ruined fort, and informed us that this well was used by the inhabitants of the fortress 'until Fingal, one day, drove them out, and placed a large stone over the well, which has ever since kept the water from oozing up, after which he jumped to the other side of the [Strathpeffer] valley'. There being considerable rains for some days previous to our visit, water could be seen in the 'well'. One of the boys drove down a stick until it struck the stone, producing a hollow sound which unmistakably indicated the existence of a cavity beneath. 'Coinneach Odhar foretold', said the boy, 'that if ever that stone was taken out of its place, Loch Ussie would ooze up through the well and flood the valley below to such an extent that ships could sail up to Stathpeffer and be fastened to Clach an Tiompain; and this would happen after the stone had fallen three times. It has already fallen twice', continued our youthful informant, 'and you can now see it newly raised, strongly and carefully propped up, near the end of the doctor's house.' And so it is, and can still be seen, on the right, a few paces from the roadside, as you proceed up to the Strathpeffer Wells.

～·～·～

Other predictions that remain unfulfilled ominously include: Loch Shiel becoming 'so narrow that a man can leap across it, the salmon shall desert the Loch and the River Shiel'. Loch Shiel had indeed been getting rapidly narrower at a particular point by the action of the water on the banks and bottom. In 1977 Elizabeth Sutherland wrote with regard to this, that 'if it goes on as it has done in recent years it can easily be leaped at no distant date. Prudence would suggest a short lease of these Salmon Fishings.' Fortunately, this is yet to be the case. In fact, the author was recently faced with the problem of needing to cross the Shiel

*Scotland's Nostradamus*

when a friend's dachshund ran off up the side of the glen and we were faced with the problem that we could only cross where there were bridges. While the River Shiel today should produce up to fifty salmon in a season, however, stocks of sea trout have collapsed in recent years.

According to A.B. MacLennan (the author of *The Petty Seer*), 'With reference to some great revolution which shall take place in the country, Coinneach Odhar said that "before that event shall happen, the water of the river Beauly will cease to run. On one of these occasions a salmon, having shells instead of scales, will be found in the bed of the river."' Macintyre gives another version: 'When the river Beauly is dried up three times, and a "scaly salmon" or royal sturgeon, is caught in the river, that will be time for a great trial.' According to Elizabeth Sutherland, the river had already dried up twice by 1977, the last time in 1826, and a *Bradan Sligeach*, or royal sturgeon, measuring nine feet in length, had been caught in the estuary of the Beauly about two years beforehand.

Biodiversity is currently an immense challenge in the United Kingdom, and there should be no greater anxiety facing the Highlands today than the potential impact of climate change and rising sea levels (as it should for the entire world). Concern with global warming makes the threat of local flooding a very genuine one, and should the valley below Loch Ussie be flooded as far as Strathpeffer, this particular prophecy could well be widely spoken of as having been fulfilled. As the two young herdsmen informed the Clach, the Eagle Stone has already fallen twice and is now firmly concreted in place to ensure that it does not fall down again. So, here we have yet another example of how the Brahan Seer's name became attached to a variety of stories from the ancient past that were so deep-rooted in the local consciousness that even in modern times people have thought it necessary to take precautions, lest his prophecy be fulfilled.

As I was in the process of writing this book, on 24 October 2023, following the devastating impact of Storm Babet, the *Ross-shire Journal* reported in a headline: 'Flooding of Castle Leod grounds as River Peffery bursts banks prompts Ross-shire clan chief call for "radical solutions" as extreme weather events become new normal'. Shortly thereafter John Cromartie shared with me on WhatsApp a number of photographs that showed how unprecedented the extensive flooding had been. Should circumstances see the Eagle Stone for some reason fall for a third time, and climate change allow the valley to be flooded beyond the Castle and right up to the village of Srathpeffer, it would not surprise me if some people chose to regard such events as evidence of a further fulfilled prophecy. Indeed, those who follow recent advances in physics could feasibly now seek new explanations that draw on the possibility of there being further dimensions, multiple universes and added sensory perceptions that other species are known to have, for example.

For current physicists, time is a complex topic and many regard it as something that is only experienced as a psychological construct to help us differentiate between the present and our perception of the past; while to other physicists

142

*'I see into the far future ...' Prophecies Believed to Have Been as Yet Unfulfilled*

time remains an unsolved mystery, at least in some respects because it does not behave in the same way under all circumstances. Support for a multiverse theory comes from a scientifically valid Big Bang theory called Cosmic Inflation, which refers to a faster-than-light expansion of the universe that may be responsible for spawning an unlimited number of disconnected universes that eternally issue from one another. Although that theory contradicts the basic laws of thermodynamics and remains controversial, many respected scientists regard it as helpful in being able to explain certain features of the universe that are otherwise difficult to explain, such as Einstein's theory of relativity, which famously makes mass bend space and time. It has been suggested that such a multiverse could also allow so-called 'time slips' in reality, as well as in popular fiction. Surprisingly, such things are being seriously discussed by modern scientists who are questioning fundamentally the way we see the world. The very nature of the scientific process demands that there is no such thing as a final definitive explanation and that there should always remain room for continued evidence-based debate. In what is expected to be an increasingly uncertain world, could we expect the 'occult laboratory' to be revisited by men of science a third time at some point in the near future?

~·~·~

Perhaps the best-known prophecy that still resonates today is, 'Sheep shall eat men, men will eat sheep, the black rain will eat all things; in the end old men shall return from new lands.' The longer version is as follows:

> The day will come when the jaw-bone of the big sheep, or *caoirich mhora*, will be put the plough on the rafters (*air an aradh*); when sheep shall become so numerous and the bleating of the one shall be heard by the other from Conchra in Lochalsh to Bun-da-Loch in Kintail, they shall be at their height in price, and henceforth will go back and deteriorate, until they disappear altogether, and be so thoroughly forgotten that a man finding the jaw-bone of a sheep in a cairn, will not recognise it, or be able to tell what animal in belonged to. The ancient proprietors of the soil shall give place to strange merchant proprietors, and the whole Highlands will become one deer forest; the whole country will become so utterly desolate and depopulated that the crow of the cock shall not be heard north of Druim-Uachdair; the people will emigrate to Islands now unknown, but which shall yet be discovered in the boundless oceans after which the deer and other wild animals in the huge wilderness shall be exterminated and browned by horrid black rains (*siantan dubha*). The people will then return and take undisturbed possession of the lands of their ancestors.

The emigration to 'Islands now unknown' was a clear reference to Australia and New Zealand. Emigration to Australia from the Northwest of Scotland in

*Scotland's Nostradamus*

particular came into the picture in a prominent way in the late 1830s, and then again more significantly in the 1850s, when the Highlands and Islands Emigration Society assisted in the region of 5,000 emigrants to go to Australia, particularly from Skye, ensuring that there was a replacement pastoral workforce in the parts of Australia from which people had fled to the gold fields, which had just been discovered in New South Wales and Victoria. This bounty scheme that gave people varying degrees of assistance from the late 1830s came at an opportune time as it coincided with the potato famine (the initial outbreak was in the 1830s, but it became more significant in the late 1840s and 1850s).

Interestingly, a comparable prophecy was purported to have been made by the Rev John Morrison, the 'Petty Seer', who predicted,

> Large as the Ridge of Petty is and thickly as it is now populated, the day will come, and is not far off, when there will be three smokes in it, and the crow of the cock at each cannot be heard, owing to the distance, at either of the others. After a time, however, the lands will again be divided, and the parish of Petty become as populous as it is at this day.

While the decline in population in the Highlands had been proceeding at pace when Alexander Mackenzie was writing in 1877, the recent reversal of this decline in the vicinity around Petty would have been less predictable. Notably, in January 2023, the Free Church of Scotland launched its plan to rent Petty Church to serve the newly founded community of Tournagrain, a new town built near Inverness Airport on the A96 road, between Inverness and Nairn, with plans for 5,000 homes and 10,000 people. In the words of the Rev Innes Macsween, 'Unlike some new housing developments, Tornagrain is being built with a very clear vision of creating a "community" rather than just new houses, something we are emphasising as part of our own vision for the new church.' This particular region just to the east of Inverness has indeed seen marked changes in fortune since the start of the eighteenth century when the author's ancestor, Daniel *Og* McKenzie, was a tenant in MidCoul on the estate of the Inverness merchant William Dunbar, who was married to Daniel's great-aunt. One drives past this small white farmhouse immediately on leaving the airport, when turning right on to the A96 towards Petty, Tournagrain and Inverness. Even since Elizabeth Sutherland edited her 1977 edition of *The Prophecies of the Brahan Seer*, Inverness airport has become an important hub for air travel, operating regional services around the Highlands and Islands, scheduled services to Edinburgh, Glasgow, London and Manchester, together with charter services to the Mediterranean. The consequence has been considerable development of the surrounding parishes of Dalcross and Petty.

In September 2018, a report was published that was commissioned by the Highlands and Islands Enterprise and Highlands and Islands Airports Limited to make an economic and social impact study of Inverness Airport. It concluded, 'Inverness Airport has been critical for regional economic development and

144

*'I see into the far future ...' Prophecies Believed to Have Been as Yet Unfulfilled*

growth, contributing to confidence in the local economy, supporting businesses with day-to-day operations and attracting and retaining staff, helping to attract inward investment, supporting the tourism industry and contributing to population growth and retention.' The report outlines how the airport has brought more tourists to the area, 'reducing the sense of isolation for communities, and raising the profile of the region'. In 2017, more than 6,000 general aviation passengers landed at Inverness Airport, which is a source of well-paid high-quality jobs across a range of functions and there are opportunities for further development of jobs on-site if the number of passengers using the airport further increases and reaches the 1 to 1.25 million levels expected. This, it is believed, would attract interest from a range of hotel and retail operators, which would further improve on-site facilities, and would, in turn, attract more passengers, jobs and employment. The airport currently accounts for 748 direct and indirect jobs.

> Most stakeholders and a large proportion of businesses were of the view that the airport is a very significant factor in contributing to population retention and growth. The Highlands and Islands attracts people who are retiring, working in business, setting up a lifestyle business or even high net worth individuals who live in the region and commute to work elsewhere.

One is reminded of Morrison's prediction that 'the lands will again be divided, and the parish of Petty become as populous as it is at this day', along with the Brahan Seer's prophecy that the 'ancient proprietors of the soil shall give place to strange merchant proprietors'!

So much of the Seer's best-known prophecy appears to be an account of the most devastating occurrences that took place in the Highlands and Islands in the last half millennium, transforming the lives of its inhabitants beyond recognition: the witch-crazes of the late sixteenth century and seventeenth, the Clearances and consequent introduction of sheep on an unprecedented scale; depopulation and mass emigration to once unknown territories, such as Australia and New Zealand, accompanied by the sale of land by families that had for centuries been a reassuring presence, to outsiders; the transformation of much of the landscape to deer-stalking estates owned by rich industrialists; the stocking of vast estates by absentee landowners with game so that they could indulge their paying guests in an orgy of slaughter for just a handful of months in the year; and, most recently, the disappearance of many indigenous species under that transformation of their natural habitat. It is understandable, therefore, that the final part of the prophecy that refers to 'black rain' should still be quoted today with such fear and foreboding. This has been interpreted by some as predicting a great underwater explosion due to the finding of oil in the North Sea; to be connected with the oil refinery in Nigg Bay; or – the darkest fear of all in recent times – nuclear fall-out. It can't be denied, on the other hand, that such

*Scotland's Nostradamus*

organisations as the Highlands and Islands Development Board and a flourishing and more sophisticated tourist industry has brought renewed employment and prosperity to the Highlands and Islands, while such innovations as the aluminium works at Invergordon and the building of oil-rig platforms north of the Black Isle at Nigg Bay might encourage a ray of light at the end of the Seer's dark psychological tunnel: the foretelling that 'old men shall return from new lands' and that 'the people will then return and take undisturbed possession of the lands of their ancestors' may indeed be happening already!

~·~·~

What is more, in the modern psyche there seems every reason why the Brahan Seer's story should remain current, as perceptions of upheaval in the Highlands continue, which may well account for the way in which the Seer's currency has survived unabated in what is supposedly a more rational age.

Marjory Harper of the University of Aberdeen and Visiting Professor at the University of the Highlands and Islands, has pointed out that, in the 1920s, there was almost a re-run of the post-Napoleonic crisis in emigration, particularly in the Outer Hebrides: the sense of Highlanders being powerless and passive – rather than active – participants in emigration was something that lingered. The grievances surrounding the Highland Clearances have also remained in the forefront of politics: Willie Ross, when he was Secretary of State for Scotland in 1965 and introduced the Bill that led to the Highlands and Islands Development Board, stated: 'For two hundred years the Highlander has been the man on Scotland's conscience.' 'Clearance' itself has been used as a term to describe almost any national tragedy in Scotland, with de-industrialisation having been described as a 'new Clearance'. The Highland Clearances have also played a prominent part in the popular literature of the twentieth century: such as Neil M. Gunn's *Butchers Broom* of 1934, and *The Silver Darlings* of 1941, which was made into a film in 1947, addressing the success of the fishing industry overcoming the Clearances; also Ian Crichton-Smith's *Exiles* of 1991; and John Magra's play *The Cheviot, the Stag and the Black Black Oil*, which premiered at Aberdeen Arts Centre in 1973 and was about the continuing exploitation of the Highlands and Northern Scotland, being part of a wider literary perception that employed the word 'Clearance' as a metaphor for anything that went wrong in industrial and commercial policy, or in social deprivation, becoming a classic concept to describe the Scottish experience. Equally, Peter Watkins's television docudrama for the BBC in 1964, *Culloden*, repeated John Prebble's popular and emotive depiction of that notorious battle that was predicted in such emotional terms by the Seer. It is no wonder that the subject matter embedded in the Coinneach *Odhar*'s prophecies continue to play on the modern Scottish psyche.

I have already explained the Romantic, Jacobitical depiction of the Highlands as a land of mystique and loss, popular among those in the cosmopolitan, literary, professional and landowning classes in the mid- to late nineteenth

*'I see into the far future ...' Prophecies Believed to Have Been as Yet Unfulfilled*

century; and the myth might still be seen as remaining as potent as ever among American émigrés who are fans of Diana Gabaldon's *Outlander* novels and the subsequent television series. There are now clan societies in the United States, Canada, Australia, New Zealand and in northern Europe, which meet and dress up in what has been described as 'military tartanry', and an interesting point that Tom Devine made in an episode of BBC Radio 4's *In Our Time* was that, when one of his former students at Edinburgh University chose that phenomenon as the subject for his doctoral thesis, when they considered who to supervise him, they discussed whether they should include a psychologist, as well as a historian, as part of the team.

# Conclusions

In my Preface, I mentioned two questions that were raised in recent Clan Mackenzie Podcasts. The first one effectively asked whether the Brahan Seer was a real person. I started my quest from a somewhat sceptical stance, since I had found no evidence for the second-sighted labourer on the Brahan estate that Elizabeth Sutherland suggested might have been the authentic figure to whom a number of other stories became attached. I had been well aware that there was much written discussion of second sight at the time when Countess Isobel was supposed to have had him executed, and so I was confident that, if he had existed, he would have been mentioned in surviving documents. I was, however, more convinced by William Matheson's discovery of a genuine Coinneach *Odhar*, who was Katherine Ross's 'principal Enchanter' in the 1570s witch trials, as the likely source of the name that became attached to the Brahan Seer. My brother Kevin's further observation that there was a Coinneach *Mhor*, in the person of Countess Isobel's husband, the Third Earl of Seaforth, who was said to have had second sight and whose seat was Brahan Castle, and could therefore easily have been described at the time as the 'Brahan Seer', seemed to further explain how that man could have been conflated in the oral stories shared among locals about Coinneach *Odhar*, a man who seems likely to have been executed on Chanonry Point.

This was precisely the same methodology that my brothers and I employed as children when we made up stories about the characters who in our imaginations inhabited the model village we built in the loft of our house. These stories combined real characters that we knew (who were mostly parents of our friends, or friends and associates of our parents) with myths, fairy tales and archetypes. Perhaps there is something in our family's genes when it comes to storytelling! Or, more likely, there is simply something in human nature that loves to combine the familiar with the romantic when relaying stories for entertainment.

When I started writing this book, that is how I had expected to conclude my story. However, by attempting to answer the second question that was raised in these podcasts – which was why a belief in second sight survived for so long in this part of the world – my mind turned to the wider issues surrounding Highland culture in the early modern period and whether it was as backward and isolated culturally as some commentators have suggested. In doing so, I have surprised even myself, since my best guess in answering that question now is that I believe, in a sense, that the Brahan Seer probably did exist and was a very remarkable man, in the person of the thirteenth-century seer and proto-scientist Michael Scot. This is not least because he was the earliest and most widely known person

*Conclusions*

about whom a number of later stories surrounding the Brahan Seer had clearly been associated. It is my proposition that he then went on to be conflated with both Coinneach *Odhar*, the 'principal Enchanter' in Katherine Ross's trial in Chanonry in the 1570s, and, in the following century, with the husband of the Brahan Seer's nemesis, Countess Isobel, in the person of the second-sighted Earl of Seaforth, Coinneach *Mhor*, who was resident at Brahan. It could also very well have been that the account James Fraser gave us in the Wardlaw Manuscript regarding Hugh Lord Lovat's prophecy, which foretold the near extinction of the Frasers' chiefly line and, in particular, how a younger son was to outlive his older brothers, was remembered among the local community and parallels were later drawn at the time of the last Lord Seaforth's own death, when his promising sons tragically predeceased him. When the last Lord Seaforth was seen to be deaf and dumb, it would have been easily conflated with the memory of another widely known local prediction, which had supposedly been fulfilled when the birth of 'Blackspotted Lovat' in 1666 was seen to coincide with '4 considerable chieftains in the North born with signall marks'. It is the very nature of Highland oral storytelling that allowed a variety of other stories, such as those relating to Thomas the Rhymer and the two John Morrisons from Lewis, both factual and fictional, as well as those stories that follow psychological archetypes, then to have been attached to the Brahan Seer's name as well in due course over the centuries.

~·~·~

A further unexpected discovery that I made in the course of investigating this second question was that there were three serious attempts in the history of the Highlands to explain second sight by observational, empirical, scientific and non-magical explanations. This very much reinforced those findings that I had already made when previously researching my own ancestors, confirming that the Highlands was an extraordinarily cosmopolitan and open-minded place, not at all a backwater of superstition.

It seems now all the more appropriate that Michael Scot is one of the earliest thinkers to have investigated what might be termed paranormal activity from an observational approach, consciously shunning magic. In his day, there was no awareness of what we would now term the social sciences of psychology, anthropology and sociology, but, as I was impressed to discover, his enquiring mind showed that he had a precocious interest in the sort of issues those modern academic disciplines address. Some of Michael's successors who attempted a scientific explanation for second sight also stressed the importance of psychology when carrying out their research into it. As we have seen, in the seventeenth century, Robert Boyle showed an awareness of the need to understand such matters when dealing with second sight, when he wrote of this psychic phenomenon as 'an intermediate region, bounded on the north by psychology'. In this statement, he will no doubt have been aware of what Sir Francis Bacon, who formulated the requirements for making the careful, systematic observations

*Scotland's Nostradamus*

necessary to produce quality facts as a means of studying and interpreting natural phenomena, wrote about prophecy earlier in the century. Bacon specified three things that gave prophecies 'grace and credit', which were: 'First that men mark when they hit and never mark when they miss, as they do,' he adds, 'generally also in dreams.' The second is that 'probably conjectures or obscure traditions many times turn themselves into prophecies, while the nature of man which coveteth divination thinks no peril to foretell that which they do but collect'. 'The Third and last (which is the great one) is, that almost all of them being infinite in number, have been, impostures, and by idle and crafty brains merely contrived and feigned after the event passed.'

It is somewhat appropriate that one of the Brahan Seer's prophecies concerned the fate of the estate of Rosehaugh on the Black Isle, since its former owner, Sir George Mackenzie, was the founder of the Advocate's Library in Edinburgh, of which I have already quoted the statement, 'Anthropology, sociology, ethnography: almost all our modern social sciences got their start from the volumes assembled on the shelves at the Advocates' Library in Edinburgh.' Later, in the 1890s, Campbell and Hall's analysis of the study of Highland second sight concluded: 'What was wanted for the Enquiry, apart from the absence of newspaper publicity, was a trained psychical researcher with a knowledge of Gaelic, of psychology and of the values of evidence.' When discussing second sight, neither Michael Scot in the thirteenth century, nor the members of the Royal Society in the seventeenth century, nor the members of the SPR in the late nineteenth century had time for what they deemed to be superstition and magic.

It was precisely such considerations of psychology, sociology and anthropology that I believe best explain the ongoing belief in the Brahan Seer's prophecies in the Highlands right up to the present day. As Karen Douglas, a Professor of social psychology at the University of Kent, has recently observed in relation to today's conspiracy theories, there is a collective repertoire of stories and story parts that we can rely on as we try to fit a new event or a new experience into our collective world view: 'Everybody has the potential to believe in conspiracy theories: it's just a natural by-product of the way we process information when we're uncertain and feel threatened.'

I recognise that such an explanation is unlikely to be the final word on the subject and may not account for every instance of second sight that has been so widely recorded over the last four centuries in the Highlands and Islands. Indeed, in my last chapter I suggested that the world is now in such a state of uncertainty that there is every possibility that we may expect the Highland 'occult laboratory' to be the focus of men of science a third time at some point in the not-too-distant future.

Between the time that Hugh Miller was collecting his tales about 'Kenneth Ore' from 1815 to 1830, and the time that the Clach published his *Prophecies of the Brahan Seer* in 1877, James MacPherson, Sir Walter Scott, Queen Victoria and Sir Edwin Landseer had between them made the Highlands the most

150

*Conclusions*

fashionable cultural go-to place in Europe, if not the world, and for many people it has remained so ever since. Prior to that, far from being the fictional contrivance of a superstitious backwater, the Brahan Seer can now be seen as the collective creation of minds that were at the heart of every great European intellectual movement that scholars have regarded as contributing to the forging of the modern world: the germs of the mediaeval Renaissance in the eleventh and twelfth centuries, the Renaissance itself in the fifteenth and sixteenth centuries, the religious upheaval of the Reformation that followed, the Scientific Revolution in the seventeenth century, the period of Enlightenment and Romanticism in the eighteenth century, and, finally, the full impact of the Industrial Revolution in the nineteenth century. When it comes to explaining many of the predictions recently attributed to the Brahan Seer, I would like to think that the psychological explanation I have given would also have appealed to all those thoughtful predecessors of mine who have sought a non-magical explanation for second sight, not least Michael Scot, the very man whom I suggest was Scotland's earliest 'Nostradamus' and the initial inspiration for the Brahan Seer.

—·—·—

Those experts who have attempted to explain conspiracy theories have compared their creation to constructing a necklace, by means of stringing together separate and unrelated beads. I also hope, therefore, that I have identified many of the beads in the necklace that make up the story of Scotland's Nostradamus, along with some of those all-important links that tie the beads of that necklace together. In doing so, I would be pleased should people think I have come further in answering the first of the two initial questions that inspired this study, by helping to piece together the historical identity (or identities) of the Brahan Seer. In answering the second podcast question, which was why second sight survived for so much longer in Scotland, I believe that the reason ultimately lies in a particular aspect of the cultural genius that was relatively unique to Highland culture, yet that can also be regarded as participating in what might be termed 'high-brow' European cultural traditions.

The truth behind the Brahan Seer is far more than about a distant memory of an extraordinary man (or men) in history. Having tried to see how the ever-shifting kaleidoscope of history became intertwined with folktales, it has become apparent to me that, as a result of the genius of generation after generation of ordinary people in Ross-shire, those valuable lessons that Michael Scot first gave to Scotland (and, in fact, to European civilisation as a whole) were personalised and moulded into a figure who mattered to them and who was portrayed as having concerns about the things they most cared about. What many people might at first dismiss as a nonsensical piece of local superstition can, when studied more closely, shed a great deal of light on the past, not least in allowing us a window on those concerns that truly mattered to an otherwise voiceless population. Not only that, but by recognising that these stories were

151

*Scotland's Nostradamus*

rooted in such concerns about social and material conditions and were not pure fiction, they become far more than just stories. In this respect I should quote the particularly appropriate words of Marina Warner on the subject of folktales:

> Charting the circumstances of their making and remaking, analysing the politics and history embedded in the tales, does not mean trampling, I hope, on the sheer exuberance of their entertainment, or crushing the transcendent pleasures they so often give. For these are stories with staying power, as their antiquity shows, because the meanings they generate are themselves magical shape-shifters, dancing to the needs of the audience.

In Hugh Cheape's 2023 paper to the Royal Society of Edinburgh, he made the following remark:

> One almost universal comment – or complaint – of the historian embarking on their study of the Highlands and Islands has been the absence of documentation for a satisfactory narrative, and the lack of archival sources for any systematic analysis. The inference of this cry of despair has been: 'No Documents, No History'! So, this too-prevalent excuse had tended to a default position in a Highland history of cultural and ideological stereotypes. From today's standpoint, what I see for our students in the schools and universities is a narrative that is well-worn, staid and compiled elsewhere. That is not to suggest that it is other than a substantial body of scholarship in its own right, but it is not without its own crop of theories and dogmas – and its own gaps in competencies.

In relation to Hugh's point about the supposed dearth of sources that might lend us an insight into the mindset of the ordinary Highlander, is a statement made by the renowned folklorist, Calum Iain Maclean, in his major publication, *The Highlands*, which made its appearance a year before his untimely death in 1960: 'There are two histories of every land and people, the written history that tells what is considered politic to tell and the unwritten history that tells us everything.' For him, therefore, 'My sources of information were not to be guide-books, travellers' accounts or the prejudiced writings of formal historians. They had to be living sources breathing the air and treading the soil of Lochaber. They are, of course, the people who know most about Lochaber.' That was why he devoted his life to collecting the songs and stories of some of the country's finest traditional storytellers, people whose remarkable tales would otherwise have been lost forever. And that is why we owe a similar debt to Hugh Miller and Alexander Mackenzie, who were doing the same thing in the nineteenth century, recording those valuable sources that breathed the air and trod the soil of Ross-shire.

When writing of the local oral traditions that he was recording for posterity, Miller said: 'They abounded with what I deemed as true delineations of character, as pleasing exhibitions of passion, and as striking instances of the vicissitudes of human affairs – with the vagaries of imaginations as vigorous, and the beliefs of superstitions as wild.' He continued: 'Human nature is not exclusively displayed in the histories of only great countries, or in the actions of only celebrated men; and human nature may be suffered to assert its claim on the attention of the beings who partake of it, even though the specimens exhibited be furnished by the traditions of an obscure village.'

Echoing Hugh Cheape's words,

> Surely we can mount a challenge to conventional Highland and Island history with the varied sources we have to hand and adopt an innovative and open approach with multi-disciplinary and interdisciplinary studies; we can draw on sociology, ethnology, history, human geography, cultural anthropology – and, of course, language and literature, and drawing into the pool new elements such as the *Tobar an Dualchais* sound archive.

That sound archive was an invaluable record of oral storytelling, of precisely the type that recorded Coinneach *Odhar*'s story and that is what I have attempted in this book in my own small way.

~·~·~

To sum up my findings: far from being dismissed as mere fiction, or simply as the remnants of a more superstitious age, I believe the stories surrounding the Brahan Seer offer us just such a precious insight into what were many of the most significant concerns in the mindset of local people, many of them illiterate, others highly educated, whose worries and priorities we would not otherwise have access to. And these concerns were not those of a backward region, cut off from civilisation; they were, on the contrary, a reflection of the uniquely rich and imaginative culture of the Highlands of Scotland – a part of the world that I would describe as both an intellectual and cultural powerhouse. The very reason for these stories' survival was owing to the collective genius of Highland oral tradition, weaving its patchwork of colourful memories, of tales that originated in both fact and fiction, all of which addressed what mattered most to a community hungry for the best kind of entertainment. It is the genius of those tales that no doubt explains my original childhood love for them, and that spurred my lifetime's quest for Scotland's Nostradamus. And that is why I believe the wonder tales of the Highlands deserve our attention and should still be shared and treasured by one and every one of us.

# Selected Bibliography

**MANUSCRIPTS**

**British Library, Additional Manuscripts (Add.)**

*Lauderdale Papers*, Add. 23117;

Sir George Mackenzie, first Earl of Cromartie, *History of the Family of Mackenzie*, 1849 transcript with annotations by Lewis Mark Mackenzie, Add. 39205; The Rev. John MacRa, *A Brief Geneological* [sic] – *Historical Account of the Origin, Rise, and Growth of the Family and Surname of Mackenzie from Colin the First Baron of Kintail, to Kenneth the Third Earl of Seaforth's death, which happened 16th September, 1678 – written first in several letters to a friend, and now collected into one continued discourse, by J.M.*, transcript of 1865, Add. 40721 (1).

*Seaforth Papers*, Add. 28151, 28238, 28239, 28250 and 61624.

**Dundee City Archive**

'The true start of Sir George Mackenzie's affairs, Octr 1673', GD/WH *Wharncliffe Estate Papers*.

**Edinburgh Public Library**

*Mackenzie Family Manuscript*, RBR QX DA7583MK 37.

**Glasgow, Mitchell Library**

*A Deduction of the Family of Seafort from its first Settlement in Scotland down to the present time 1755*, MS 591699.

**National Archives of Scotland, Register House, Edinburgh**

*Commission under the Quarter Seal appointing Lauchlan Makintosche of Dunnachtane, Colin McKenzie of Kintaill, Robert Monro of Foulis, Walter Urquhart, sheriff of Cromartie, Hugh alias Hucheoun Ross of Kilraok (Kilravock) and Alexander Falconar of Halkartoun, justiciaries within the bounds of the earldoms of Ross and Moray and lordship of Ardmanach*, 23 January 1577–78, GD 93/92.

*Cromartie Family Muniments*, GD 305.

*Exchequer Records*, E1/7, ff67–68.

*Seaforth Papers*, GD 46.

**National Library of Scotland**

*Mackenzie of Delvine Papers*, MSS 1118–5209.

*Selected Bibliography*

## National Register of Archives of Scotland
*Mackenzie of Gairloch Papers*, 143.

## PRIMARY PRINTED

Aubrey, John, *Miscellanies upon the following subjects collected by J. Aubrey, Esq*, 1696.

Boswell, James, *Journal of a Tour to the Hebrides*, 1785.

Brodie, Alexander and James, *The Diary of Alexander Brodie of Brodie 1652–1685, and his son, James Brodie of Brodie, 1680–1685: consisting of extracts from the existing manuscripts, and a republication of the volume printed at Edinburgh in the year 1740*, Vol. 33, 1863.

Boyd, Allan, *Prophecies of Thomas the Rhymer: The Ancient Scotch Prophet, Containing the Wonderful fulfilment of many of his Predictions; and those not yet accomplished*, 1828.

Cameron, Ewen, *The Fingal of Ossian, an Ancient Epic Poem in Six Books. Translated from the original Galic Language, by Mr James Macpherson, and now rendered into Heroic Verse by Ewen Cameron*, 1776.

Craven, J.B. (ed.), *Journals of the Episcopal Visitations of the Rt Rev Robert Forbes, MA with a History of the Episcopal Church in the Diocese of Ross*, 1923.

Dante Alighieri, *Inferno*, circa 1308–21.

Defoe, Daniel, *A Tour Thro' the whole Island of Great Britain*, 1724.

Defoe, Daniel, *A Political History of the Devil*, 1726.

Defoe, Daniel, *A System of Magick*, 1726.

Defoe, Daniel, *An Essay on the History and Reality of Apparitions*, 1727.

*The Exchequer Rolls of Scotland*, Vol. 20, 1899.

Ferguson, Adam, *Essay on the History of Civil Society*, 1767.

Fraser, William, *The Earls of Cromartie, their Kindred, Country and Correspondence*, 1876.

Gordon, Sir Robert, *A genealogical history of the Earldom of Sutherland, from its origin to the year 1630, by Gilbert Gordon, published from the original manuscript by H. Weber, edited by G.G.L. Gower*, 1813.

Grant, Elizabeth of Rothiemurchus, *Memoirs of a Highland Lady*, 1815.

Healey, G (ed.), *The letters of Daniel Defoe*, ed. by G Healey, 1955.

Johnson, Samuel, *A Journey to the Western Islands of Scotland*, 1775.

Mackay, William, *Records of the Presbyteries of Inverness and Dingwall 1643–1688*, 1896.

Mackay, William. (ed.), *Chronicles of the Frasers: the Wardlaw Manuscript*, 1905.

Mackenzie, Alexander, *History of the Highland Clearances*, 1883.

Mackenzie, Donald Alexander, *Wonder Tales from Scottish Myth and Legend*, 1917.

Mackenzie, Sir George, *Pleadings in remarkable cases*, 1672.

Mackenzie, Sir George, *Lawes and Customes of Scotland in Matters Criminal*, 1678.

Mackenzie, Sir George, *The Works of the Eminent and Learned Lawyare, Sir George Mackenzie of Rosehaugh, Advocate to King Charles II and James VII*, 1716.

MacLennan, A.B., *The Petty Seer*, 1894.

MacNaughton, Colin, *Church Life in Ross and Sutherland from the Revolution, 1688, to the present time (compiled chiefly from the Tain Presbytery records)*, 1915.

*Representations of the Family of Seaforth*, 1829.

MacPherson, James, *Fingal, an Ancient Epic Poem in Six Books, together with Several Other Poems composed by Ossian, the Son of Fingal, translated from the Gaelic Language*, 1760.

MacPherson, James, *Temora*, 1763.

MacPherson, James, *The Works of Ossian*, 1765.

McInnes, C. T. (ed.), *Calendar of Writs of Munro of Foulis, 1299–1823*, 1940.

Miller, Hugh, *Scenes and Legends of the North of Scotland: Or the Traditional History of Cromarty*, 1834.

Necker de Saussure, Albertine-Adrienne, *A Voyage to the Hebrides*, 1822.

Nostradame, Michel de, *Les Prophéties*, omnibus edition, 1568.

Pennant, *A Tour of Scotland*, 1769.

Pitcairn, Robert, *Criminal Trials in Scotland*, 1833.

Tanner, J.R., (ed.), Samuel Pepys, *Private Correspondence and Miscellaneous Papers, 1679–1703*, 1926.

Thompson, Francis, *The Supernatural Highlands*, 1999.

Urquhart, Sir Thomas, *Pantochronochanon, or, A Peculiar Promptuary of Time and Ekskubalauron, or, The Discovery of a most Exquisite Jewel*, 1652.

Wodrow, Robert, *Analecta, or, Materials for a history of remarkable providences, mostly relating to Scotch ministers and Christians*, ed. M. Leishman, Maitland Club, 60, 1842–3.

Wodrow, Robert, *The History of the Sufferings of the Church of Scotland*, 1829.

*Selected Bibliography*

## SECONDARY PRINTED

Michael Barkun, *A Culture of Conspiracy: Apocalyptic Visions in Contemporary America*, 2003.

Bettelheim, Bruno, *The Uses of Enchantment: The Meaning and Importance of Fairy Tales*, 1976.

Brown, James Wood, *The life and legend of Michael Scot*, 1897.

Burke, Peter, *Popular Culture in Early Modern Europe*, 2001.

Campbell, John L. and Trevor H. Hall, *Strange Things*, 1968.

Cannadine, David, 'Aristocratic indebtedness in the Nineteenth Century', *Economic History Review, 2nd Series*, Vol. XXX, 1977.

Cannadine, David, *Aspects of Aristocracy*, 1994.

Clough, Monica, *Two Houses*, 1990.

Craven, Rev. J.B., *History of the Episcopal Church in the Diocese of Moray*, 1889.

Craven, Rev. J.B., *History of the Episcopal Church in the Diocese of Orkney*, 1893.

Craven, J.B. (ed.), *History of the Episcopal Church in the Diocese of Moray*, 1908.

Cromartie, Earl of, *A Highland History*, 1979.

Cruickshanks, Eveline, and Corp, Edward (eds.), *The Stuart Court in Exile and the Jacobites*, 1995.

Cumming, Laura, 'Fabritius, my Father and me: how art has shaped my life', *The Guardian*, 25 June, 2023.

Devine, T.M., *Clanship to Crofters' War: The social transformation of the Scottish Highlands*, 1994.

Devine, T M, *The Scottish Clearances: A History of the Dispossessed, 1600–1900*, 2018.

Dixon, J.H., *Gairloch and Guide to Loch Maree*, 1886.

Finlayson, Clarence, *The Strath. The biography of Strathpeffer*, 1979.

Gaskill, Howard, Editor, *Ossian Revisited*, 1991.

Gregory, David, *History of the Western Highlands and Islands*, 1836.

Herman, Arthur, *The Scottish Enlightenment: The Scot's Invention of the Modern World*, 2001.

Grundlingh, Albert, 'Probing the Prophet: The Psychology and Politics of the Siener van Rensburg Phenomenon', *South African Historical Journal*, 34 May, 1996.

Highlands and Islands Enterprise, *The social and economic influence of Inverness Airport*, 11 September, 2018.

*Scotland's Nostradamus*

Hunter, James, *Last of the Free: A Millennial History of the Highlands and Islands of Scotland*, 1999.

Hunter, Michael, *The Royal Society and its Fellows 1660–1700: the Morphology of an Early Scientific Institution*, 1994.

Hunter, Michael, *The Occult Laboratory, Magic, Science and Second Sight in Late Seventeenth-Century Scotland*, 2001.

Jackson, Clare, 'The paradoxical virtue of the historical romance: Sir George Mackenzie's *Aretina* (1660) and the civil wars' in *Celtic dimensions of the British civil wars*, ed. John R. Young, 1997.

Kay, Billy, *Knee Deep in Claret*, 1994.

Kirk, Robert, *The Secret Commonwealth of Elves, Fauns and Fairies*, 1815.

Lang, Andrew, *Sir George Mackenzie, King's Advocate, of Rosehaugh, His Life and Times 1636(?)–1691*, 1909.

Lockhart, John Gibson, *The Life of Sir Walter Scott*, 1837–8.

Lockyer, Roger, *James VI and I*, 1998.

Mackenzie, Alexander (ed.), *The Celtic Magazine*, no. XXV, Vol. III, November 1877.

Mackenzie, Alexander, *Historical Tales and Legends of the Highlands*, 1878.

Mackenzie, Alexander, *History of the MacLeods*, 1889.

Mackenzie, Alexander, *History of the Mackenzies and the Principal Families of the Name*, 1894.

Mackenzie, Alexander, *The Prophecies of the Brahan Seer with a Foreword and Commentary by Elizabeth Sutherland*, 1981.

Mackenzie, Dr. George, *The Lives and Characters of the most Eminent Writers of the Scots Nation*, 1711.

Mackenzie, Hector, 'Flooding of Castle Leod grounds as River Peffery bursts banks prompts Ross-shire clan chief call for "radical solutions" as extreme weather events become new normal', *Ross-shire Journal*, 24 October, 2023.

Mackenzie, John H. Dixon, *Gairloch and Guide to Loch Maree*, 1886.

McKenzie, Andrew and Kevin, *May we be Britons? A History of the Mackenzies*, 2012.

MacLeod, Rev. Donald, *Memoir of Norman MacLeod*, 1876.

McLeod, Rev. Donald, *A Treatise on the Second Sight, Dreams and Apparitions*, 1763.

Macrae, Norman, *Highland Second Sight with Prophecies of Coinneach Odhar and the Seer of Perth*, 1908.

Martin, Martin, *A Description of the Western Islands of Scotland*, 1703.

Matheson, William, 'Traditions of the Mackenzies', *Transactions of the Gaelic Society of Inverness*, 1963), Vol. XXXIX.

## Selected Bibliography

Matheson, William, 'The Historical Coinneach Odhar and some Prophecies Attributed to Him', *Transactions of the Gaelic Society of Inverness*, 1968.

Matheson, William, ed., *The Blind Harper: the songs of Roderick Morison and his music*, 1970.

Morrison, Leonard, Allison, *The history of the Morison or Morrison family with most of the 'Traditions of the Morrisons' (clan MacGillemhuire), hereditary judges of Lewis, by Capt. F. W. L. Thomas, of Scotland, and a record of the descendants of the hereditary judges to 1880*, 2010.

Normand and Roberts (eds.), 'Witchcraft in Early Modern Scotland', *Scottish Historical Review* 81 (2), 267–269, 2002.

Prebble, John, *Culloden*, 2002.

Rampini, Charles, *A History of Moray and Nairn*, 1847.

Richards, Eric and Clough, Monica, *Cromartie: Highland Life 1650–1914*, 1989.

Richards, Eric, *The Highland Clearances: People, Landlords and Rural Turmoil*, 2000.

Scott, Tony, 'Michael Scot and the Four Rainbows', *International Journal for the Historiography of Science*, 2, 2017.

Scott, Sir Walter, *Letters on Demonology and Witchcraft*, Addressed to J. G. Lockhart, Esq., 1830.

Scott, Sir Walter, *The Lay of the Last Minstrel: Canto II*, 1805.

Thomas, Keith, *Religion and the Decline of Magic*, 1971.

Thorndike, Lynn, *Michael Scot*, 1965.

Thorndike, Lynn, 'Manuscripts of Michael Scot's *Liber introductorius*', *Didascaliae: studies in honor of Anselm M. Albareda*, 1961.

Warner, Marina, *From the Beast to the Blonde: On Fairy Tales and Their Tellers*, 1994.

Westwood, Jennifer, and Sophia Kingshill, *The Lore of Scotland: A guide to Scottish legends*, 2009.

White, Gregor, Free Church of Scotland reaching out in Inverness and Tornagrain, *The Inverness Courier*, 8 February, 2023.

Wilby, Emma, *The Visions of Isobel Gowdie*, 2012.

Wilson, Damon, *The Mammoth Book of Nostradamus and Other Prophets*, 1999.

Wormald, Jenny, *Court, Kirk and Community*, 1983.

Yeoman, Louise, 'Witchcraft in early modern Scotland: James VI's "Demonology" and the North Berwick witches', *Scottish Historical Review* 81 (212), 2002.

*Scotland's Nostradamus*

## BROADCASTS, LECTURES AND ONLINE ARTICLES

BBC Radio 4, 'The Highland Clearances', *In Our Time*, 8 March, 2018.

Cheape, Hugh, '"The folk who did all the business" – *a' mhuinntir do rinn an t-seirbhis uile*. Revisiting the Past in the Islands', unpublished lecture to the Royal Society of Edinburgh in their *Islands – Past* event, 28–29 April, 2023.

Clan Mackenzie Podcasts: *The Brahan Seer, Part 1*, October 2022; *The Brahan Seer, Part 2*, November, 2022; *Caroline Stanford from The Landmark Trust on the Mackenzies and Fairburn Tower*, February, 2023.

'Dornie Manuscript' (Manuscript History of the Mackenzies transcribed by Colin Mackenzie of Newburnside, 1760: online version: http://www.castles. org/Chatelaine/EDC/edc-history.htm).

Goodare, J., Yeoman, L., Martin, L. and Miler, J., *Survey of Scottish Witchcraft, 1563–1736*, University of Edinburgh. School of History, Classics and Archaeology, online database, 2010.

Jack, R.D.S., 'Urquhart [Urchard], Sir Thomas, of Cromarty (1611–1660)', *Oxford Dictionary of National Biography*, online edition.

McKenzie, Andrew, *The Mackenzies and Artistic Patronage*, Grantown Museum lecture for the symposium, *Richard Waitt: New Perspectives on Culture and Context*, 2017.

McKenzie, Andrew, *Friendship, Wine, Poetry and Music: The Social Life of the Mackenzies in the 17th and 18th Centuries*, YouTube video, 2024.

Reddit article by Ucumu in *Did Moctezuma II really believe Cortes was "an armor-clad God"?*: Ask Historians, 28th April 2015.

Schuchard, Marsha, 'Swedenborg, Yeats and Jacobite Freemasonry', Revised and up-dated version of lectures given at Livingston Masonic Library, New York City, 2010, and Yeats Summer School, Sligo, Ireland, 2012.

Salerno, Rosarie, online article (in *Rocky Point Times Newspaper*) 'Did Montezuma think Cortez was the God Quetzalcoatl?', 8 December 2011.

Tinline, Phil, *Conspiracies: The Secret Knowledge*, BBC Radio 4 Series, 2023.

# Index

Aberdeen  127
Aberdeen Arts Centre  146
Addison, Joseph  60
Advocate's Library  47, 150
Albany, Duke of, *see* Stewart, John
Albermarle, First Duke of, *see* Monck,
    George
Alexander III, King  112
Al-Kamil, Sultan  78
America  110
American War of Independence  110
Annales School  57, 132
Anne, Queen  32
Antichrist  6–7, 9
Apollo moon landing  6
Arabia  46
Ard-a-chaolais  135
Ardersier  76–77
Ardmore  22–23
Ardnamurchan  104
Ardross  20
Ardvreck Castle  74
Aristotle  78, 80
Arpafeelie  136
Assynt (in Easter Ross)  20
Atbara, Battle of  138
Aubrey, John  12, 15, 87
Auld Alliance  54
Auldearn  29
Aulnoy, Baroness d', *see* Barneville, Marie-
    Catherine Le Jumel de
Ault-nan-Torcan  135
Aurengzeb  46
Australia  67, 111, 143–144, 147
Averroes  78
Avicenna  78
Avoch  106
Aztecs  9, 67

Babington, Anthony  8
Bacon, Sir Francis  149–150
Baddiel, David  131
Badenhorst, Anna  129
Bailen a Caillich, *see* Nunton House

Baile-na-Cille  2–3, 67, 72–73
Baker, Henry  16
Balmoral Castle  64
Baltic  45
*Bannatyne Manuscript*  1, 72, 121
Barkun, Michael  131
Barneville, Marie-Catherine Le Jumel de,
    Baroness d'Aulnoy  87
Barra  122
Barra Seer  105
Barret, William F.  101
BBC Radio 4  131–132, 147
Beauly  77, 125, 139, 142
Benbecula  104
Benet, St  66
Bennetsfield  66
Berwick  70
Bettelheim, Bruno  85–86
Bible  6–7, 31, 59
Biden, President Joe  8
Bidpai  84
Big Bang theory  142
Birmingham  126
Black Isle  1, 5, 27, 31–32, 45, 63, 66, 71,
    106, 120, 136, 138, 146
Black Watch  88
Black, J.D.S.  50
Blair, Archibald  16
Bleau, Joan  46
Blunt-Mackenzie, Sybil Lilian, Third
    Countess of Cromartie  99–100
Boers  128–129
Bohemia  88
Bologna, Mary of  79
Bonar Bridge  69
Book of Genesis  10
Book of Jeremiah  9
Book of Revelation  6
Bordeaux  54
Borders  69, 71, 89
Boreraig  69
Boswell, James  16–18, 25, 53, 89
Botha, General Louis  129
Boyd, Allan  69–70

161

*Scotland's Nostradamus*

Boyer, Alexandre Jean-Baptiste de, Marquis d'Éguilles  116
Boyle, Robert  12, 57–58, 61, 63, 149
Bragar  72
Brahan Castle  ix, x, 1, 26, 32–33, 51, 56, 63, 93, 115–116, 118–119, 148
Brahe, Tycho  59, 79
Bridlington, John, of  70
Brodie, Alexander, of Brodie  26, 28, 32
Brodie, David  138
Buchan, John  132
Bun-da-Loch  68, 123, 143
Burghley, Lord, *see* Cecil, William
Burke, Professor Peter  xiii, 25, 57, 87, 89
Burns, Robert  54, 90
Bush, President George W.  7

Cadell, Christian  27
Caesar, Julius  6
Caithness  23
Caithness, Fifth Earl of, *see* Sinclair, George
Caledonian Canal  viii, 119, 124, 126
California Gold Rush  79
Callanish  xi, 82
Calrossie  20
Cambridge University  8, 57–58, 132–133
Cameron, James, Rev Canon  101
Campbell, Angus, of Ensay  137–138
Campbell, Gavin, First Marquis of Breadalbane  137
Campbell, John L.  18, 101, 103, 150
Campbell, John, Fourth Earl of Loudon  117
Campbell, Marjory  21, 23
Canada  45, 69, 111, 138, 147
Cannadine, Professor Sir David  xiii, 57
Caribbean  84
Cassindonisch *see* Thomas McAnemoir McAllan McHenrik
Castle Craig  138
Castle Leod  ii, viii–ix, 94, 98–100, 126, 140, 142
Catherine de Medici, Queen  6
Cavendish-Scott-Bentinck, William Henry, Fourth Duke of Portland  125
Cecil, William, Lord Burghley  8
*Celtic Magazine*  134
Celtic Renaissance  100
*Challenger* space shuttle  6
Channel Tunnel  xii, 127

Chanonry  x, 5, 20, 23, 25, 27, 31, 33, 34, 43, 51, 54–55, 63, 71, 76–78, 82, 94, 117–118, 125, 148–149
Charles I, King  xii, 9
Charles II, King  8, 26, 32, 50, 139
Charles III, King  129
Cheape, Professor Hugh  xiii, 51, 152–153
Chesterton, J.K.  132
Christian IV, King  59
Clach an Tiompain, *see* Eagle Stone
Clach an t-Seasaidh  136
Clach an Tuindain, *see* Eagle Stone
Clach Dubh an Abain  72
Clach Mhor  118, 136
Clan Ranald  104
Clanranald of Glengarry  141
Clootie Well  66
Cnoc-a-Clachain  137
Collace, Katherine  29
Conchra  68, 123, 143
Condillac, Étienne Bonnot de  56
Conon  140
Conon Bridge  139
Conon, River  125, 139
Conspiracy Theories  131–133, 151
Contin  26
Coole Park  100
Copenhagen  88
Copernicus  79
Corelli, Marie  99
Cornwall  70
Corp, Edward  52
Cortés, Hernán  9
Cotswolds  45
Covenanters  26, 30
COVID-19 pandemic  xii, 8, 99, 131
Coyleford-green  70
Craven, J.B.  29
Crichton-Smith, Ian  146
Crichton-Stuart, John Patrick, Third Marquis of Bute  101–102
Crofting Commission  124
Cromartie, Third Countess of, *see* Blunt-Mackenzie, Sybil Lilian
Cromartie, Countess of, *see* Mackenzie, Eve
Cromartie, First Earl of, *see* Mackenzie, Sir George
Cromartie, Third Earl of, *see* Mackenzie, George

162

*Index*

Cromartie, Fourth Earl of, *see* Mackenzie, Roderick
Cromartie, Fifth Earl of, *see* Mackenzie, John
Cromarty 63, 138–139
Cromarty Firth 138, 140
Cromwell, Oliver 9, 11, 26, 118
Crookes, Sir William 101
Crowley, Aleister 99–100
Cruickshanks, Evelyn 52
Crusade, Sixth 79
Cudworth, Ralph 58
Culloden, Battle of viii, 18, 43, 52, 72, 110, 116, 121, 123, 146
Cumberland, Willam, Duke of 52, 72, 123
Cumbria 75
Cumming, James xi, 38, 82
Cumming, Laura xi, xiii, 82
Curetán, St 66

Daan 20
Dalcross 144
Dante Alighieri 66, 75, 77
Davy, Sir Humphrey 5, 107, 114
*De Chiromantia*, by Michael Scot 78
Dee, John 8, 59, 66–67, 79, 99
Defoe, Daniel 45–46, 60
Delphi 6
Devil 59, 72, 75, 77, 125
Devine, Tom 111, 124, 147
Dewar, Peter, Rev 101
Diana, Princess of Wales 6
*Dick Whittington and his Cat* 113
Dickson, John, *see* Cadell, Christian
Diffusionism 84
Dingwall 5, 140
Dornie 122
Dornoch 25
Dornoch Firth 2
Douglas, Gavin 50
Douglas, Karen 150
Doyle, Arthur Conan 99
*Dracula*, by Bram Stoker 99
Druim-Uachdair 143
Drumossie Moor 72, 123
Dryden, John 47
Dunbar family 138
Dunbar, Alexander, of Westfield 138
Dunbar, Katherine 138
Dunbar, William 144
Dunean 125

Dunrobin Castle 11
Dunvegan 137

Eagle Stone 97, 140–142
Earlston 69
*Edda* 75
Edinburgh 27, 48–49, 53, 55, 144
*Edinburgh Daily Review* 118
Edinburgh University 147
Edward VII, King xi
Edward VIII, King xi
Eguilles, Marquis d', *see* Boyer, Alexandre Jean-Baptiste de
Egyptians 67
Eidseal 135
Eilean Donan Castle 66, 93, 113–114, 116, 119, 122
Einstein 142
*Electric Scotland* 18
Elgin 21, 27–28
Elizabeth I, Queen 8–9, 59, 70
Elizabeth of Bohemia, Queen 9
Emigration 110–112, 123, 143–146
Enlightenment 45, 47, 52–54, 56, 89, 151
Eoligarry 105
Ercildoun, Sir Thomas de, *see* Thomas the Rhymer
Eriskay 101
Evans, Richard 132
Evans-Pritchard, E.E. 29
Evelyn, John 47, 58

Fáfnir 75
Fairburn Tower x, 37, 106, 119
Fairy Flag 137
Falconer, Alexander, of Halkerston 21
Far East 46
Farqhuar, Sir Robert, of Mounie 139
Farquharson, Anne, Lady Mackintosh 116
*Fearchair a Ghunna* 125
Fénelon, François de Salignac de La Mothe-Fénelon, known as the Abbé Fénelon 86
Fenwick, Sir William, of Meldon 75
Ferguson, Adam 47, 53–54, 88
Ferguson, Robert 54
Ferrintosh 120, 125
Ficino, Marsilio 79
Fillan, St, pool of 65
Fingal 141

163

*Scotland's Nostradamus*

Fletchers 106
Flowerdale House 121
Fodderty 115
Fontaine, Jean de la 84, 86
Forbes, Lord President Duncan, of Culloden 18, 115
Fordoun, John of 52
Forfar 27
Forres 21
Fort George 77
Fortrose Town Hall 51
Fortrose, *see* Chanonry
Fortrose, Viscount, *see* Mackenzie, Kenneth
Fortrose, Viscountess, *see* Stewart, Lady Mary
France 45, 51–52, 57
François II, King 70
Fraser, Catherine 11
Fraser, Finlay 28
Fraser, Flora, Twenty-First Lady Saltoun 109
Fraser, Hugh, Seventh Lord Lovat 10–11, 63, 149
Fraser, James, Rev 10–11, 28, 32, 62–63, 149
Frederick II, Emperor 59, 78, 80
Frederick of the Palatinate, King 9, 59
Free Church of Scotland 124, 144
Freer, Ada Goodrich 101–103, 105
French Revolution 6
Freud, Sigmund 13

Gabaldon, Diana 44, 56, 147
Gairloch 15, 113, 117, 121
Gairloch, Lady, *see* Grant, Anne
Garden, Professor James 15–16, 53, 59
Geikie, Sir Archibald 69
Glack 115
*Glasgow Evening News* 101
Glashach, Donald 11
Glastullich 20
Glen Shiel, Battle of 55, 116
Goethe, Johann Wolfgang von 54
Gogha Ban, an 135
Goodyear, Professor Julian 25
Gordon, Alexander, Third Earl of Huntly 136
Gordon, Cosmo George, Third Duke of Gordon 9
Gowdie, Isobel 15, 26, 29

Graham, James, First Marquis of Montrose 9
Grant, Anne, Lady Gairloch 15
Grant, Elizabeth, of Rothiemurchus 108
Grant, Isabel 14–15
Grantown Museum 50–51
Great Fire of London 6
Great Plague 68
Greeks 67
Greene, Graham 132
Greenyards 69
Gregory, Augusta, Lady 100
Gregory, Professor James 58
Grimm, Jacob and Wilhelm 89
Gunn, Neil M. 146
Gustavus Adolphus, King 9, 45

Hag stones 99
Hall, Trevor H. 18, 101, 103, 150
Hamilton, Emma, Lady 52
Hamilton, Sir William 52
Hannah, Phyllis x
Hardenberg, Georg Philipp Friedrich Freiherr von 87
Harper, Marjory 146
Harris 134
Hastings 99
Hebrides 89, 104, 112, 146
Helvétius, Claude Adrien 56
Heraclitus 6
Herbert, Lady Frances, Countess of Seaforth x, 32–33
Herculaneum 52
Hermetic order of the Golden Dawn 99–100
Hickes, George 58, 62
High Political School of History 132
Highland Clearances viii, 69, 71, 110–111, 123–124, 146
Highland Line 52
Highlands and Islands Airports Limited 144
Highlands and Islands Development Board 146
Highlands and Islands Emigration Society 144
Highlands and Islands Enterprise 144
Hiroshima 6
*Historia animalium*, by Aristotle 80
Hitler, Adolf 6, 127

164

*Index*

Hobbes, Thomas 54
Holy Land 79
Home, Henry, Lord Kames 52
Home, John 54, 114
Homer 54
Hood, Lady, *see* Stewart-Mackenzie, Hon.
 Mary Frederica
Hume, David 47
Hunter, Michael 58, 60–61
Huntly, Third Earl of, *see* Gordon, Alexander
Hussain, Saddam 130

India 46
Industrial Revolution 126, 151
*Inferno*, by Dante Alighieri 66, 75
Innes, Barbara 27
Innes, John 27
Inverness 126–127, 144
Inverness Airport 144–145
*Inverness Courier* 127
Inverness Gas and Water Company 127
Ireland 70
Isla Seer 11, 71, 82, 123
Isle Maree 65–66
Italy 52–53

Jacobite Rebellions 56, 60, 70, 114, 116–
 117, 119, 146
James V, King 119
James VI and I, King 24, 70
James, William 101
Johnson, Samuel, Dr 16–18, 25, 53, 89
Jung, Carl 13, 84

Kames, Lord, *see* Home, Henry
Kay, Billy 55
Keanoch *Odhar*/Ower 20–21, 23–24
Kellie, Margaret 27
Kelly, Rose Edith 99
Kennedy, President J.F. 131
Kilchrist 140–141
Kilcoy Castle 93, 106, 120–121
Kilduich 137
Kintail 55, 68, 106, 112–113, 119, 122–
 123, 136–137, 143
Kirk, Robert, Rev 15, 85
Kneep 135
Knock of Alves 27
Knockfarrel 94, 115, 140–141
Königsberg, Johannes Müller von 8

Koos de la Rey, *see* Herculaas de Rey, Jacobus
Kotter, Christopher 9

Laden, Osama bin 7, 130
Landmark Trust x, 119
Landseer, Sir Edwin 112, 150
Lang, Andrew 18, 67, 101
Lauderdale, First Duke of, *see* Maitland, John
*Legend of the Birds* 67–68, 75, 84, 112
*Legend of the Son of the Goat* 66, 113
Leith 27, 48–49
Leod, Jarl of Orkney 140
Leslies of Findrassie 138–139
Leveson-Gower, George, First Duke of
 Sutherland 69
Lewis, C.S. viii, 135
Lewis, Isle of ix, xi, xii, 55, 71, 72–73, 94,
 99, 115, 134–136, 149
Leyden 29
Lhuyd, Edward 12, 14
*Liber Introductorius maior in astrologiam*,
 by Michael Scot 80
*Liber Physiognomiae*, by Michael Scot
 80–81
Lipari islands 79
Livorno 45
Loch Maree 64–66, 113
Lochaber 152
*Lochaber No More*, by John Watson Nicol
 90–91
Lochalsh 55, 68, 123, 143
Lockhart John Gibson 5, 107, 107, 114
Lodge, Sir Oliver 101
Logie Easter 20
Lohengrin 71
Lombard League 78
London 48, 58, 144
Long Meg 75
Lordship of the Isles 134
Loskoir Longert/Lonskie Loncart, *see*
 McAlester, Mariota Neynaine
Lothian 29
Louis XIV, King 51, 87
Lovat Estate 109
Lovat, Seventh Lord, *see* Fraser, Hugh
Lowlands 116, 123

Mabus 7, 130
*Mac a' Chreachair* 11
MacAulay, Clan 135–136

165

*Scotland's Nostradamus*

MacAulay, Donald  77, 135
MacAulay, Donald *Cam*  135–136
MacAulay, Iain *Ruadh*  136
MacAulay, Margaret  ix, 135
MacBeth MacFinlay, King  140
*MacBeth*, by William Shakespeare  6, 27
MacCoinnich, Aonghas  54
MacDonald, Alexander, of Kingsburgh  16
MacDonald, Allan, Father  18, 101, 104, 121
MacDonald, Clan  140
MacDonald, Colin, of Boisdale  104, 121
MacDonald, Donald *Dubh*  134, 136
MacDonald, Somerled, Fifth Lord MacDonald of Sleat  69
MacDonnells of Glengarry  141
Macgillivray, William  23
MacGregor, Alexander, Rev  64–66
MacInnes, Angus  104
Macintyre, Donald  136–137, 142
Macintyre, Donald  4
MacKay, Donald, First Lord Reay  9, 15, 27, 45, 59, 99
Mackenzie tartan  88
Mackenzie, Alexander, Sir, of Gairloch  121
Mackenzie, Alexander, the Clach  x, 2, 5, 18, 20, 57, 61, 64, 72, 85, 88–89, 99, 106–109, 115, 119, 125, 134–136, 139, 141–142, 144, 150, 152
Mackenzie, Caroline, Hon.  ix, 35
Mackenzie, Clan  viii–ix, 5, 9, 25, 44, 46, 50–51, 54–57, 62, 66–68, 84, 88, 104, 106, 112–120, 135–136, 139–141
Mackenzie, Coinneach *Odhar*  viii, x, xi–xii, 1–4, 6, 10, 14, 20, 23–24, 31, 33, 46, 61–63, 67–68, 72, 74–76, 82, 85, 90, 104, 107, 108, 116, 119, 124–127, 130, 134, 136, 138, 140–142, 146, 148–149, 153
Mackenzie, Colin, Captain  115–116
Mackenzie, Colin, First Earl of Seaforth  25, 28, 51, 121
Mackenzie, Colin, of Kintail  21
Mackenzie, Colin, Rev  115
Mackenzie, Donald Alexander  64, 84, 87
Mackenzie, Eve, Countess of Cromartie  xiii, 99
Mackenzie, Francis Humberston, Lord Seaforth  ix, 5, 8, 21, 57, 92, 110, 114, 118–119, 149

Mackenzie, George, in Baile-na-Cille  72
Mackenzie, George, Second Earl of Seaforth  9
Mackenzie, George, Sir, of Rosehaugh  28–31, 41, 46–50, 86, 106, 150
Mackenzie, George, Sir, of Tarbat, First Earl of Cromartie  26, 28–29, 31–32, 58, 60, 62–63, 99
Mackenzie, George, Third Earl of Cromartie  116
Mackenzie, Hector, Sir, of Gairloch  109
Mackenzie, Henry  54, 107, 114
Mackenzie, Isobel, Countess of Seaforth  viii, 5, 26, 29, 31–33, 39, 46, 62–63, 74, 82, 86, 130, 148–149
Mackenzie, James, Dr  52–54, 59
Mackenzie, John, Fifth Earl of Cromartie  xiii, 99, 142
Mackenzie, John, Lord MacLeod  117
Mackenzie, John, of Delvine  53
Mackenzie, John, of Fairburn  x, 119
Mackenzie, John, of Findon  118
Mackenzie, John, Sir, of Tarbat  32, 46
Mackenzie, Kenneth *Mhor*, Third Earl of Seaforth  10, 25, 29, 32–33, 40, 46, 59, 62–63, 73–74, 82, 130, 148–149
Mackenzie, Kenneth, Fourth Earl of Seaforth  32
Mackenzie, Kenneth, last Earl of Seaforth  51–52, 54
Mackenzie, Kenneth, Sir, of Gairloch  65
Mackenzie, Kenneth, Viscount Fortrose  115–117
Mackenzie, Mary, Lady  55
Mackenzie, Roderick, Fourth Earl of Cromartie  viii, 99
Mackenzie, Thomas, Major  116
Mackenzie, Thomas, of Pluscarden  9, 27
Mackenzie, William *Dubh*, Fifth Earl of Seaforth  32–33, 51, 55, 116, 119
Mackintosh, Isobel, Lady Balnagowan  22–23
Mackintosh, Lachlan, of Dunachton  20
Mackintosh, Lady, *see* Farquharson, Anne
Maclean, Calum Iain  152
MacLennan, A.B.  2, 66–67, 71, 20, 142
MacLennan, Clan  136–137
MacLeod, Donald, Rev  137
MacLeod, General Norman, of Dunvegan  17

166

# Index

MacLeod, John *Breac*, of Dunvegan 137–138

MacLeod, Lord, *see* Mackenzie, John

MacLeod, Torquil, of Lewis 136

MacLeods of Lewis 121, 128, 135–137

MacMathan, Kenneth 113

MacMillan, Clan 137

MacNeils of Barra 122

MacPherson, Andrew, of Cluny 15

MacPherson, Duncan, of Cluny 15

MacPherson, James 54, 64, 100, 107, 114–115, 140, 150

MacRae, Clan 136–138

Macrae, Norman 103–104

Macsween, Innes, Rev 144

Magra, John 146

Maitland, John, First Duke of Lauderdale 58, 62

Maories 67

Marshall, Neil 130

Martin, Martin 13–14, 16, 18, 58, 73

Mary Queen of Scots 8, 70

Matheson, Murdoch 55

Matheson, William 20–21, 24, 57, 67–68, 72, 134, 148

McAlester, Mariota Neynaine 20–22

McHenrik, Thomas McAnemoir McAllan 20, 23

McKenzie, Alexander, in Strathnaver 15–16, 53, 69

McKenzie, Chris ix, xiii, 148

McKenzie, Daniel *Og* 144

McKenzie, Daniel x, 28, 32, 45

McKenzie, Hector, Rev 16

McKenzie, James, Captain 77

McKenzie, John xiii, 122

McKenzie, Kevin viii, xiii, 27, 43, 66, 68, 71, 84, 99–100, 113, 148

McKenzie, Murdo, Bishop of Moray and Orkney ix, 9, 15, 26–29, 32, 45, 77

McKenzie, Patricia xiii

McKenzie, William 45, 126

McLeod, Donald, of Hamer 16

Mediterranean 45, 144

Melville, Daniel 55

*Memoirs of a Highland Lady*, by Elizabeth Grant of Rothiemurchus 108

Merlin 8, 71

MidCoul 144

Middleburg 50

Milla, Cristina 20–21

Milla, Robert 20–21

Miller, Hugh iii, 1, 2, 5, 20, 66, 85, 89–90, 117, 140, 150, 152–153

Monck, George, First Duke of Albermarle 58

Montesquieu, Charles Louis de Secondat, Baron de 56

Montezuma II, Emperor 9

Montrose, First Marquis of, *see* Graham, James

Moray Firth 56, 71, 76–77, 126

Moray, Sir Robert 62

More, Henry 58

More, Marie Murdoch 22

Morpeth 75

*Morrison Manuscript* 73

Morrison, Donald 73

Morrison, John, in Bragar 71, 73, 82, 85, 130, 149

Morrison, John, Rev 56, 71–74, 130, 144, 145, 149

Morrison, Roderick 56, 73, 138

Morritt, John Bacon Sawrey 5, 107, 114

Mozart, Wolfgang Amadeus 52

Muir of Ord 119, 125, 136

Munlochy Bay 66

Munro, Clan 9 21–23, 29, 72, 140

Munro, Hector, of Foulis 23–23

Munro, Robert 21–22

Munro, Robert, of Foulis 20–21

Mussman, Boy 129

*My Heart is in the Highlands*, by Robert Burns 90

Nagasaki 6

Nairn 21, 29, 144

Napoleon, Emperor 6

Napoleonic Wars 88, 110–112, 146

National Gallery, Edinburgh 112

National Portrait Gallery, Edinburgh 51–52

National Trust for Scotland 119

Necker de Saussure, Albertine-Adrienne 18

Neo-Platonism 79

Ness in Lewis 72, 121, 134

Ness, River xi, 77, 82, 126–127

New South Wales 144

New York City 7

New York Stock Exchange 129

*Scotland's Nostradamus*

New Zealand 111, 143, 147
Newton, Sir Isaac 12, 59, 61, 80
Nieuwenhuizen, C.P. 129
Nigg 20, 145–146
North Berwick witches 24–25
North Sea 45, 127, 145–146
Northumberland 70, 75
Norway 88–89
Nostradame, Michel de 6–8, 129–130
Nostradamus, *see* Nostradame, Michel de
Novalis *see* Hardenberg, Georg Philipp
	Friedrich Freiherr von
Nunton House 104
Nur ad-Din al-Bitruji 78

O'Neill, Hugh, Earl of Tyrone 135
*Oban Times* 101–102
Occitan 88
Occult Revival 100
Oickel, River 2
Oldenburg, Henry 58
*One Thousand and One Nights* 84, 113
Ord House 20
Ossian 54, 64, 88–89, 107, 114, 140
*Outlander*, by Diana Gabaldon 44, 147
Oxford University 78–79

Paracelsus 9
Paris University 78
Paris x, 32, 84
Parsifal 71
Patterson, James 28
Peffery, River 142
Pennant, Thomas 1, 18
Penrith 75
Pentagon 7
Pepys, Samuel 8, 58, 59, 62
Perrault, Charles 87
Persia 70
Peterhouse School of History, *see* High
	Political School of History
Petty 56, 144
Petty Seer, *see* Morrison, Rev John
Pilpay, *see* Bidpai
Piper Alpha xi, 82, 127
Pitcairn, Robert 21, 23, 26
Pittock, Professor Murray 111
Pliny 46
Pluscarden 118
Poland 45, 82, 126–127

Portland, Fourth Duke of, *see* Cavendish-
	Scott-Bentinck, William Henry
Pompeii 52
Poolewe 115
Pope, Alexander 47, 55
Portmaguran 135
Prebble, John 146
Prestonpans, Battle of 18, 70
Protocols of the Elders of Zion 132
Pyranees 84

Queen of Elfland 70
Quetzalcoatl 9

Raasay, Island of 108
Rabelais, François 50
Railways 124–126
Reay, First Lord, *see* MacKay, Donald
Redcastle 106, 120–121
Reformation 24, 26, 117, 151
Reitz, Deneys 128–129
Remus 66
Renaissance 78–79, 151
Rensburg, Siener van 128–129
Rey, General Jacobus Herculaas de la 128–
	129
Rhodes 137
Riach, Christian 25, 29
Richet, Charles 101
Rig, William, of Adernie 138
Robert Bruce, King 138
*Robinson Crusoe*, by Daniel Defoe 45, 60,
	89
Robinson, Sir Tony 55
Romantic Movement 45, 53, 87, 146, 151
Romulus 66
Rose, Hugh, of Kilravock 21
Rose, Hugh, Rev 29
Rosehaugh 106, 150
Ross, braes of 118
Ross, Christian 22, 23
Ross, Clan 23
Ross, George, of Balnagown 21–22
Ross, Katherine 20–23, 29, 33, 130,
	148–149
Ross, Willie 146
Ross-shire ix, 1–2, 10, 15, 20, 24–25, 27,
	32–33, 66–67, 71, 75, 89, 108, 114,
	121–124, 127, 140, 151–152
*Ross-shire Journal* 126, 142

*Index*

Roup, Julian xiii, 128
Roy, Agnes 23
Royal Society 12–15, 53, 57–58, 61, 82, 87, 99, 101, 105, 150
Royston House 46
Rupert of the Rhine, Prince 8
Russia 52

Sahara 79
Salem witch trials 29
Sampson, Agnes 25
Schiller, Friedrich, 54
Schuchard, Marsha Keith 100
Scientific Revolution 45, 59, 62
Scot, Michael iv, 75–83, 85, 99, 113, 130, 148–151
Scot, Sir Michael, of Balwearie 78
Scott, Sir Walter 5, 21, 50, 54, 64, 70, 75, 77–79, 89–90, 106–107, 114, 150
Scottish Parliament xii, 127
Scudéry, Madeleine de 47
Seaforth, Countess of, *see* Herbert, Lady Frances
Seaforth, Countess of, *see* Mackenzie, Isobel
Seaforth, First Earl of, *see* Mackenzie, Colin
Seaforth, Second Earl of, *see* Mackenzie, George
Seaforth, Third Earl of, *see* Mackenzie, Kenneth *Mhor*
Seaforth, Fourth Earl of, *see* Mackenzie, Kenneth
Seaforth, Fifth Earl of, *see* Mackenzie, William *Dubh*
Seaforth, last Earl of, *see* Mackenzie, Kenneth
Seaforth, Lord, *see* Mackenzie, Francis Humberston
Seaforth, Lord, *see* Stewart-Mackenzie, James Alexander Francis Humberston
Seaforth's Doom viii, ix, 4, 8, 21, 44–45, 84–86, 104, 106–123, 127
Seaforth's Highlanders 88
Second Sight x, xi, xii, 5, 11–19, 31–33, 44, 54, 56–63, 67, 75–76, 79, 82, 84–85, 86–87, 100–103, 125, 133, 148–151
Second World War viii, xi, 82, 126–129
Selby, Margaret 75
Selkirk, Alexander 89
Sellar, Patrick 69

Seton 70
Seven Years' War 110
Sheriffmuir 70
Shiel River 141–142
Shipton, Mother 8
Sicily 79–80
Sidgewick, Henry 101
Siegfried 75
Simpson, Margaret 28, 63
Sinclair, George, Fifth Earl of Caithness 23
Sinclair, John, Sir, of Dunbeath 11
Skye, Isle of 14, 16, 69, 111, 144
Smart, Jared x, xiii, 131
Smith, Patrick, of Braco 138
Smoo Cave 59
Snyman, Adam van 129
Society of Psychical Research (SPR) 18, 82, 100–103, 105, 150
Somoyeds 67
South Africa 128
Southeil, Ursula, *see* Shipton, Mother
Spain 52
Spanish Armada 8
Spartans 53
*Speranza, see* Wilde, Jane, Lady
Spynie Palace 27
St Andrew's Cathedral 118
Stanford, Caroline x
Steele, Richard 60
Stevenson, David 56
Stewart, John, Duke of Albany 70
Stewart, Lady Mary, Viscountess Fortrose 116
Stewart-Mackenzie, Hon. Mary Frederica, Lady Hood ix, 107, 114, 118
Stewart-Mackenzie, James Alexander Francis Humberston, Lord Seaforth 120
St-Germain-en-Laye 55
Stoker, Bram 99
Storm Babet 142
Stornoway xii, 73, 116, 135
*Strange Things,* by John L. Campbell and Trevor H. Hall 103
Strath, Skye 69
Strathnaver 15, 53, 59
Strathpeffer xi, 94, 99, 119, 126, 140–142
Stuart, Prince Charles Edward 56, 115–117
Sturgeon, Nicola 25
Suisnish 69, 94
Sutherland 2, 11, 15, 53, 59

169

*Scotland's Nostradamus*

Sutherland, First Duke of, *see* Leveson-
 Gower, George
Sutherland, Elizabeth  x, 57, 72, 125–126,
 139, 141–142, 144, 148
Syl, Nellie van  129
Syria  137

Tacitus  6
Tain  20, 27
Tarbat House  45
Tarbert, Harris  134
Tarradale  125
Tavernier, Jean-Baptiste  46
Telford, Thomas  124, 126
*The End of the Song*, by the Countess of
 Cromartie  100
*The Guardian*  xi, 82
*The Happy Prince*, by Oscar Wilde  iii, 87
*The Hound of the Baskervilles*, by Arthur
 Conan Doyle  99
*The Last of the Clan*, by Thomas Faed
 90–91
*The Lay of the Last Minstrel*, by Sir Walter
 Scott  75, 77
*The Selfish Giant*, by Oscar Wilde  87
*The Sorrow of Satan*, by Marie Corelli  99
*The Wanderings of Oisin*, by Jack Butler
 Yeats  100
Theseus  66
Thirty Years War  9, 45, 59
Thomas the Rhymer  69–71, 82, 85, 106,
 114, 123, 130, 149
Thomas, Professor Sir Keith  8, 62, 71, 112,
 132–133, 136
Thomson, Francis  12
Thorfinn II Sigurdsson, Jarl  140
Tinline, Phil  131–132
Toledo  78–79
Tolkien J.R.R.  viii
Tomnahurich Hill  124
Tonkaways  67
Tour, Anna de la  70
Tournagrain  144
Tower of London  139
*Transactions of the Gaelic Society*  134
Troy, François de  51
Trump, President Donald J.  8
Tuarag people  79
Twelfth Century Renaissance  79, 151
Tyne  70

Tyrone, Earl of, *see* O'Neill, Hugh

Uig  ix, 2–3, 36, 66, 72, 99, 135–136
Ullapool  xii
United States  x, 7, 129, 131, 138–139, 147
Urquhart, Colonel Wilins Fisk, of Urquhart
 138
Urquhart, Major Beauchamp  138
Urquhart, Sir Thomas, of Cromarty  42,
 49–50, 138–139
Urquhart, Walter, of Cromarty  20, 21, 138
Urray  56, 140
Ussie, Loch  3, 140–142

Velázquez, Diego  xii
Versailles  51
Victoria, Australia  144
Victoria, Queen  64–65, 150
Villandon, Marie-Jeanne L'Héritier de  87
Voltaire, François-Marie Arouet  56

Wagner, Richard  66, 70–71
Waitt, Richard  50
Wales  70
Walpole, Horace  67
Wardlaw Manuscript  10–11, 32, 63, 149
Warner, Marina  84, 86, 152
Watson, Bessie  28, 63
*Waverley*, by Sir Walter Scott  90
Webster's Census  111
West, Benjamin  51, 112
White Lady of Lawers  11
Wilby, Emma  15, 29
Wilde, Jane, Lady  87
Wilde, Oscar  iii, 87
William III, King  8
Windsor  139
Wodrow, Robert  12
Worcester, Battle of  139
World Trade Center  6–8, 129

Yates, Frances  9
Yeats, Jack Butler  100
Yeoman, Professor Louise  25
Young, Ian C.  126

Zulus  66

170